For Dave Came:
the "unsung hero" behind so many
publications on The Divine Mercy,
including this one

DIVINE MERCY

A Guide from Genesis
to Benedict XVI

DIVINE MERCY

A Guide from Genesis to Benedict XVI

Revised Edition

Robert A. Stackpole, STD
Director of the John Paul II Institute
of Divine Mercy
Professor of Theology, Redeemer Pacific College

MARIAN PRESS
STOCKBRIDGE MA 01263

John Paul II Institute of Divine Mercy
An Imprint of Marian Press
2014

Available from:
Marian Helpers Center
Stockbridge, MA 01263

Prayerline: 1-800-804-3823
Orderline: 1-800-462-7426
Website: www.marian.org

Imprimi Potest:
Very Rev. Daniel Cambra, MIC
Provincial Superior
The Blessed Virgin Mary, Mother of Mercy Province
April 29, 2009

Library of Congress Catalog Number: 2009927760
ISBN: 978-1-59614-208-4

Cover Art: Composite rendering of artwork in strip © copyright Congregation
of Marians of the Immaculate Conception. Inset: Photo by Arturo Mari.

Design of Cover and Pages: Kathy Szpak

Editing and Proofreading: David Came and Dan Valenti

For texts from the English Edition of *Diary of St. Maria Faustina Kowalska*

Nihil Obstat:
George H. Pearce, SM
Former Archbishop of Suva, Fiji

Imprimatur:
Joseph F. Maguire
Bishop of Springfield, MA
April 9, 1984

Printed in the United States of America

CONTENTS

FOREWORD

It has been said that love is what makes the world go round. In reality, it is love and mercy that make the world go round, because it is love and mercy that brought the world into existence and daily sustain it. Without love poured out in the form of mercy, the world would lose hope. This is why Divine Mercy is at the heart of the Gospel of Jesus Christ. In this book, Dr. Robert Stackpole, Director of the John Paul II Institute for Divine Mercy and Professor of Theology at Redeemer Pacific College, presents to the reader a "theological history" of Divine Mercy, as it has been revealed from Genesis to Pope Benedict XVI. Holding a Doctorate in Theology from the Angelicum in Rome and having lectured at conferences around the world, Dr. Stackpole is an expert in teaching others about the riches of Divine Mercy as found in Divine Revelation and the lives of the saints.

As a result of his being a close collaborator in The Divine Mercy apostolate of the Marians of the Immaculate Conception, I first met Dr. Stackpole shortly after entering the Marian community. Along with such men as Fr. Seraphim Michalenko, MIC, and Fr. Kazimierz Chwalek, MIC, Dr. Stackpole has played a key role in transmitting to the Marians in formation a familiarity with and love for the theology and spirituality of The Divine Mercy message and devotion.

I consider myself truly blessed because, during my seminary studies at the Dominican House of Studies in Washington, D.C., Dr. Stackpole was invited as a visiting professor to teach a full-semester class on the history, theology, and spirituality of Divine Mercy. I thoroughly enjoyed that class and learned so much about Divine Mercy that I truly believe it equipped me to be an apostle of mercy and bring the message of mercy to others.

As I discovered the broader historical perspective on mercy as a seminarian in Dr. Stackpole's classroom, I realized anew the urgency of the message of Divine Mercy given to St. Faustina for our own time. That kind of understanding is now available to everyone through this very readable and thought-provoking study of Divine Mercy.

In fact, in this revised edition, Dr. Stackpole includes an expanded chapter on the great theologian St. Augustine, a new chapter on the spiritual master St. Bernard of Clairvaux, and a full chapter on Pope Benedict XVI and his commitment to Divine Mercy. The chapter on Pope Benedict highlights his involvement at the first World Apostolic Congress on Mercy in April 2008.

My prayer is that everyone who reads this book comes to a greater appreciation of the mystery of God's mercy and seeks to bring the message of mercy to others.

Divine Mercy is for everyone.

Fr. Donald Calloway, MIC, STL
Marian House of Studies

INTRODUCTION

This book is a guide to a message that the world desperately needs to hear. This message comes from "above," "right from the top," from the Maker of the universe Himself. It is the central message of God's revelation to His human creatures: the message of God's merciful love.

One might well ask: "Why does this book say 'from Genesis to Benedict XVI'? If the message is so important, why didn't God reveal the whole thing to human beings right from the start? Why do you have to cover all of history, from Genesis to Pope Benedict today, to tell us about it?" Of course, if humanity had been willing and able to listen to this message, perhaps God could have revealed it to us all at once. However, as a result of the fall of humanity into sin, our minds were clouded and our hearts darkened. For this reason, God's revelation of His merciful love could only be communicated to the human race one step at a time. As century followed century, God progressively revealed Himself more and more, and there was also an increasing appreciation of His mercy down through the ages.

That is the focus of the first part of this book: the progressive revelation of God's message of mercy, as recorded in the Bible. Moreover, as we shall see, the message of God's merciful love is not just something He wanted to send to us in words, but *Someone* He wanted to give to us *in person*: Himself, in the person of His Son, Jesus Christ. That was His main message (or "Word") made flesh, so that we could know and experience His mercy in the most clear and comprehensible way. Saint John summed it all up for us in His first epistle: "In this the love of God was made manifest among us, that God sent his only Son into the world, that we might live through him" (1 Jn 4:9).

The second part of this book focuses on those who did "live through him" — namely, the best friends of God, the saints. We shall see that the saints of God in the Catholic Tradition focused their reflections, their prayers, and their witness to the world on the biblical revelation of Divine Mercy. Sometimes they wrote theological reflections about it. Sometimes God manifested His mercy to them in the form of special revelations, such as supernatural apparitions, visions, and locutions. Always, the praises of God's mercy were on their lips and manifest in their lives.

Finally, in the third part of this book, we shall show that God has done something new in our time. Beginning with the life and witness of a simple Polish sister back in the 1930s, St. Faustina Kowalska, He has expressed His mercy for the world in a new way, re-presenting the biblical and traditional message in a way that human beings in our time can hear it afresh. As this new "Devotion to The Divine Mercy" began to spread around the world, obstacles were thrown into its path, and then God did another new thing: he raised up from that same Catholic land a pope, John Paul II, who would teach the message of mercy to the world with startling clarity and power, and consecrate the world to The Divine Mercy at the dawn of the third millennium.

This part of the story is not over. It will be written by the Holy Spirit in the hearts and lives of present and future generations. In fact, it can be written in the lives of those who read this book. That is why study questions and discussion starters are included at the end of sections of material in the chapters — to help both individual readers and groups reflect on how they can take part as the story of Divine Mercy unfolds in their own lives.

In this revised edition, new material has been added to tell even more fully the story of Catholic devotion to The Divine Mercy. For example, there is a brand new chapter on St. Bernard of Clairvaux, since no account of the unfolding of the message of Divine Mercy in the Church would be complete without including his contribution. A full chapter has been developed on Pope Benedict XVI , given the important things that our present Pope has both said and done to call the Church and the world to the merciful love of God — especially at the first World Apostolic Congress on Mercy. Finally, the chapter on St. Augustine has been revised and expanded to give a more comprehensive presentation of his thought.

Indeed, St. Augustine probably should be named the patron saint of all revised book editions, since, near the end of his life, he was one of the few theologians in history humble enough to write a whole book entitled simply *Retractions,* containing nothing but revisions and corrections of all of his previously published work. May our Savior grant that all of us who work on books concerning His merciful love will become as humble and willing to correct and revise our own work as St. Augustine was!

With all this in mind, the author, the publisher, and the Congregation of Marians of the Immaculate Conception, who sponsored this publication as part of their mercy apostolate, hope and pray that we all may take our part in the spread of the merciful love of Jesus Christ, in a world that needs that mercy now more than ever.

Robert Stackpole, STD
Director, John Paul II Institute of Divine Mercy
Professor of Theology, Redeemer Pacific College

PART ONE

Understanding Divine Mercy
and Its Foundation
in Scripture

CHAPTER ONE

What Is Divine Mercy?

Before we can walk through the story of God's merciful love for the human race, we need to have some knowledge of what "Divine Mercy" actually means. The phrase presents us with a semantic problem right from the start. After all, the word "mercy" in contemporary English has a very restricted meaning. It is usually used to refer to an act of pardon, as in "Let me off, judge; have mercy!" or "He threw himself on the mercy of the court." In the Catholic tradition of theology, however, mercy means more than just the cancellation of punishment, far more than that.

Divine Mercy is God's love reaching down to meet the needs and overcome the miseries of His creatures. The Bible, the teachings of St. Thomas Aquinas, and Pope John Paul II all assure us that this is so.

The Old Testament provides us with many images of human misery and of God in His mercy seeking to relieve it. One of most poignant images of such misery is that of a woman suffering the aching loneliness of having no husband and no children — of being completely bereft in the world. This is the spiritual plight of all of us without God. It was used by the Old Testament prophets to signify Israel being reduced to utter misery because of her sins and unfaithfulness to the Lord. But this is not the end of the story. The Lord Yahweh Himself has compassion on the woman by marrying her and making her fruitful. He reaches down to the woman in her misery and raises her up. Where there was only despair, loneliness, and heartache come joy, fruitfulness, and abiding love.

An inspiring example of such steadfast divine love relieving human misery is found in the Old Testament prophet known as Second Isaiah. As he writes, he is encouraging the Jews who are exiles in Babylon not to give up hope that God in His compassion will deliver them:

"Sing, O barren one, who did not bear; break forth into singing and cry aloud, you who have not been in travail! For the children of the desolate one will be more than the children of her that is married, says the Lord. Enlarge the place of your tent, and let the curtains of your habitations be stretched out; hold not back, lengthen your cords and strengthen your stakes. For you will spread abroad to the right and to the left, and your descendants will possess the nations and will people the desolate cities.

"Fear not, for you will not be ashamed; be not confounded, for you will not be put to shame; for you will forget the shame of your youth, and the reproach of your widowhood you will remember no more. For your Maker is your husband, the Lord of hosts is his name; and the Holy One of Israel is your Redeemer, the God of the whole earth he is called. For the Lord has called you like a wife forsaken and grieved in spirit, like a wife of youth when she is cast off, says your God. For a brief moment I forsook you, but with great compassion I will gather you. In overflowing wrath for a moment I hid my face from you, but with everlasting love I will have compassion on you, says the Lord, your Redeemer.

"For this is like the days of Noah to me: as I swore that the waters of Noah should no more go over the earth, so I have sworn that I will not be angry with you and will not rebuke you. For the mountains may depart and the hills be removed, but my steadfast love shall not depart from you, and my covenant of peace shall not be removed, says the Lord, who has compassion on you" (Is 54:1-10).

In the Old Testament, there are two principal Hebrew words that we usually translate as mercy. First, there is the word *hesed*, which means "steadfast love, covenant love." Someone who has the attribute of *hesed* is someone you can always count on, someone who never lets you down. According to the Catholic Biblical scholar John L. Mckenzie, the word *hesed* is often used in Hebrew in connection with other words which bring out its meaning, such as *hesed-emet* (steadfast, dependable love), *hesed-sedekah* (righteous, holy love) and *hesed-yesua* (rescuing, saving love). In a remarkable endnote to his encyclical *Dives in Misericordia (Rich in Mercy)*, Pope John Paul II teaches that *hesed* contains the meaning of faithfulness to oneself, to one's own promises and commitments to others (Thus, Prof. Scott Hahn's popular book on the Bible is entitled *The Father Who Keeps His Promises*). The Holy Father writes:

> When in the Old Testament the word *hesed* is used of the Lord, this always occurs in connection with the covenant that God established with Israel. This covenant was, on God's part, a gift and a grace for Israel ... God had made a commitment to respect it ... [this divine *hesed*] showed itself as what it was at the beginning, that is, as a love that gives, love more powerful than betrayal, grace stronger than sin (no. 52).

As we have seen in our opening example, in a sense, the whole experience of Israel with God is an experience of His *hesed*-love (Is 54:10): "For the mountains may depart and the hills be removed, but my steadfast love [*hesed*] shall not depart from you, and my covenant of peace shall not be removed, says the Lord who has compassion on you." As John L. Mckenzie has written: "The entire history of the dealing of Yahweh with Israel can be summed up as *hesed*; it is the dominating motive which appears in his deeds, and the motive which gives unity and intelligibility to all His dealings with men" (*Dictionary of the Bible*).

The second most common word for God's mercy in the Old Testament is the Hebrew word *rachamim*: tender, compassionate love, a love that springs from pity. Someone who has *rachamim* is someone who feels for your plight and is moved with compassion to help you. *Rachamim* is often used in conjunction with *hesed*. It comes from a root word *rechem*, which means a mother's womb. Thus, there is a special intimacy and responsiveness about this kind of love, and a special concern for the sufferings of others. The Holy Father sees *hesed* as, in a sense, a masculine form of love (steadfast, dependable, righteous, being true to oneself and to one's promises), while *rachamim* is more feminine (tender, responsive, compassionate, like a mother responding in love to the sufferings of her child).

In the New Testament, the Greek word that is usually translated as "mercy" is the word *eleos*. It can also be translated as loving kindness or tender compassion. The Greek word comes from a root word meaning oil that is poured out. Thus, when the Church sings in her liturgy the Greek words *Kyrie Eleison* and *Christie Eleison*, she is praying that the merciful love of God will be poured out upon her children, like holy oil from above. According to the ancient Fathers of the Church, the Church herself was born from the wounded side of Christ, when out of His heart there poured out blood and water, symbolic of all the graces of the two chief Sacraments, Baptism and the Eucharist (Jn 19:34). In short, *eleos* is God's love poured out upon His people.

In the Latin tradition, the principal word for mercy is *misericordia*, which means, literally "miserable heart." Father George Kosicki, CSB, the great Divine Mercy evangelist, once summed up the meaning of this Latin word as follows: *misericordia* means "having a pain in your heart for the pains of others and taking pains to do something about their pain."

The most comprehensive statement by the Magisterium on the meaning of Divine Mercy can be found in Pope John

Paul II's encyclical letter *Dives in Misericordia* (*Rich in Mercy*, 1981). In that encyclical, the Holy Father made two very important statements about mercy. First, he wrote, "Mercy is love's second name." Secondly, he taught that mercy is "the greatest attribute of God."

Let us look at each of these statements in turn.

1. MERCY IS LOVE'S SECOND NAME

Here the Pope was not saying anything new. According to the Catholic theological tradition, mercy is a certain kind of love, a certain expression of love.

Love in general might be defined as a sharing and giving of oneself to another, a selfless seeking of the good of another. According to the Polish theologian Ignacy Rozycki:

> Traditional Catholic moral theology treats of the virtue of mercy as flowing from love of neighbor. Namely, it is that virtue which inclines us to offer assistance to a person suffering from want or misery. This being so, "mercy" in moral theology ... is not love itself but love's result and extension (quoted in *Pillars of Fire in my Soul: the Spirituality of St. Faustina*, Marian Press, 2003, p. 95).

Thus, playing games with one's children, enjoying and sharing conjugal love with one's spouse, or singing the praises of the Lord at Holy Eucharist, while each of these acts would be considered acts of "love" of various kinds, ordinarily we would not call them acts of "mercy." On the other hand, giving bread to the hungry, drink to the thirsty, clothes to the naked, and shelter to the homeless — or indeed bringing the Good News of Jesus Christ to the lost and the broken — these are all acts of merciful love: love reaching down to lift people out of their physical and spiritual miseries.

2. MERCY IS THE GREATEST
ATTRIBUTE OF GOD

Pope John Paul II wrote in *Dives in Misericordia*: "The Bible, Tradition, and the whole faith life of the People of God provide unique proof ... that mercy is the greatest of the attributes and perfections of God" (no. 13). As we shall see later in this book, the Pope was reiterating here the teaching of St. Augustine and St. Thomas Aquinas. But we still may want to know how this can be true. How can any of God's perfections be "greater" than any other? According to the Christian philosophical tradition and the definition of God given at the First Vatican Council, God is one, simple, spiritual, infinitely perfect act of Being. He does not have "parts" as bodily creatures do. Rather, each of His perfections — such as His love, His goodness, His power, and His wisdom — is just another name for what He is. The Polish theologian Fr. Ignacy Rozycki explained it like this:

> In this sense, all of God's attributes are God, one and the same. For this reason, all are absolutely equal to each other. Divine Mercy is as infinitely perfect as His Wisdom or Power, for it is likewise God, and the same God, just as Divine Wisdom and Divine Power are God (*Pillars of Fire*, p. 96).

In other words, God does not just do merciful things sometimes, nor does He have a merciful "side" to His character, as a human being might have. On the contrary, He is always and everywhere and at all times merciful. Everything He does is an expression of His Mercy — and of all of His other attributes too, all at once. All of His attributes are eternally in action! But then Fr. Rozycki goes on to write:

> If, on the other hand, mercy is understood in the Biblical sense as functional, then, even though it is

called an attribute, it first of all denotes the results of the infinite and eternal love of God in world history, and especially in the history of mankind's salvation. In fact, both *hesed* (mercy in the Old Testament), as well as *eleos* (mercy in the New Testament) signify active manifestations of God's love toward mankind. In the Old Testament the manifestations found their expression in the calling and directing of the chosen people, and in the New Testament they were found in the sending of the Son of God into the world and in the entire work of redemption. This Biblically formulated relationship between love and mercy is expressed by [St.] Faustina in the words: 'Love is the flower, mercy the fruit' (*Diary*, 948).

So, if we understand mercy in the Biblical sense, then without any fear of error contrary to the faith, it can be said that mercy is the greatest attribute of God ... [in other words] within this Biblical understanding, the results of the activity of merciful love are the greatest in the world and in this respect, mercy surpasses all other Divine attributes (*Pillars of Fire*, p. 96).

Another way to express this insight would be as follows: Divine Mercy is supremely manifest in all of God's actions toward mankind, and to show mercy must be the motive and intention behind all of God's actions in the world.

Drawing upon the biblical words for mercy, and upon the magisterial teachings of Pope John Paul II, therefore, let us try to formulate a clear definition of what we mean by "Divine Mercy."

According to the first epistle of St. John, "God is love" (4:8). He is infinite, eternal, self-giving love within His own being, among the Three Persons of the Blessed Trinity — Father, Son, and Holy Spirit. From all eternity, therefore, within His own infinite essence, He enjoys the fullness of love given, love received, and love returned. He enjoyed that fullness of perfect love before He ever made the world — and even if He had never made any world at all, He still would have enjoyed this perfect beatitude of eternal love, for "God is love."

In the infinite, eternal love that He is, in the inner life of the Blessed Trinity, there is no need for "mercy," for there is no "want" or "misery" or "suffering" that needs to be overcome in the Infinitely Perfect Being. What then is Divine Mercy?

Saint Thomas Aquinas defined mercy in general as "the compassion in our hearts for another person's misery, a compassion which drives us to do what we can to help him" (ST II-II.30.1). Divine Mercy, therefore, is the form that God's eternal love takes when He reaches out to us in the midst of our need and our brokenness. Whatever the nature of our need or our misery might be — sin, guilt, suffering, or death — He is always ready to pour out His merciful, compassionate love for us, to help in time of need:

> In fact, God's love for His creatures always takes the form of merciful love. As we read in the Psalms (25:10) "all the ways of the Lord are mercy and truth," and again (145:9), "His tender mercies are over all His works."

> When He created the world ex *nihilo*, therefore, and holds it in being at every moment, it is an act of merciful love: His merciful love overcoming the potential nothingness, the possible non-existence of all things.

> When the divine Son became incarnate and dwelt among us, that was an act of merciful love too: His merciful love in sharing our lot, showing us the way to the Father, and making the perfect offering for our sins.

> When He sends His Holy Spirit into our hearts to refresh and sanctify us, that too is His merciful love: His merciful love pouring into our hearts the power

to grow in faith, hope, and love, and to serve him with joy. Psalm 136 says it best. While celebrating all the works of the Lord in creation and redemption, the psalm bears the constant refrain: "For His mercy endures forever" (Robert Stackpole, *Jesus, Mercy Incarnate*, Marian Press, 2000, p. 112).

Study Questions

1. What are the three main Biblical words often translated as "mercy" — and what do they mean?

2. How do we define "Divine Mercy," according to St. Thomas Aquinas and Catholic Tradition?

3. How is God's act of creating of the world an expression of His Divine Mercy?

Discussion Starter:

Pope John Paul II said that mercy is "Love's second name," in other words, a certain kind of love. When have you experienced someone's love as "merciful" love?

CHAPTER TWO

The Biblical Story of Divine Mercy — the Old Testament

The Old Testament includes many cries of the human heart to God for mercy. Perhaps none is more heart-rending than that of King David in Psalm 51 — the Church's great penitential Psalm that is known as the *Miserere*.

David's repentance is sincere and deep after he is confronted by the prophet Nathan for a double crime, which he has kept hidden. He has committed adultery with the wife of his soldier Uriah the Hittite and then has secretly arranged for Uriah to be slain in battle, so he can marry Bathsheba the wife, who is now pregnant with his own child. The prophet Nathan reveals David's guilt in a veiled story that he tells the King. At the end of the story, David tells Nathan that "the man who has done this deserves to die." Nathan then tells David, "You are the man" (2 Sam 12:6-7).

Overcome by profound emotion, David confesses his guilt before the Lord and implores His mercy in these stirring lines:

> Have mercy on me, O God, according to thy steadfast love; according to thy abundant mercy blot out my transgressions.

> Wash me thoroughly from my iniquity, and cleanse me from my sin!

> For I know my transgressions, and my sin is ever before me.

Against thee, thee only, have I sinned and done that which is evil in thy sight, so that thou art justified in thy sentence and blameless in thy judgment.

Behold, I was brought forth in iniquity, and in sin did my mother conceive me.

Behold, thou desirest truth in the inward being; therefore teach me wisdom in my secret heart.

Purge me with hyssop, and I shall be clean; wash me, and I shall be whiter than snow.

Fill me with joy and gladness; let the bones which thou hast broken rejoice.

Hide thy face from my sins, and blot out all my iniquities.

Create in me a clean heart, O God, and put a new and right spirit within me.

Cast me not away from thy presence, and take not thy holy Spirit from me.

Restore to me the joy of thy salvation, and uphold me with a willing spirit.

Then I will teach transgressors thy ways, and sinners will return to thee.

Deliver me from bloodguiltiness, O God, thou God of my salvation, and my tongue will sing aloud of thy deliverance.

O Lord, open thou my lips and my mouth shall show forth thy praise.

For thou hast no delight in sacrifice; were I to give a burnt offering, thou wouldst not be pleased.

The sacrifice acceptable to God is a broken spirit; a broken and contrite heart, O God, thou wilt not despise (Ps 51:1-17).

David speaks for all of us in our sin and misery as we cry out to God for His mercy and deliverance. With David, we all stand accused before the holiness of God, who is our Creator. At the same time, each of us — like David — can be confident that God in His merciful love will forgive and restore us if we turn to Him with repentant hearts.

To deepen our knowledge and appreciation of God's merciful love in spite of our sinfulness, let us look more closely at the whole story of God's dealings with His chosen people Israel. As the Catholic biblical scholar John L. Mackenzie claimed: "The entire history of the dealings of Yahweh with Israel can be summed up as *hesed* [steadfast love]." In this chapter, we shall show that Mackenzie's claim is, in fact, well grounded.

1. GENESIS, EXODUS, AND ON TO THE PROMISED LAND

According to the book of Genesis, God placed the first human beings, Adam and Eve, in a kind of paradise — the Garden of Eden. But they fell from that lofty state of grace when the serpent tempted them to an act of pride and disobedience, and their human nature was corrupted because they yielded to the temptation. Then what was God's response to their disobedience? On the one hand, punishment: they were cast out of the Garden of Eden, and became subject to toil, pain, and death. And yet God also tempered their sentence with a promise of mercy: God promised that of the seed of the woman would one day spring forth someone who would crush the evil serpent's head (that is, who would defeat the Devil's power, see Gen 3:15). This is called in the Catholic tradition the "*protoevangelium*" (the first hint of the Gospel), a prophetic foreshadowing of the Messiah who was to come.

Later in Genesis, there is the first homicide among the sons of Adam: Cain kills Abel. Then Cain is driven out, banished from his family to wander as a fugitive. Once again, however,

God tempers His punishments with mercy. The Lord puts His mark of protection on Cain and declares: "If anyone kills Cain, vengeance shall be taken upon him sevenfold" (Gen 4:15).

Then in the story of Noah and the Flood, we see not only Divine Justice, but Divine Mercy at work: Noah and his family are saved in the Ark from the flood, the human race is thereby given a second chance, and God places a rainbow in the sky as an abiding sign of His promise of forbearance with sinful humanity (see Gen 9:8-17).

In these early chapters of Genesis, therefore, we do not have a very well developed conception of Divine Mercy. Moses and the Israelites who first wrote and read these chapters still had more to learn about the mercy of God. Nevertheless, Divine Mercy is clearly evident. God is not just portrayed as a God of righteous wrath and punishment. Rather, His strict justice is tempered (so to speak) by His mercy.

The merciful love of God crops up in other places in Genesis as well. For example, there is the story of Abraham pleading for mercy with God upon Sodom and Gomorrah in Genesis 18. The Lord promises Abraham that if He could find only ten righteous persons in that whole city of wickedness, He would not destroy the city for the sake of the ten.

There is also the beautiful testimony to the greatness of Divine Mercy in Jacob's prayer as he went to meet his brother Esau for the first time since Jacob's long sojourn with the family of Laban. Fearing that he would meet in his brother only vengeful anger, because Jacob had tricked Esau out of the family inheritance many years before, Jacob appealed for protection to the God of Abraham and Isaac, saying: "I am not worthy of the least of all thy mercies [RSV: "I am not worthy of the least of all thy steadfast love and faithfulness" — that is, *hesed*] which thou hast shown to thy servant, for with only my staff I crossed this Jordan [many years ago], and now I have become two companies" (Gen 32:11).

It was the experience of the Exodus from Egypt that truly sealed in the minds and hearts of the Israelites that, above all, their God was a God of mercy. Pope John Paul II explains in his encyclical *Dives in Misericordia*:

> At the root of the many-sided conviction [about Divine Mercy], which is both communal and personal, and which is demonstrated by the whole of the Old Testament down the centuries, is the basic experience of the chosen people at the Exodus: the Lord saw the affliction of His people reduced to slavery, heard their cry, knew their sufferings and decided to deliver them. In this act of salvation by the Lord, the prophet [Isaiah] perceived His love and compassion. This is precisely the ground upon which the people and each of its members based their certainty of the mercy of God, which can be invoked whenever tragedy strikes (no. 4).

The Holy Father was referring here to a passage from the book of the prophet Isaiah, who summed up Israel's understanding of what the Lord had done for them as follows:

> I will recount the steadfast love of the Lord, the praises of the Lord, according to all that he has granted us, and the great goodness to the house of Israel which he has granted them according to his mercy, according to the abundance of his steadfast love. For he said, surely they are my people, sons who will not deal falsely; and he became their savior. In all their affliction he was afflicted, and the angel of his presence saved them; in his love and pity he redeemed them; he lifted them up and carried them all the days of old (63:7-9).

When the Israelites successfully crossed the Red Sea, Moses sang a hymn of praise and thanksgiving to the Lord: "Thou hast led in thy steadfast love [*hesed*] the people whom thou hast redeemed, thou hast guided them by thy strength to thy holy abode" (Ex 15:13).

When Moses brought the people of Israel through the desert to Mount Sinai, despite their unfaithfulness and faintheartedness, the Lord stressed His patient and merciful love for them in the very first of the Ten Commandments that He gave to them on the holy mount: "I the Lord your God am a jealous God, visiting the iniquity of the fathers upon the children to the third and fourth generation of those who hate me, but showing steadfast love [*hesed*] to thousands [of generations] of those who love me and keep my commandments" (Ex 20:5-6). It is clear what was gradually dawning upon the people of Israel: Divine Mercy is no longer seen as just something that "tempers" God's retributive justice—that takes the "edge" off of it, so to speak. Rather, His Divine Mercy far surpasses His justice. The sins of the people may have ill effects, even down to the third and fourth generation, but for those who follow His commandments and love Him, God promises blessings for thousands of generations.

When Moses went up to Mount Sinai again with two new tablets of stone and the Lord wrote upon them once again, He prefaced this second giving of the Law to Moses in a way that shows that His mercy is of the essence of the mystery of who He is:

> So Moses cut two tables of stone like the first; and he rose early in the morning and went up on Mt. Sinai, as the Lord had commanded him, and took in his hand two tables of stone. And the Lord descended in the cloud and stood with him there, and proclaimed the name of the Lord. The Lord passed before him and proclaimed, "The Lord, the Lord, a God merciful and gracious, slow to anger and abounding in steadfast love for thousands, forgiving iniquity and transgression and sin ... ."

And then Moses prayed to the Lord:

> "If now I have found favor in thy sight, O Lord, let the Lord, I pray thee, go in the midst of us, although it is a stiff-necked people; and pardon our iniquity and our sin, and take us for thy inheritance" (Ex 34:4-9).

Later, when the people of Israel were about to enter the Promised Land, upon hearing from the scouts that they had sent out that the land was indeed rich and fertile but inhabited by strong and valiant people who could not easily be conquered, the people again grew fainthearted and considered choosing another leader than Moses and returning to Egypt. As a result of their rebelliousness, Moses had to plead for mercy upon them again from the Lord:

> "And now I pray thee, let the power of the Lord be great as thou hast promised, saying, 'The Lord is slow to anger and abounding in steadfast love, forgiving iniquity and transgression, but he will by no means clear the guilty, visiting the iniquity of the fathers upon the children, upon the third and fourth generation.' Pardon the iniquity of this people, I pray thee, according to the greatness of thy steadfast love, and according as thou hast forgiven this people, from Egypt until now" (Num 14:19-21).

God still punished the Chosen People for their distrust and rebelliousness, stating that except for the few who remained faithful, none of the rest would make it to the Promised Land. Nevertheless, He promised that their children would enter the Promised Land, after wandering forty years in the desert. God did not abandon His Chosen People, and did not withdraw His covenant promises from them.

Moses continued to exhort the people of Israel to trust in the Lord's mercy right up until the end of his life. In the midst of his final admonition to his people, he had a prophetic vision in which he foresaw the history of his people — their infidelities, punishments, and sorrows — and yet also their conversion to God, and that the Lord would never forsake them:

> "When you are in tribulation, and all these things come upon you in these latter days, you will return to the Lord your God and obey his voice, because the Lord your God is a merciful God. He will not leave you,

nor altogether destroy you, nor forget the covenant by
which he swore to your fathers" (Dt 4:30-31).

Here we have the beginnings of another development in
the understanding of the people of Israel of the mercy of God.
As we have seen in Genesis, Divine Mercy seems to be portrayed
as something that tempers or softens God's strict, retributive
justice. On Mount Sinai, Divine Mercy is proclaimed to be, in a
sense, greater than His justice. Now in Deuteronomy, toward
the end of the life of Moses, we are told that even God's acts of
just punishment of His people are expressions of His mercy: His
mercy expressed in chastising His people, so that they will
return to faithfulness to the covenant He had graciously made
with them and so that they might enjoy all its blessings.

The Dominican Fr. Hyacinth Woroniecki, OP, summed
up these insights from the Moses story as follows:

> In this manner the mystery of Divine Mercy was
> revealed to mankind by God Himself in the most
> ancient rudiments of our faith on Mt. Sinai. We have
> learned that in the relations of God and Israel there
> was no place for indulgence, for disregard of God's
> will as expressed in His commandments. God
> demanded obedience and fidelity, and punished
> severely all iniquity, but His mercy surpassed that
> rigor, and was always ready to aid those wishing to
> revert from their evil ways and to side with the Lord
> faithfully. Even the austere punishments ... had for
> their purpose to bring [the sinner] to his senses and
> to convert him to God, so that even God's justice
> served His mercy (*Mystery of Mercy*, p. 9-10).

Study Questions

1. What is the understanding of God's mercy that we find in Genesis, the first book of the Bible?

2. What do we learn about Divine Mercy from the First Commandment that God gave to the Israelites on Mt. Sinai?

3. What can we learn about God's mercy from the final speech that Moses gave to the people of Israel?

Discussion Starter:

Have you ever wondered if God was sometimes "chastising" you by permitting you to suffer in various ways? Could these chastisements (if such they were) also be seen as acts of merciful love? Is it hard to view them in that way?

2. DIVINE MERCY IN THE PSALMS
AND THE PROPHETS

In general, the Psalms are more comprehensive than the Torah or Pentateuch (the first five books of the Bible) in their appreciation of the breadth and depth of Divine Mercy. In the Psalms, Divine Mercy applies to individuals and their struggles, as well as to Israel as a whole, and the Psalms address the need for individual, interior, spiritual renewal, and not just for the temporal blessings of the covenant.

We have seen in this chapter's opening example from the *Miserere* (Psalm 51) how King David cries out to the Lord for for moral and spiritual renewal: "Wash me thoroughly from my iniquity, and cleanse me from my sin," (verse 2), and: "Create in me a clean heart, O God, and put a new and right spirit within me" (verse 10). In other words, this is not a prayer along the lines of: "Forgive me, Lord, so that I can once again enjoy all the temporal blessings of the covenant, such as peace and prosperity and progeny." Rather, it is David's plea for the restoration of his moral and spiritual health: "Restore me to the joy of thy salvation, and uphold me with a willing spirit" (verse 12).

The theme of Divine Mercy echoes throughout the Psalter. First of all, there are Psalms devoted to the praise of Divine Mercy. Psalm 136, for example, recounts all the merciful deeds of the Lord both in creation and in rescuing Israel from slavery, bringing the Chosen People to the Promised Land. This Psalm bears the refrain: "His steadfast love (*hesed* = mercy) endures for ever." Psalms 105 and 106 are a summary of the proofs of the mercy of the Lord in leading Israel out of Egypt and into the Promised Land. Psalm 106 begins: "Praise the Lord! O give thanks to the Lord for he is good; for his steadfast love [*hesed*] endures forever." Psalm 107 gives thanks to the Lord for all of the many ways He delivers people from trouble and danger.

Secondly, several of the Psalms define the very nature of

God chiefly in terms of His merciful love. Psalm 145, for example, repeats and elaborates upon God's self-designation as the merciful one from Exodus: "The Lord is gracious and merciful, slow to anger and abounding in steadfast love. The Lord is good to all, and his compassion is over all his works" (verse 8). Psalm 103 is perhaps the most comprehensive exposition of the mercy of God: He forgives, He heals, and He is dependable, He provides for His people, and He is compassionate toward human weakness, patient and forbearing:

> Bless the Lord O my soul; and all that is within me, bless his holy name!
>
> Bless the Lord, O my soul, and forget not all his benefits,
>
> Who forgives all your iniquity, and heals all your diseases,
>
> Who redeems your life from the Pit, who crowns you with steadfast love and mercy,
>
> Who satisfies you with good as long as you live so that your youth is renewed like the eagle's.
>
> The Lord works vindication and justice for all who are oppressed.
>
> He made known his ways to Moses, his acts to the people of Israel.
>
> The Lord is merciful and gracious, slow to anger and abounding in steadfast love.
>
> He will not always chide, nor will he keep his anger forever.
>
> He does not deal with us according to our sins, nor requite us according to our iniquities.
>
> For as the heavens are high above the earth, so great is his steadfast love toward those who fear him;

As far as the east is from the west, so far does he remove our transgressions from us.

As a father pities his children, so the Lord pities those who fear him.

For he knows our frame; he remembers we are dust (Ps 103:1-14).

The Psalms also tell us how we can see the mercy of the Lord. Psalm 112:4 states: "Light rises in darkness for the upright; the Lord is gracious, merciful and just." In other words, we can only see God's mercy clearly when we are upright ourselves: a merciless and unjust heart cannot see or experience or understand the mercy of the Lord. Psalm 111 reminds us that it is through remembering His "wonderful works" that we can best appreciate Divine Mercy, for His mercy is no mere philosophical abstraction: it is proven in His deeds.

Many of the Psalms focus on the boundless extent of God's mercy. Psalm 57, for example, tells us of the greatness of Divine Mercy: "For thy steadfast love [*hesed*] is great to the heavens, thy faithfulness to the clouds" (verse 11). Psalm 33:5 states: "the earth is full of the steadfast love of the Lord." Psalm 23 tells us that the tender care of the Lord is like that of a shepherd for his flock, and that He leads us to His eternal home: "Surely goodness and mercy shall follow me all the days of my life, and I shall dwell in the house of the Lord forever" (verse 6).

Many of the Psalms also encourage us to place our trust in the Lord and to hope in Him. Psalm 32:10 promises: "Many are the pangs of the wicked, but steadfast love [*hesed*] surrounds him who trusts in the Lord." Psalm 33:18 makes a similar promise: "Behold, the eye of the Lord is upon those who fear him, on those who hope in his steadfast love [*hesed*]." Perhaps no Psalm says it better than Psalm 130, which is a cry for forgiveness and rescue from a soul cast deep into the darkness by trouble and sin:

Out of the depths I cry to thee, O Lord! Lord hear my voice!

Let thy ears be attentive to the voice of my
supplications!

If thou, O Lord, shouldst mark iniquities, Lord
who could stand?

But there is forgiveness with thee, that thou
mayest be feared.

I wait for the Lord, my soul waits, and in his
word I hope;

My soul waits for the Lord more than watchmen
for the morning, more than watchmen for the
morning.

O Israel, hope in the Lord! For with the Lord
there is steadfast love [*hesed*],

And with him is plenteous redemption.

And He will redeem Israel from all his iniquities.

It is no wonder, therefore, that one of the favorite verses
of Pope John Paul II comes from the Psalms: "I will sing of the
mercies of the Lord forever, with my mouth I will proclaim thy
faithfulness to all generations" (Ps 89:1). And generations of
English-speaking Christians of all denominations have adopted
Psalm 100 as one of their favorites:

Enter his gates with thanksgiving, go into his
courts with praise!

Give thanks to him, bless his name!

For the Lord is good; his steadfast love [*hesed*]
endures forever,

And his faithfulness to all generations.

In the Psalms, the focus of God's mercy is still very much
on the people of Israel — and understandably so, because the
Psalms were the hymns and canticles used for worship in the
Great Temple in Jerusalem. In the Prophets, on the other

hand, the biblical concept of Divine Mercy is expanded. First, there is the promise that God's mercy will be showered not only upon the Israelites but one day upon all the Gentile nations as well. Second, the People of Israel are encouraged not only to believe in Divine Mercy and to call upon the Lord, but also to be merciful, that is, to live mercifully.

The prophet Isaiah, for example, continually encourages the Israelites to trust in God's mercy: "Then a throne will be established in steadfast love [*hesed*] and on it will sit in faithfulness in the tent of David one who judges and seeks justice and is swift to do righteousness." Isaiah teaches them that they must wait patiently for God's mercy to manifest itself, even as He has waited patiently for their conversion: "Therefore the Lord waits to be gracious to you; therefore he exalts himself to show mercy to you. For the Lord is a God of justice; blessed are all those who wait for him" (38:10). When the Lord does pour out His mercy upon Israel, however, He will do so in abundance:

> He gives power to the faint, and to him who has no might he increases strength.
>
> Even youths shall faint and be weary, and young men shall fall exhausted.
>
> But they who wait for the Lord shall renew their strength.
>
> They shall run and not be weary.
>
> They shall walk and not faint (40:29-31).

Isaiah also prophesies the coming of the Suffering Servant of the Lord, the Messiah, who will obtain mercy for all by His sufferings:

> He was despised and rejected by men;
>
> A man of sorrows and acquainted with grief;
>
> And as one from whom men hide their faces.

He was despised, and we esteemed him not.

Surely he has borne our griefs and carried our sorrows;

Yet we esteemed him stricken, smitten by God and afflicted.

But he was wounded for our transgressions,

He was bruised for our iniquities;

Upon him was the chastisement that made us whole,

And with his stripes we are healed.

All we like sheep have gone astray; we have turned every one to his own way;

And the Lord has laid on him the iniquity of us all
(Is 53:3-6).

The theme of Divine Mercy recurs throughout the prophets. Through the Prophet Jeremiah, for example, the Lord promised the joyful return of Israel from exile: "I have loved you with an everlasting love, therefore I have continued my faithfulness [*hesed*] to you" (31:3). In other words, God's love is the root of His mercy; because He loves, He is merciful to Israel.

The prophet Joel repeats the refrain about the Lord's mercy that we have already seen so often, stemming from Mount Sinai:

Yet even now, says the Lord, return to me with all your heart,

With fasting, with weeping, and with mourning;

And rend your hearts and not your garments.

Return to the Lord your God,

For he is gracious and merciful,

Slow to anger and abounding in steadfast love
(Joel 2:12-13).

In the book of the prophet Hosea, however, God shows that His merciful love for His people is not just a gracious condescension on His part. It is also a passionate desire for their recovery of an intimate friendship with Himself, for their own good, like a lover longing for reunion with his beloved:

> How can I give you up, O Ephraim!
>
> How can I hand you over, O Israel! ...
>
> My heart recoils within me, my compassion grows warm and tender.
>
> I will not execute my fierce anger; I will not again destroy Ephraim;
>
> For I am God and not man,
>
> The Holy One in your midst,
>
> And I will not come to destroy (Hos 11:8-9).

3. THE STORY OF JONAH: A SUMMARY OF DIVINE MERCY IN THE OLD TESTAMENT

Symbolically, the story of Jonah captures the entire message of mercy in the Old Testament. Perhaps, most importantly, it points to God's desire to show mercy to all peoples, not only the Jews — a theme that will be more fully developed in the New Testament. The biblical scholar John L. Mckenzie, S.J., singles out the main features of this summary of mercy when he writes:

> This story has several elements that mark it as a summary of the Old Testament message of Divine Mercy. First of all, God shows His mercy to a disobedient and rebellious Jewish prophet, Jonah, by rescuing him from the belly of a whale. On one level,

this symbolizes the experience of the whole People of Israel, whom God brought to repentance and forgiveness after a time of trial and darkness in captivity and exile. Second, God calls us all to be merciful, as He was merciful to the repentant Assyrians. Third, God's mercy extends even to their most hated enemies (the Assyrians, in this story) — and even to their animals (*The Two Edged Sword: An Interpretation of the Old Testament*. Milwaukee: the Bruce Publishing Co., 1955, p. 202-203).

That is why Jonah said to God:

I pray thee, Lord, is not this what I said when I was yet in my country. That is why I made haste to flee to Tarshish; for I knew that thou art a gracious God and merciful, slow to anger, and abounding in steadfast love (Jon 4:2).

God's reply to Jonah was a crystallization of the revelation of His merciful love for all people:

The Lord said, "You pity the plant, for which you did not labor, nor did you make it grow, which came into being in a night. And should I not pity Nineveh, that great city, in which there are more than a hundred and twenty thousand persons who do not know their right hand from their left [that is, children], and also much cattle?" (Jon 4:10-11).

Throughout the entire history of Israel, and especially in the era of the prophets, at every major event or crisis point, it was the mercy of the Lord that the Israelites remembered, and on the basis of that mercy they made their prayerful appeals. For example, here is the opening line of the prayer of King Solomon at the moment of the dedication of the Great Temple in Jerusalem: "O Lord God of Israel, there is no God like thee, in heaven above or on earth beneath, keeping covenant and showing steadfast love [*hesed*] to thy servants who walk before thee with all their heart" (I Kgs 8:23). Here is the cry of the Jews for mercy when they were languishing in exile in Babylon: "Hear, O Lord, and have mercy, for we have sinned before thee. For thou art enthroned forever, and we are perishing forever" (Bar 2:11-3:8). The elderly Tobit also exalted God's mercy, in expectation of His blessings upon His scattered people:

> Make his greatness known there [before all nations], and exalt him in the presence of all the living; because he is our Lord and God, he is our Father forever. He will afflict us for our iniquities; and again he will show mercy, and will gather us from all the nations among whom you have been scattered (Tob 13:4-5).

Here are the words of the renewal of Israel's covenant with God after the return of the Jews from exile to the Holy Land: "Nevertheless, in thy great mercies thou didst not make an end of them nor forsake them; for thou art a gracious and merciful God" (Neh 9:31).

Finally, the prophets promised that through the work of the Suffering Servant, the Messiah, Israel would fulfill the full scope of her vocation: to bring the salvation of the Lord to all the Gentile nations. In Isaiah 49:6, the Lord says: "It is too light a thing that you should be my servant to raise up the tribes of Jacob and to restore the preserved of Israel; I will give you as a light to the nations, that my salvation may reach to the end of the earth."

We can sum up the message of Divine Mercy in the Old Testament with the words of Pope John Paul II from his encyclical *Dives in Misericordia*:

> Thus, in deeds and in words the Lord revealed His mercy from the beginnings of the people which He chose for Himself; and in the course of its history, this people continually entrusted itself, both when stricken with misfortune and when it became aware of its sin, to the God of mercies. ...

The Old Testament encourages people suffering from misfortune, especially those weighed down by sin — as also the whole of Israel, which had entered into covenant with God — to *appeal for mercy*, and enables them to count upon it: it reminds them of His mercy in times of failure and loss of trust. Subsequently, the Old Testament gives *thanks and glory* for mercy every time that mercy is made manifest in the life of the people or in the lives of individuals. ... Thus, it is easy to understand why the psalmists, when they desire to sing the highest praises of the Lord, break forth into hymns to the God of love, tenderness, mercy, and fidelity (no. 4).

Study Questions

1. In general, what do the Psalms add to the Old Testament appreciation of the breadth and depth of Divine Mercy?

2. What do the first 14 verses of Psalm 103 tell us about the mercy of God?

3. According to Psalm 130, why should we hope in the Lord?

Discussion Starter:

Read Isaiah 58:3-11. What kind of religious observance is most pleasing to the Lord? What does this tell us about the God of mercy?

CHAPTER THREE

The Biblical Story of Divine Mercy — the New Testament

J ust how far will the God of Israel go to pour out His merciful love upon mankind? The New Testament gives us the answer: as far as taking flesh among us as one of us and dying for us on the Cross — in other words, as far as Bethlehem and Calvary. That is how far He will go!

1. THE MERCIFUL LOVE OF JESUS

Let us look first at the many Gospel passages where the writers emphasize the compassion of Jesus, His tenderness for the lost and the broken, a tenderness which manifests His merciful love.

1. Matthew 15:32 (Christ's compassion for human physical needs): "I have compassion on the crowd because they have been with me now three days, and have nothing to eat; and I am unwilling to send them away hungry, lest they faint on the way."

2. Luke 7:13 (Christ's compassion for human emotional and social needs): "And when the Lord saw her [the widow of Nain], he had compassion on her and said to her, 'Do not weep.' And he came and touched the bier, and the bearers stood still. And he said, 'Young man, I say to you, arise.'"

3. Matthew 20:34 (Christ's compassion for the outcast, the marginalized): "And as they went out of Jericho a great crowd followed him. And behold, two blind men sitting by the

roadside, when they heard that Jesus was passing by, cried out, 'Have mercy on us, Son of David!' And Jesus stopped and called them saying, 'What do you want me to do for you?' They said to him, 'Lord, let our eyes be opened.' And Jesus in pity touched their eyes, and immediately they received their sight and followed him."

4. Mark 1:40 (Christ's compassion for those needy in every respect): "And a leper came to him, beseeching him, and kneeling said to him, 'If you will, you can make me clean.' Moved with pity, he stretched out his hand and touched him, and said to him, 'I will; be clean.' And immediately the leprosy left him, and he was made clean."

5. Mark 10:17-22 (Christ's compassion for those sincerely seeking to do God's will): "And as he was setting out on his journey, a man ran up and knelt before him and asked him, 'Good teacher, what must I do to inherit eternal life?' And Jesus said to him. ... 'You know the commandments: Do not kill, Do not commit adultery, Do not steal, Do not bear false witness, Do not defraud, Honor your father and mother.' And he said to him, 'Teacher, all these have I observed from my youth.' And Jesus looking upon him loved him and said to him, 'You lack one thing; go, sell what you have, and give to the poor, and you will have treasure in heaven; and come and follow me.'"

6. Mark 6:34 (Christ's compassion for those hungry for the Word of God): "As Jesus went ashore he saw a great throng, and he had compassion on them, because they were like sheep without a shepherd; and he began to teach them many things."

7. Luke 19: 41-42 (Christ's tender compassion for His people and His country): "And when he drew near and saw the city he wept over it, saying, 'Would that even today you knew the things that make for peace! But now they are hid from your eyes. For the days shall come upon you, when your enemies will cast up a bank about you and surround you, and hem you in on every side, and dash you to the ground, you and your children within you, and they will not leave one stone upon another in you, because you did not know the time of your visitation.'"

8. John 11:32-36 (Christ's tender compassion for human

grief and mortality): "Then Mary, when she came where Jesus was and saw him, she fell at his feet, saying to him, 'Lord if you had been here, my brother would not have died.' When Jesus saw her weeping, and the Jews who came with her also weeping, He was deeply moved in spirit, and troubled: And he said, 'Where have you laid him?' They said to him, 'Lord, come and see.' Jesus wept. So the Jews said, 'See how he loved him.'"

The Gospel writers are trying to tell us that merciful, compassionate love was a consistent and abiding characteristic of the whole life of Jesus of Nazareth, the Son of God. And this tells us something very important about the God who sent Him, the God whose very self-manifestation or "Word" made flesh, Jesus truly is.

If the Son of God Himself is overflowing with merciful love, it is no wonder that the New Testament encourages everyone to place all their trust in Him and in His heavenly Father. In St. Matthew's story of Jesus walking on the water, for example, the underlying message is not only that Jesus manifests His divine power over nature by this miracle, but also that Christians are encouraged to trust in Him in the midst of all the raging waters and threatening waves of this trouble-filled life:

> So Peter got out of the boat and walked on the water and came to Jesus; but when he saw the wind, he was afraid and beginning to sink he cried out, "Lord, save me." Jesus immediately reached out his hand and caught him, saying to him, "O man of little faith, why did you doubt?" And when they got into the boat, the wind ceased. And those in the boat worshipped him, saying, "Truly, you are the Son of God" (Mt 14:29-33).

In Matthew 6:26, Jesus called His disciples to trust in the merciful providence of God, whose tender care is even manifested to some extent in nature: "Look at the birds of the air: They neither sow nor reap nor gather into barns, and yet your heavenly Father feeds them. Are you not of more value than they?"

Another important mercy theme in the life of Jesus is his exhortation to be merciful to others as God is merciful to us: "Be merciful, as your Father is merciful" (Lk 6:36). Divine Mercy is not just to be received for oneself; it is to be shared with others. Indeed, our Lord teaches that this is one of the most important aspects of the moral law: "Woe to you scribes and Pharisees, hypocrites! For you tithe mint and cumin, and have neglected the weightier matters of the law: justice, and mercy, and faith" (Mt 23:23). In fact, it is a recurrent theme in the teaching of Jesus that if we refuse to pass on the mercy we have received, we are in danger of judgment: "Blessed are the merciful, for they [the Greek here implies "only they"] shall obtain mercy" (Mt 5:7).

All this is vividly illustrated for us in Jesus' Parable of the Unforgiving Servant, in which a servant who was forgiven a huge debt by his Master then turned around and had one of his fellow servants thrown into prison for the latter's inability to pay him what he owed. The Master summoned the unforgiving servant and said to him: "You wicked servant! I forgave all that debt because you besought me; and should not you have had mercy on your fellow servant, as I had mercy on you?" (Mt 18:32-33). Indeed, to forgive the sins of others is a truly Christlike manifestation of merciful love. As Jesus said: "Take heed to yourselves; if your brother sins, rebuke him, and if he repents, forgive him; and if he sins against you seven times in the day, and turns to you seven times and says, 'I repent,' you must forgive him" (Lk 17:3).

2. ST. LUKE: THE GOSPEL OF MERCY

One Gospel in particular, the Gospel according to St. Luke, has traditionally merited the title "the Gospel of Mercy." First of all, the theme of God's merciful love ties the whole book together from beginning to end. Second, the Gospel contains a cluster of parables in chapter 15 that is unique to St. Luke's Gospel, and that especially highlights the merciful love of God. Finally, St. Luke places special emphasis on the universal scope of Divine Mercy, portraying it as a distinctive characteristic of the kingdom of God dawning upon the world through Jesus Christ.

Let us begin with a look at how the theme of God's merciful love runs through the entire book.

In its opening chapter, St. Luke's Gospel begins with two great canticles in praise of Divine Mercy: the *Magnificat* and the *Benedictus*. The Magnificat is essentially a hymn of thanksgiving to the God of *hesed*-mercy: The God of steadfast love and faithfulness. In verses 46-50, for example, Mary praises God for showering His mercy upon her:

> My soul magnifies the Lord,
>
> And my spirit rejoices in God my Savior,
>
> For he has regarded the low estate of his handmaiden.
>
> For behold, henceforth all generations will call me blessed; For he who is mighty has done great things for me,
>
> And holy is his name;
>
> And his mercy is on those who fear him
>
> From generation to generation.

Mary then praises God in verses 51-55 for His mercy upon the faithful poor of Israel, who trusted Him to keep His promises to send the Messiah:

> He has shown strength with his arm,
>
> He has scattered the proud in the imagination of their hearts,
>
> He has put down the mighty from their thrones,
>
> And exalted those of low degree;

He has filled the hungry with good things,
and the rich he has sent empty away.

He has helped his servant Israel,

In remembrance of his mercy,

As he spoke to our fathers,

To Abraham and to his posterity forever.

In the *Benedictus*, Zechariah praises God for keeping His covenant promises to Israel: "As he spoke by the mouth of his holy prophets from of old, that we should be saved from our enemies and from the hand of all who hate us; to perform the mercy promised to our fathers, and to remember his holy covenant" (Lk 1:70-72). Zechariah rejoices that the true Israel will be established, just as God had promised through His prophets. But Zechariah also recognizes that the New Israel will not be exactly the same as the old one; in verse 77 he acknowledges that the New Israel will be built upon deliverance from sin: "To give knowledge of salvation to his people, for the forgiveness of their sins." The New Israel will be spiritually renewed in every respect, and this will be a manifestation of the Lord's tender mercy: "Through the tender mercy of our God, when the day shall dawn upon us from on high to give light to those who sit in darkness and the shadow of death, and to guide our feet into the way of peace" (vv. 78-79).

Here also the phrase about giving "light to those who sit in darkness" is probably an allusion to Isaiah 9: "The people who walked in darkness [that is, the Gentiles] have seen a great light; those who dwelt in a land of deep darkness, on them has the light shined." In short, God will keep His promises to restore the Kingdom of Israel, but it will be a spiritually renewed Israel, and somehow the Gentiles will be brought in as well. All this comes from the "tender mercy" of God. The phrase used here in the Greek original text of St. Luke's Gospel is *splagchna eleous*, which literally means through the "bowels" or "guts" of God's "mercy" — a phrase that expresses how deep the mercy of the Lord for us really is.

It is clear from the opening canticles in the first chapter of St. Luke's Gospel, the *Magnificat* and the *Benedictus*, that the evangelist wants to show us that it is the God of Israel, the God of the Old Testament, the God of Mercy, who is active in the whole story about the "good news" of His Son. His *hesed* is at work as he fulfills His messianic promises to His people, and His *rahamim* is expressed as a tender mercy so deep that it even reaches out to embrace the Gentiles, lost in darkness, in order to bring them too into the new, renewed Israel.

Much of the message of Divine Mercy in St. Luke's Gospel has its parallels in the other Gospel accounts. Thus, when Jesus teaches, "Be merciful, as your Father is merciful" (Lk 6:36) this finds its echo in the Gospel according to St. Matthew — in the Sermon on the Mount ("Blessed are the merciful, for they shall obtain mercy," Mt 5:7), and in the parable of the Unforgiving Servant (Mt 18:23-35). In St. Luke's Gospel, however, the merciful love of God takes center stage as a defining characteristic of the kingdom that Jesus, the Son of God, is bringing into the world. Indeed, Jesus points to the miracles of compassionate love that He is performing as signs not only of His messianic identity, but also as signs that God's kingdom of mercy is dawning upon the world through His ministry:

> And Jesus came to Nazareth where he had been brought up, and he went to the synagogue, as his custom was, on the Sabbath day. And he stood up to read; and there was given to him the book of the prophet Isaiah. He opened the book and found the place where it was written, "The Spirit of the Lord is upon me, because he has anointed me to preach good news to the poor. He has sent me to proclaim release to the captives, and recovery of sight to the blind, to set at liberty those who are oppressed, to proclaim the acceptable year of the Lord." And he closed the book and gave it back to the attendant, and sat down; and the eyes of all in the synagogue

were fixed on him. And he began to say to them, "Today this scripture has been fulfilled in your hearing"(Lk 4:16-21).

And when the men had come to him, they said, "John the Baptist has sent us to you saying, 'Are you he who is to come, or shall we look for another?' In that hour he cured many diseases and plagues and evil spirits, and on many that were blind he bestowed sight. And he answered them, 'Go and tell John what you have seen and heard: the blind receive their sight, the lame walk, lepers are cleansed, the deaf hear, the dead are raised up, and the poor have the good news preached to them. And blessed is he who takes no offence at me'"(Lk 7:20-23).

The Parable of Lazarus and the Rich Man in Luke 16:19-31 also has its parallel in St. Matthew's Gospel. The story about Lazarus shows us that unless we practice mercy ourselves, we shall not find mercy in the time of judgment. Although the parable concerning Lazarus is unique to the Gospel according to St. Luke and the Parable of the Sheep and the Goats is unique to St. Matthew's Gospel, both convey a similar message: "I was hungry and you gave me no food. ... Truly I say to you, as you did it not to one of the least of these, you did it not to me" (Mt 25:31-46). On the other hand, for those who fail to practice mercy toward one another, God's mercy is always available if they are truly contrite. Anyone who is able to say with the publican in our Lord's Parable of the Pharisee and the Publican, "Lord, have mercy on me a sinner," will come away "justified," that is, set right with God, restored to fellowship with Him, and enriched with His grace (see Lk 18:9-14).

Study Questions

1. How does Jesus illustrate in His teachings and parables the importance of being merciful to others as our heavenly Father is merciful to us (Lk 6:36)?

2. Why is St. Luke's Gospel additionally called "The Gospel of Mercy"?

3. In what ways is God's mercy manifested in the *Magnificat* and the *Benedictus?*

Discussion Starter:

Read the Parable of The Sheep and the Goats (Mt 25:31-46) and that of The Pharisee and The Publican (Lk 18:9-14). What kind of actions and attitudes does Jesus say we need to have to be in harmony with God's merciful love, receive "justification" and attain everlasting life?

3. THE PARABLES OF MERCY

While the message of God's merciful love permeates St. Luke's Gospel, there is one section of the book that is generally known as the "parables of mercy," a cluster of parables in chapter 15 unique to this Gospel that centers upon the theme of Divine Mercy: the Lost Sheep, the Lost Coin, and the Prodigal Son. In all three parables, what is "lost" is the sinner, because of his sins, and the one who finds him is the merciful Savior-God. These three parables, therefore, focus on one particular form of God's mercy, namely, His mercy that meets our needs for forgiveness and moral renewal.

Let us look at two themes that are common to all three parables.

First, in each one, Jesus emphasizes that He not only welcomes the penitent sinner back — He actively goes out and seeks the sinner until He finds him. God is the "Hound of Heaven," so to speak. This comes out most clearly in the parable of the Lost Sheep:

> What man of you, having a hundred sheep, if he has lost one of them, does not leave the ninety-nine in the wilderness, and go after the one which is lost, until he finds it? And when he has found it, he lays it on his shoulders, rejoicing. And when he comes home, he calls together his friends and his neighbors, saying to them, "Rejoice with me, for I have found my sheep which was lost." Just so, I tell you, there will be more joy in heaven over one sinner who repents than over the ninety-nine righteous persons who need no repentance (Lk 15: 4-7).

Commenting upon the parables in Luke 15, the great Jewish scholar C.G. Montefiore held strongly that these parables emphasize the one absolutely new thing that Jesus came to say: "The idea of a God who will invite the sinner back is not new; the idea of a God who will welcome the sinner back is not new; but the idea of a God who will go and seek for the sinner, and who wants men to do the same, is something completely new." Montefiore would therefore find the very center and soul of the Christian Gospel in Luke 15:1-10, in the story of the shepherd searching for the lost sheep, and the woman searching for the lost coin" (See Rick Torretto, "St. Luke: The Gospel of Divine Mercy," in R. Stackpole, ed., *Divine Mercy: The Heart of the Gospel*, Marian Press, 1999).

We have seen so far that the New Testament does not substantially alter the Old Testament definition of Divine Mercy, but it does show us just how deep and all-encompassing God's merciful love for us really is. The parables of mercy in St. Luke's Gospel reflect this appreciation for the depth of God's mercy shown in the Incarnation and the Redemption of the world through Christ. As St. John wrote in his first epistle: "In this the love of God was made manifest among us, that God sent his only Son into the world that we might live through him. In this is love, not that we loved God, but that he loved us, and sent his Son to be the expiation for our sins"(1 Jn 4:9-12). In other words, God is not just sitting patiently in heaven, waiting for penitent sinners to come home to Him. Rather, our heavenly Father sent His Son into the world to seek us out and find us, like a shepherd seeking his lost sheep, or like the father of a prodigal son who runs down the road to meet his lost son at the first sign of his appearing.

We find the same theme echoed beautifully in the writings of St. Maria Faustina Kowalska (1905-1938). She heard Jesus teach her this same basic Gospel message:

> **My mercy is greater than your sins and those of the entire world. Who can measure the extent of My goodness? For you I descended from heaven to earth; for you I allowed Myself to be nailed to the cross; for you I let My Sacred Heart be pierced with a lance, thus opening wide the source of Mercy for you. Come, then, with trust to draw graces from this fountain** (*Diary*, 1485).

A second theme common to all three parables of mercy in Luke, chapter 15, is the great joy our Lord manifests whenever He is able to rescue lost sinners and bring them home to His Heart:

Luke 15:5:   When he finds his lost sheep he "lays it on his shoulders *rejoicing*."

Luke 15:6:   "And then when he got home, he called together his friends and neighbors, saying to them, "*Rejoice* with me, I have found my sheep that was lost.""

Luke 15:9:   "And when she had found it [the lost coin], she called together her friends and neighbours, saying to them, "*Rejoice* with me, I have found the drachma that I lost.""

Luke 15:32: "But it was only right that we should *celebrate and rejoice*, because your brother here was dead and has come to life; he was lost and is found.""

So God in Christ "rejoices" and is "filled with joy" whenever He finds His lost sheep! This implies an intimacy between our Savior-God and His creatures, an intimacy of which mere hints are given in the Old Testament. It also implies a depth of commitment in God to the good of human beings. In a way similar to St. Luke's use of the phrase *splagchna eleous* (tender mercy), we see how completely God is committed to care for us, a depth of caring love that springs from the very depths of who He is.

A similar truth is echoed in the writings of St. Faustina. Jesus said to her:

> **With My mercy, I pursue sinners along all their paths, and My Heart rejoices when they return to Me. I forget all the bitterness with which they fed My Heart and rejoice in their return. ... What joy fills My Heart when you return to Me. Because you are weak, I take you in My arms and carry you to the home of My Father** (*Diary*, 1728 and 1486).

Let us focus more directly now on the parable of the Prodigal Son. Pope John Paul II, in his encyclical *Dives in*

Misericordia (Rich in Mercy), section 5, focuses explicitly on this parable as portraying for us how Divine Mercy overcomes human sin.

First, the son in the parable begins by asking for his inheritance early. Basically, he says to his father: "I really wish you were dead so that I could have my inheritance; just give me my inheritance now, and I will go off with it and forget all about you — just as if you were dead!"

Second, the father (no doubt sadly) acquiesces and gives his son the inheritance. Then the son goes off and wastes his father's (doubtless hard-earned) gift of money on immoral living. The result is that the son ends up losing most of his human dignity, for the parable says that he finds himself ultimately in a condition lower than the pigs he takes care of just to survive.

Then, verse 17 says, "But when he came to himself" — that is, when he saw something of the truth about himself — he saw into the depths of his "squandered sonship." Pope John Paul II writes:

> He seems not to be conscious of it even now, when he says to himself: "How many of my father's hired servants have bread enough to spare, but I perish here with hunger." He measures himself by the standards of the goods that he has lost, that he no longer 'possesses,' while the hired servants of his father's house 'possess' them. These words express above all his attitude to material goods; nevertheless, under the surface is concealed the tragedy of lost dignity, the awareness of squandered sonship (no. 5).

Up until this point in the parable, the prodigal son's repentance does not appear to be very genuine. There is a strong element of self-seeking calculation — what Catholicism has traditionally called "imperfect contrition" — in his words, "treat me as one of your hired servants," a speech obviously designed just to get him a few decent meals. Nevertheless, he also seems to have gained some kind of appreciation for the offense that he has done to his father, and in addition, an aware-

ness of the fact that he has squandered something precious —
his relationship of sonship to his father — because the speech he
rehearses begins with the words, "Father ... I am no longer
worthy to be called your son." Deep down, he knows that by his
actions he has thrown away more than good food. He has
thrown away a treasured relationship, and he knows as well what
that sin justly deserves.

Then Jesus says: "But when he was still far off" — that
is, when the prodigal son's repentance was still half-hearted
and imperfect — "his father saw him." The father must have
been gazing down the road constantly, hoping and praying to
see his son return one day (which is why he caught sight of
him when he was still "far off"); the father had compassion on
him (*splagchna eleous* again — compassion from the "guts"),
and ran and embraced and kissed him" (literally in the Greek
text: "showered him with kisses").

That was no way for a Middle-Eastern father to behave!
By rights, he should have made the son who had offended him
at least grovel in the dust before forgiving him. But that would
not be in accord with this father's merciful heart. In fact, by
running out to embrace him with tenderness, the father
obviously moves to the depths the heart of his son, enabling
and assisting his son to make his contrition more perfect. This
is clear from the fact that when the son recites his prepared
speech — "Father, I have sinned against heaven and before you;
I am no longer worthy to be called your son" — he leaves out
the last line: "Treat me as one of your hired servants!"

There is no longer any selfish calculation involved: In the
light of his father's boundless, tender love for him, he just
acknowledges his grievous sin and pleads to his father for a full
restoration of their broken relationship. Moreover, there is no
longer any doubt in his mind about his father's merciful love.
He "throws himself on the mercy of the court," so to speak,
trusting now that this court — his father's merciful heart — is
full of compassion and love.

What we see in the story of the Prodigal Son, therefore,
is a father who reflects both aspects of Divine Mercy:

1. His faithfulness to himself, to his commitments as a father to care for his children, and thus his *hesed*, and

2. His passionate pity for his lost son's plight; in other words his *rachamim*.

Pope John Paul II, therefore, concludes in his encyclical *Dives in Misericordia* that what we see happen to the prodigal son in this parable is a grace-assisted repentance that restores his true dignity as a son of his father:

> Mercy — as Christ has presented it in the parable of the prodigal son — has the interior form of the love that in the New Testament is called *agape*. This love is able to reach down to every prodigal son, to every human misery, and above all to every form of moral misery, to sin. When this happens, the person who is the object of mercy does not feel humiliated, but rather found again and "restored to value." The father first and foremost expresses to him his joy that he has been "found again" and that he has "returned to life." This joy indicates a good that has remained intact: even if he is a prodigal, a son does not cease to be truly his father's son. It also indicates a good that has been found again, which in the case of the prodigal son was his return to the truth about himself (no. 6).

4. DIVINE MERCY IS FOR EVERYONE

The third thing that makes St. Luke's Gospel the Gospel of Mercy is its special emphasis on the universal scope of Divine Mercy: God intends to embrace all people with His mercy, through Jesus Christ. We have already seen this theme in the canticles in the first chapter of the Gospel, especially in the *Benedictus* of Zechariah, where he sings a hymn of praise to the Lord who gives "light to those who dwell in darkness, and the shadow of death"—that is, to the Gentiles. We find the same theme in the *Nunc Dimittis* of old Simeon in chapter two. Simeon speaks of Christ as a light for everyone: "For mine eyes have seen thy salvation, which thou has prepared before the presence of all peoples, a light for revelation to the Gentiles, and for glory to thy people Israel."

The universality of Divine Mercy is a recurrent theme in St. Luke's Gospel. In chapter three, for example, he quotes Isaiah 40:3-5 as a prophecy about the coming of John the Baptist ("the voice of one crying in the wilderness"), but unlike St. Matthew (who quotes the same prophecy), Luke quotes its final line: "And all flesh [that is, all humanity] shall see the salvation of God." Saint Luke also traces the genealogy of Jesus in chapter three not just back to Abraham — the father of the Jewish nation according to the Bible — as St. Matthew had done, but all the way back to Adam, the father of all mankind. Luke ends his genealogy with the words, "the son of Adam, the son of God," thereby identifying God as Adam's father. In short, Luke seems to be saying that all descendents of Adam are children of God, and this is another sign that Jesus' saving mission is intended to be universal in scope.

Another way that St. Luke emphasizes this theme is by including in his Gospel stories of how Jesus reached out to all kinds of people, of every gender, class, race, and moral character. In his essay "St. Luke, the Gospel of Mercy" (in *Divine Mercy: The Heart of the Gospel*, Marian Press, 1999, p. 25), Rick Torretto points out that if we confine ourselves to material unique to St. Luke's Gospel, we can see that he deliberately included many stories about Jesus that stress this theme. We find:

1. The cure of the servant of a centurion, who was a military officer from the dreaded Roman army occupying Palestine.

2. A son is raised to life because he was the only son of a widow who would be left destitute without him.

3. A woman of questionable reputation who anoints Jesus.

4. Female disciples who travel with and supported Jesus in His ministry; women were considered second-class citizens in ancient Israel.

5. Jesus cures a demoniac, at the very least a psychologically challenged person!

6. He tells the parable of the Good Samaritan; Samaritans were considered heretical, sectarian half-breeds.

7. In another parable, Lazarus, a homeless, poor, sick individual, is welcomed into Abraham's bosom in heaven.

8. Jesus touches and cures lepers: medical, social, and religious outcasts.

9. In another parable, a Pharisee is criticized, while a Publican (a tax collector and collaborator with the Roman occupation) is praised for his faith and humility — so, "politically correct" ideas are turned upside-down!

10. Jesus dines with the tax collector Zacchaeus.

11. He even asks forgiveness for those who crucify Him.

Torretto concludes:

Each of these people is a complete outsider either socially or religiously. The Kingdom of God, Divine Mercy, is freely given to each as a gift. The only thing that stops them from accepting the gift of God is their own refusal to repent and seek forgiveness.

Lest we miss the point, Luke reiterates it in recording Jesus' final commission to His disciples — and this material is unique to Luke:

Jesus said to them: "So it is written that the Christ would suffer and on the third day rise from the dead, and that in his name, repentance for the forgiveness of sins would be preached to all nations, beginning with Jerusalem" (Lk 24:46-47; also see Mt 28:18-20).

Here we see a theme that will later find an echo in the *Diary of St. Faustina*. Jesus said to her:

Urge all souls to trust in the unfathomable abyss of My mercy, because I want to save them all. On the cross, the fountain of My Mercy was opened wide by the lance for all souls — no one have I excluded! (*Diary*, 1182).

Study Questions

1. What "absolutely new thing" do we learn about Divine Mercy from the three "parables of mercy," according to C.G. Montefiore?

2. How does Jesus illustrate in the three "parables of mercy" the joy in the Heart of God — that is, in His own Heart — at the return to Him of penitent sinners?

3. What does the prodigal son recover through his repentance? How does his father's reaction to his return home help him recover it?

Discussion Starter:

Was Jesus "soft" on sin? In other words, if He taught that Divine Mercy is for everyone, does that mean that Jesus does not care whether or not unjust "tax collectors" and "adulterers" and other genuine sinners actually repent? (Read Lk 19:1-10 and Jn 8:1-11). What is the difference between the universality of Divine Mercy and divine "permissiveness" or "indifference" to sin? Discuss how the attitude and actions of the father of the prodigal son might be reflected in our own toward those who wrong us (see Lk 6:36).

5. THE CROSS AND THE RESURRECTION

Although the message of Divine Mercy is prominent in the teachings of Jesus and expressed through His works of healing throughout His ministry, the Gospel writers emphasize that the Cross and the Resurrection of Jesus, above all, is the most decisive breakthrough of God's merciful love in the world. For example, after St. Peter's confession of faith in Christ in chapter 9 of St. Luke's Gospel, the rest of the book tells the story of Jesus' final missionary walk from Galilee to Jerusalem, His arrest, trial, crucifixion, and Resurrection. In other words, the story of the Cross and of Easter really begins at Luke 9:22, and continues right to the end of the Gospel in chapter 24. This clearly illustrates the overwhelming importance to St. Luke of these events in the story of God's merciful love.

When our Lord was dying on the Cross, He never ceased to shower his merciful love upon those around Him. For example, He prayed for His persecutors: "Father, forgive them, for they know not what they do" (Lk 23:34). He gave the hope of pardon and eternal peace to the penitent thief crucified alongside Him: "Truly I say to you, today you shall be with me in paradise" (Lk 23:43). He even made provision for the care of His mother from the Cross, and gave her to us as Mother of all Christians: "Woman, behold your son ... son, behold your mother!" (Jn 19:26-27).

By dying on the Cross for our sins, Jesus satisfied the requirements of Divine Justice for us — but He went way beyond justice, obtaining for us an infinite ocean of graces of His merciful love. Pope John Paul II explained this in *Dives in Misericordia*:

In the Passion and Death of Christ — in the fact that the Father did not spare His own Son, but "for our sake made him sin"— absolute justice is expressed, for Christ undergoes the passion and cross because of the sins of humanity. This constitutes even a "superabundance" of justice, for the sins of man are "compensated for" by the sacrifice of the Man-God. Nevertheless, this justice, which is properly justice "to God's measure," springs completely from love: from the love of the Father and the Son, and completely bears fruit in love. ... The divine dimension of the redemption is put into effect not only by bringing justice to bear upon sin, but also by restoring to love that creative power in man thanks to which he once more has access to the fullness of life and holiness that come from God. In this way, redemption involves the revelation of mercy in its fullness (no. 7).

The Gospel according to St. John reports a detail of the death of Jesus that manifests God's mercy in an especially vivid way. In chapter 19 of his Gospel, St. John writes:

One of the [Roman] soldiers pierced His side with a spear, and at once there came out blood and water. He who saw it has borne witness — his testimony is true (19:34-35).

On the one hand, a flow of blood and water (plasma) is precisely what medical science would expect to observe issuing from the pierced heart and lung of a crucified human being. Yet the meaning of this passage goes far beyond the physiological facts. As the Second Vatican Council put it: "The origin and growth of the Church are symbolized by the blood and water which flowed from the open side of the crucified Jesus" (*Lumen Gentium*, no. 3). As Adam's bride, Eve, was taken from his side while he slept (Gen 2: 21-22), so the Bride of Christ, the Church, was born from the wounded side of Jesus, the Second Adam. God the Son, in His mercy, betrothed Himself to the human race through His Church, giving His life for her on the Cross (Mt 25:1-13; Mk 1:18-20; Eph 5: 21-33; Rev 19:9; 21: 1-5; 22:17). In fact, as we shall see later in the writings of St. Catherine of Siena and St. Faustina Kowalska, there are even deeper layers of meaning in this symbolic blood and water that flowed from the side of the crucified Savior.

According to John Paul II, the Resurrection is a testimony to Divine Mercy through and through. For the Resurrection shows us not only that Christ's love was more powerful than sin and death, but more powerful than OUR sin and OUR death! His Resurrection is for US, not just for Himself: He rises to new life in order to be with us always, to the end of time (see Mt 28:20), to fill us with His new life and thereby enable us to share in His Easter triumph. Pope John Paul II writes of this in *Dives in Misericordia*:

> Here is the Son of God, who in His resurrection experienced in a radical way mercy shown to Himself — that is to say, the love of the Father, which is *more powerful than death*. And it is also the same Christ, the Son of God, who at the end of His messianic mission ... reveals Himself as the inexhaustible source of mercy, of the same love that, in a subsequent perspective of the history of salvation in the Church, is to be everlastingly confirmed as more powerful than sin. The paschal Christ is *the definitive incarnation of mercy*. ... In the same spirit, the liturgy of Eastertide places on our lips the words of the psalm: '*Misericordia Domini in aeternum cantabo.*'

> 'I will sing of the mercies of the Lord forever!' (no. 8)

6. THE GOSPEL OF THE COMING KINGDOM

Throughout the Gospels, we find another important theme which is an integral part of "the good news" Jesus came to bring. Central to His preaching was Jesus' promise of the coming of "the kingdom of God." By "the kingdom" He meant the reign of God over all of creation and over every aspect of human life: God's reign over sin by His forgiveness and grace, over suffering by healing, over slavery by liberation, and over by death by everlasting life. Wherever Jesus, the rightful King, is present God's kingdom begins to dawn. That is why Jesus opened His public ministry with the words: "The kingdom of God is at hand; repent and believe in the gospel" (Mk 1:15). The fact that He cast out demons was already a sign that God was beginning to liberate people from Satan's tyrannical hold on human life: "If it is by the finger of God that I cast out demons, then the kingdom of God has come upon you" (Lk 11:20).

Of course, Jesus was well aware that the kingdom of God had not yet come to earth in its fullness during the time of His earthly ministry. He promised that it would grow like a tiny mustard seed into a great tree (Mt 13: 31-32), and gradually leaven the world as yeast leavens a new loaf of bread (Mt 13:33) — and all this would be a free gift of God's grace and merciful love. "Fear not, little flock," He said, "for it is your Father's good pleasure to give you the kingdom" (Lk 12:32), and He taught His disciples to pray with hope and expectation: "Father ... thy kingdom come" (Lk 11:2). Moreover, Jesus knew it would take more than just gradual growth and "leavening" for God's kingdom to come to the world in all its fullness. On the road to God's final victory over the forces of evil, there would be cataclysmic events, Jesus predicted: earthquakes, plagues, wars, famines, the fall of the Great Temple in Jerusalem, and the worldwide persecution of His followers. God's ultimate triumph, however, was assured, and Jesus promised that one day He would return to earth with all the angels of heaven to bring the kingdom to its consummation:

> Immediately after the tribulation of those days the sun will be darkened, and the moon will not give its light, and the stars will fall from heaven, and the powers of heaven will be shaken; then will appear the sign of the Son of Man in heaven, and then all the tribes of the earth will mourn, and they will see the Son of Man coming on the clouds of heaven with power and great

glory; and he will send out his angels with a loud trumpet call, and they will gather his elect from the four winds, from one end of heaven to the other (Mt 24:29-31).

For those who are cruel and impenitent to the end, they have only the justice and wrath of God to look forward to, but for those who are faithful, the Second Coming of Jesus is the final triumph of His mercy: "Now when these things begin to take place, look up and raise your heads, because your redemption is drawing near" (Lk 21:28).

7. THE MERCY MESSAGE OF ST. PETER AND ST. PAUL

If the Gospels show us God's mercy expressed in decisive acts for our salvation (such as the Incarnation, Cross, and Resurrection of His Son), the Apostolic letters in the New Testament are the praise and proclamation of that mercy, and an exhortation to practice it.

Saint Paul gives us the most comprehensive doctrine of Divine Mercy. For him, Divine Mercy, considered as God's merciful love toward human beings, is essentially synonymous with God Himself. For example, he begins his second epistle to the Corinthians with the words: "Blessed be the God and Father of our Lord Jesus Christ, the Father of mercies and the God of all comfort" (2 Cor 1:3). According to St. Paul, it was from out of the depths of God's merciful love that the Father brought us back from spiritual death to new life in Christ:

> But God, who is rich in mercy, out of the great love with which he loved us, even when we were dead through our trespasses, made us alive again with Christ (by grace you have been saved), and raised us up with him, and made us sit with him in the heavenly places in Christ Jesus, that in the coming ages he

might show the immeasurable riches of his grace in kindness toward us in Christ Jesus (Eph 2: 4-7).

Perhaps most memorable of all of St. Paul's words in this regard are his words regarding the merciful love of Jesus Christ manifested in His death on the Cross for us:

> While we were still weak, at the right time Christ died for the ungodly. Why, one will hardly die for a righteous man — though perhaps for a good man one will dare even to die. But God shows his love for us in that while we were yet sinners, Christ died for us. Since, therefore, we are now justified by his blood, much more shall we be saved by him from the wrath of God. For if while we were enemies we were reconciled to God by the death of his Son, much more, now that we are reconciled, shall we be saved by his life. Not only so, but we also rejoice in God through our Lord Jesus Christ, through whom we have now received our reconciliation (Rom 5:6-11).

In fact, St. Paul's thoughts here find an echo in the book of Hebrews, which describes Jesus as "a merciful and faithful High Priest before God" (2:17), precisely because Jesus has made the perfect atoning sacrifice for our sins on the Cross.

Saint Paul then bases the moral imperatives that he teaches on this Gospel of Mercy — as God through Christ has been merciful to us, so we also ought to be merciful to one another: "Let all bitterness and wrath and anger and clamor and slander be put away from you, with all malice, and be kind to one another, tenderhearted, forgiving one another, as God in Christ forgave you" (Eph 4:31-32). Similarly, St. Paul writes in Colossians: "Put on then, as God's chosen ones, holy and beloved, compassion [the Greek phrase here is *splagchna eleous*, mercy from the very depths or guts], kindness, lowliness, meekness, and patience, forbearing one another, and, if one has a complaint against each other, forgiving each other; as the Lord has forgiven you, so you must also forgive" (Col 3:12).

Finally, for St. Paul, God's mercy is seen in the epistle to the Romans as the only possible explanation of why He allowed the whole human race — both Jew and Gentile alike — to fall into sin: "For God has consigned all men to disobedience, that he might have mercy on all" (Rom 11:32). In other words, God permitted evil, sin, and unfaithfulness in order to show a mercy that was even greater than sin and death. Thus, even sin and death results in God being glorified in the end, even more so than if He had not permitted human beings to fall.

Saint Peter also focuses his teaching on the merciful love of God. We need to remember that Peter was the apostle who denied three times that he knew Jesus on the night of his Master's arrest, despite boasting that he would never forsake Jesus, even if all the other apostles did. Thus, when St. Peter writes of the "mercy" of the Lord manifest on Easter morning, he is speaking from his own personal experience:

> Blessed be the God and Father of our Lord Jesus Christ! By his great mercy we have been born anew to a living hope through the resurrection of Jesus Christ from the dead, and to an inheritance which is imperishable, undefiled, and unfading, kept in heaven for you, who by God's power are guarded through faith for a salvation ready to be revealed in the last time (1 Pet 1:3-5).

Notice that where St. Peter emphasizes the Resurrection-aspect of the paschal mystery as the principal manifestation of God's merciful love for us, St. Paul often emphasized the Cross. Saint Peter focuses on Easter as the foundation of Christian hope, for in the Resurrection God has shown the unfading, imperishable, eternal destiny that He has prepared for us.

Also, for St. Peter, the Church itself, the New Israel of God, is a people that by definition have received the mercy of God:

> But you are a chosen race, a royal priesthood, a holy

nation, God's own people, that you may declare the wonderful deeds of Him who called you out of darkness into His marvelous light. Once you were no people, but now you are God's people; once you had not received mercy, but now you have received mercy (1 Pet 2: 9-10).

In the light of this Gospel of Mercy, St. Peter then enumerates the virtues that he expects the disciples of Christ to practice:

Finally, all of you, have unity of spirit, sympathy, love of the brethren, a tender heart and a humble mind. Do not return evil for evil or reviling for reviling; but on the contrary bless, for to this you have been called, that you may obtain a blessing (1 Pet 3:8).

We find a similar teaching in the epistle of St. James, where, in passing, he reminds his hearers that "judgment is without mercy to one who has shown no mercy" (2:13). In other words, "Blessed are the merciful, for they shall obtain mercy" (Mt 5:7). Later, St. James sums up his exhortations with a call for living a mercy that comes from above:

But the wisdom from above is first pure, then peaceable, gentle, open to reason, full of mercy and good fruits, without uncertainty or insincerity. And the harvest of righteousness is sown in peace by those who make peace (Jas 3:17).

8. CONCLUSION

The Gospel message of Divine Mercy "in a nutshell" is summed up for us in the Gospel according to St. John: "God so loved the world [that is, with merciful love, a love seeking to meet the needs and overcome the miseries of his creatures] that he gave his only Son, that whoever believes in him should not perish, but have eternal life" (Jn 3:16). In other words, if we "believe" in Him (that is, not just with our minds, but with a total entrustment of our hearts and lives to Him) then we shall have the gift of eternal life. "Thanks be to God, who gives us the victory through our Lord Jesus Christ!" (1 Cor 15:57).

Study Questions

1. According to Pope John Paul II in *Dives in Misericordia*, what did the Son of God accomplish on the Cross for us?

2. According to this same document, what did Jesus Christ accomplish by His Resurrection from the dead?

3. Why did St. Paul claim that Christians should be compassionate, tender-hearted, and forgiving toward one another?

Discussion Starter:

Saint Peter teaches that Christians are, by definition, people who have "received mercy" (1 Pet 2:10). Do you think that most Catholics think of themselves that way? What would you say to one who doesn't?

PART TWO

Divine Mercy in the Lives
of the Saints

CHAPTER ONE

St. Augustine

"Though I am but dust and ashes, suffer me to utter my plea to Thy mercy; suffer me to speak, since it is to God's mercy that I speak and not to man's scorn. From Thee too I might have scorn, but Thou wilt return and have compassion on me. ... I only know that the gifts Thy mercy had provided sustained me from the first moment. ... All my hope is naught save in Thy great mercy. Grant what Thou dost command, and command what Thou wilt" (St. Augustine of Hippo, *Confessions*, 6, 19).

The man who wrote these lines in his autobiography had reason enough to praise the infinite mercy of God.

Saint Augustine was born in 354 in a small town in what is now Algeria, North Africa. His father was a pagan, but his mother was a devout Christian believer who was later canonized and is known to the whole Catholic world as St. Monica. As a young man, Augustine prepared for a career as a teacher of Rhetoric and subsequently taught in Carthage and Rome. Unfortunately, despite having a saint for a mother, as his career progressed he wandered far from his Christian upbringing, and his life sank into an abyss of pride and lust. Like many young pagan men of his time, he lived with a mistress and conceived a child with her out of wedlock. However, the Lord did not want to lose hold of this lost sheep altogether: thus, inspired by the writings of the Roman philosopher Cicero (and, no doubt, prompted by the Holy Spirit), Augustine began what would prove to be a lifelong search for wisdom. This search took him first to the religious cult called the "Manichees," a strange sect that believed the material world is the product of the powers of "darkness," while the spiritual realm is the realm of "light."

After becoming disillusioned with the bizarre theories of the Manichees, Augustine adopted the philosophy of the Neo-Platonists. This was a school of philosophy centered on the writings of the ancient philosopher Plotinus, who described the mystical journey that all people ought to undertake as "the flight of the alone to the Alone," in other words, as a mystical, solitary search for the ineffable Source of all things.

In 386, Augustine moved to Milan to a new teaching post, and there, by divine providence, he encountered the preaching of the archbishop of the city, the great theologian St. Ambrose. As a result of the example and preaching of this great saint, as well as the prayers and tears of his saintly mother, Augustine was quickly plunged into a profound inner struggle, wrestling with his sins of the flesh and with temptations to intellectual pride. The turning point of this struggle came in the summer of 386 when Augustine was sitting in a garden, recollecting his past life and gazing into the depths of his own soul. He describes what happened next in his autobiographical *Confessions* (written in 397):

> Such things I said, weeping in the most bitter sorrow of my heart. And suddenly, I heard a voice from some nearby house, a boy's voice or a girl's voice, I do not know: but it was a sort of sing-song repeated again and again, "Take and read, take and read." I ceased weeping and immediately began to search my mind most carefully as to whether children were accustomed to chant these words in any kind of game, and I could not remember that I had ever heard any such thing. Damming back the flood of my tears I arose, interpreting the incident as quite certainly a divine command to open my book of Scripture and read the passage at which I should open. ... I snatched it up, opened it, and in silence read the passage upon which my eyes first fell:

"Not in rioting and drunkenness, not in chambering and impurities, not in contention and envy, but put ye on the Lord Jesus Christ and make no provision for the flesh in its concupiscences" (Rom 13:13). I had no wish to read further, and no need. For in that instant, with the very ending of the sentence, it was as though a light of utter confidence shone in my heart, and all the darkness of uncertainty vanished away.

Then we [Augustine and his friend Alypius] went in to my mother and told her, to her great joy. We related how it had come about: she was filled with triumphant exultation, and praised You who are mighty beyond what we ask or conceive: for she saw that You had given her more than with all her pitiful weeping she had ever asked. For You converted me to Yourself ... (*Confessions*, 8.11-12).

1. ST. AUGUSTINE'S INTELLECTUAL LIFE AFTER HIS CONVERSION

Saint Augustine's intellectual development after his conversion can be divided into several phases. In the first phase, he was still a follower of the philosophy of Plotinus and sought to interpret and defend the Christian faith with the help of this philosophy (St. Clement of Alexandria in the East had tried much the same thing). After he became a bishop, however, he became more interested in Scriptural study, especially the letters of St. Paul and the Psalms. Divine Revelation became for Augustine more than just the mystical philosophy of Plotinus with the doctrines of Creation (*creatio ex nihilo*) and the Incarnation thrown in for good measure. Rather, in this period Augustine began to plumb the depths of what it means for God's grace to come to the aid of a sinful soul through prayer and the Sacraments.

This is the period in his life that produced written works that "moderate Augustinians" would refer to so often. Here Augustine emphasizes that God in His mercy always takes the initiative with the sinner, because the sinner is too weak even to stretch out his hands to God in prayer on his own. Augustine taught that salvation cannot be gained merely by the soul receiving proper moral and doctrinal instruction and by following the example of Jesus and the saints. Rather, salvation involves the entire inner renewal of the soul by divine grace, received as a free gift from God through prayer and the Sacraments of the Church. The teachings of this period of St. Augustine's life, such as his treatise "On Forgiveness and the Just Deserts of Sins, and the Baptism of Infants," became standard fare for theology in the West, both Catholic and Protestant, and were largely endorsed by the Western Council of Orange in 529.

Reflections on Divine Mercy can be found in St. Augustine's writings that come from this period of his life. For example, here is his commentary on Psalm 58, from the phrase in the Latin Vulgate version of the Psalm, "My God is my mercy":

> Lastly, considering that every type of good thing we may possess — either as gifts of nature, or through education or social relationships, or through the gifts of faith, hope, and charity, or moral goods such as justice, or fear of God — are nothing but [God's] gifts, [the Psalmist] concludes thus: "My God is my mercy."... Now, since none is better than You, none more powerful than You, and none is more generous in mercy than You from whom I received that I exist, from You I received [the grace] that I [can] be good.

Later in his life, however, St. Augustine's view of human nature and its corruption took a more pessimistic turn. It is not hard to see the roots of his discouragement with the human species. For example, as Bishop of Hippo he had to contend first with the Donatist schism, which split the North African Church for over a century. The Donatists taught that only Sacraments administered by pure and holy priests were valid — which meant that no Christian could ever be sure he was receiving valid Sacraments and the grace those Sacraments contain, since no one can have an in-depth knowledge of the hearts of the priests performing them. In essence, the Donatists undermined the confidence of Catholics in the Sacraments as means of grace. In the end, imperial military force was called in to support the Catholic side in the dispute.

Augustine's attempts to deal with this ecclesiastical conflict were long, tiring, and largely futile. In the end, he reluctantly agreed to support the imperial policy of coercion, as long as it was limited to the use of pressure and "rebuke" rather than crude physical force. However, no sooner was the Donatist situation under control than Augustine faced another mounting heresy, the Pelagian heresy, which denied the need for inner regeneration of the soul by God's invisible, divine grace. This controversy would involve St. Augustine in theological labors that would last most of the rest of his life.

In addition to these ecclesiastical and theological trials and tribulations, Augustine had to contend with the horrors of the barbarian invasions. The whole of Western Roman civilization was rapidly crumbling around him. In 407, barbarian tribes overran Roman Gaul, then crossed into Spain in 409, bringing pillage, rape, and murder wherever they went. In 410, the city of Rome itself was sacked by Alaric and the Goths. Refugees poured into North Africa and the safer Christian East. To gain an appreciation of what Augustine and his fellow bishops had to face in those dark times, here is a passage from the historian Henry Chadwick's book *The Early Church* that vividly describes the scene:

> Augustine's last letters dealt with the problem of conscience whether clergy might join with the refugees and flee [the oncoming barbarian armies]. In Gaul and Spain the bishops of many cities, such as

Toulouse, had been the principal organizers of resistance to the invaders; but some bishops had gone with
those who fled before the murdering, plundering
hordes. What were the African clergy to do? Augustine
did not want all the best priests to be lost in the
oncoming massacre. Yet there was a clear duty to be
there to minister to those who would be clamoring for
baptism or for the last rites before the cruel invaders
cut their throats. Augustine recommended that some
should go and some should stay, and that to avoid
invidious decisions the clergy should cast lots. He
himself stayed in Hippo for the Vandal siege, but died
on August 28, 430, before the barbarians broke
through the defenses (Pelican edition, 1967, p. 24).

It was in the midst of this dreadful situation that St.
Augustine finished writing his most famous work, *The City of
God*, in which he tried to show that although human history
is a record of war and strife, still, by the mercy of God, the city
of God (the kingdom of heaven) endures, and it is built up
through the means of grace that God gives to us in the
Church, which will abide forever, and whose duty it is now to
convert the barbarian invaders to the Christian faith.

This was also the time in Augustine's life when he put
the final form on his doctrine of salvation as a manifestation
of the mercy of God. Whether or not Augustine's doctrine in
this regard truly manifests God's merciful love in the way that
he intended, however, remains a contentious theological
point in the Christian world to this very day.

2. SALVATION AND PREDESTINATION

Let us return to the writings of the Patristics scholar
Henry Chadwick, and his summary of St. Augustine's fully
developed doctrine of salvation. Chadwick writes:

According to the doctrine that Augustine opposed to the Pelagians, the entire [human] race fell in Adam. ... The transmission of hereditary sinfulness is bound up with the reproductive process. The general belief that virginity is a higher state than marriage proved for Augustine that the sexual impulse can never be free of some element of concupiscence [that is, of disordered passion, lust]. In any event, the practice of infant baptism for the remission of sins presupposes that infants arrive polluted by sin; since they have committed no actual sin, remission must be for the guilt attaching to a fault in their nature. Therefore, if babies die unbaptized, they are damned, even though [Augustine says] it will be a "very mild" form of damnation. Mankind is a lump of perdition, incapable, without redeeming grace, of any act of pure good will, and all the virtues of the good pagan are vitiated by sin. ... If all humanity were consigned to hell, that would be nothing but strict justice. Nevertheless, God's mercy is such that, inscrutably, He has chosen a fairly substantial minority of souls for salvation by a decree of predestination, which is antecedent to all differences of merit. To complain that this election is unjust is to fail to consider the gravity of the guilt attaching to original sin, and yet more to actual sin.

A necessary corollary of this doctrine of predestination is that [saving] grace is irresistible. If man is so corrupt that he no longer has free will to do good, grace must do all; and that this power is irresistible is a plain deduction from the divine decree of predestination, which otherwise would be frustrated. It is the purpose of God to bring His elect, infallibly, to a certain end. Accordingly, the empirical test of the operation of grace lies in man's consistent goodness of character right through to the end of his life, a "final perseverance" which is a foreordained gift of God, independent of merit (p. 232).

While Chadwick's summary is true as far as it goes, he does not give St. Augustine sufficient credit for seeking to preserve the reality of human free will in the process of salvation, or for recognizing that this whole matter of predestination is a deep and unfathomable mystery. Patristics scholar Richard Price rounds out the picture for us:

[According to Augustine,] man in his fallen state is only capable of evil, but God is able to rescue him not by overriding his free will but precisely by empowering it. Evil is not something concrete and positive, but a mere deficiency, an absence of the good. Every created being in virtue of his mere existence has some share of the good; every conscious and rational being has some potential to respond to the grace of God. In fallen man this potential is so weakened as to be wholly dormant. But divine grace is able to bring this potential to realization, to reawaken and reanimate the natural powers within the soul of every human being: this it does by acting through both external stimuli [for example, preaching, the Sacraments, and the good example of Christ and the saints] and inner assistance within the will itself. As beings endowed with free will, we could choose to resist the healing action of God; but God can so work on us that we have not the faintest inclination to exercise this freedom. ...

Since [Augustine] was sure that God is able to save whomever he pleases, and yet believed that not all are saved, he concluded that God does not wish to save everyone. How is this compatible with the Christian doctrine that God is love? Augustine argued that because of the guilt of original sin everyone deserves eternal damnation. The amazing thing is not that many are damned but that any at all are saved. While the damnation of the many is required by the justice of God, the salvation of the few is proof of the depths of his mercy. God does not choose to damn anyone: in the case of the majority he simply allows the effect of sin to take its natural course. Meanwhile, he shows his love by rescuing the few; he uses all the resources of his grace to ensure their salvation, despite the effects of original sin. ...

He insists that God must have good reasons for making the selection he does, even if these reasons are for us an inscrutable mystery, hidden in the secret abyss of divine wisdom (*Augustine*. Liguori Press, 1996, pp. 52, and 56-57).

The Catholic Church has never endorsed some aspects of this full-blown Augustinian doctrine of salvation and predestination — and for good reason, for it is hard to see how it entirely fits with the Church's faith in the merciful love of God. For example:

(a) The Church has never taught that the corruption of the soul from original sin is transmitted to each infant by the inordinate passions involved in the sexual intercourse that conceived it (see the *Catechism of the Catholic Church*, 402-406). Saint Augustine's view here contradicts God's mercy because it seems to imply that He has permitted sin completely to corrupt the natural process by which He brings new life into the world.

(b) The Church has certainly defined that the Baptism of infants is a good ecclesiastical tradition because it pours sanctifying grace into the child's soul right from the start of its earthly pilgrimage, the grace that enables the infant to overcome the effects of its inheritance from Adam: the inner disorder and inclination to sin in every human heart coming from "original sin" (*Catechism*, 1250). But the Church has never taught that the inheritance of original sin ascribes to each new generation the kind of "guilt" that involves personal moral responsibility for that state of original sin, and therefore it would in no way be just for God to condemn unbaptized infants even to a "mild form of damnation" on account of an inherited sin that involved no voluntary fault on the part of the infants themselves (see *Catechism*, 1257-1261). Saint Augustine's view here contradicts the Church's understanding of God's compassion for our fallen condition and His merciful love for unbaptized infants.

(c) The Church has always taught that in order for us to be saved, our sinful souls, weakened and corrupted by original and actual sin, must be prompted, strengthened, and assisted by divine grace to enable us to take any and every step on the road to salvation. But the Church has never taught that God's saving grace is irresistible. As the Council of Trent clearly taught, salvation is a work of grace, but it does not happen without the free consent of the souls of the elect (*Catechism*, 1993 and 2002). Saint Augustine's view here seems to contradict God's merciful love because it seems to imply that in some way God compels certain sinners — the elect — to repent and be saved.

Again, we need to acknowledge that St. Augustine had no real intention of entirely eliminating human free consent in the salvation process. As he said in one of his sermons: "He who created you without your cooperation does not justify you without your cooperation. He created you without your knowing it, He does not justify you without your wanting it" (Sermon 11, 13). The paradox in Augustine's theory is that our "wanting it" (if we are among God's "elect") is somehow solely the result of divine action on our will without violating our freedom. The great Augustine scholar Agostino Trape, OSA, explains that behind this aspect of St. Augustine's theology lies the principle of "the omnipotence of the divine action which, although no one can be saved who does not wish to be, can transform every person, without violating his freedom, from one who does not wish to be saved into one who does. ... God always has in reserve a grace which no heart, no matter how hard, resists, since it is given precisely for taking away the hardness of the heart" (*De praed.* s. 8, 13). This is the doctrine of "irresistible grace" (to use Chadwick's phrase) that the Church has hesitated to endorse. One reason for the Church's hesitation here is that "love" as we know it in human personal relationships is not "irresistible": when authentic love is offered, it always respects the real freedom of the beloved not to return that love. A love that irresistibly causes a free response of love, therefore, might be a contradiction in terms. Moreover, the idea of irresistible grace inevitably raises another question. Trape explains:

> The question then arises as to why [God] does not use this grace for all, but permits that some be lost? This is the torturous question which Augustine asks himself, and to which he confesses that he does not know how to respond. ... He therefore bows humbly to the mystery (Serm. 27, 7) ... adding "Grace cannot be unjust, nor can justice be cruel" (De Civ. Dei 12, 27) ("Saint Augustine," in Johannes Quasten, Ed., *Patrology*. Westminster, Maryland, Christian Classics, 1992, p. 443).

(d) The Church has never taught that the solid majority of the human race is destined for hell. The most one could say with any confidence is that only very few enter heaven immediately upon their death (Mt 7:13-14) and therefore vast numbers must have their purification completed in purgatory, by God's great mercy, before they are ready for heaven (Catechism, 1030-1032). Again, St. Augustine's view seems to contradict God's merciful love, for God's mercy would be weak and ineffective if the great mass of humanity is eternally lost.

Despite the extremes of St. Augustine's teaching in his later years, however, we can still trace within his theology a deep appreciation for the merciful love of God. After all, since he sincerely believed that all human beings (apart from divine grace) are worthy of eternal damnation (even unbaptized infants), and since none of us has any capacity at all on our own to repent of our sins and seek divine aid and forgiveness, the fact that anyone at all repents and is saved can only be the work of God's merciful love, pouring out His saving grace upon those who do not deserve it. Moreover, while St. Augustine did call the human race a "lump of perdition" ("*massa damnata*"), Fr. Trape points out that he also wrote of the human race as, in essence, a lump of redemption ("*massa redempta*"): "Through this Mediator [Jesus Christ] there is reconciled to God the mass of the entire human race which is alienated from Him through Adam" (Sermon 293, 8). In fact, St. Augustine's sermons are filled with passages that vividly portray for us God's compassionate, healing love for sinners. For example, he takes the parable of the Good Samaritan as an allegory of God's healing, sanctifying love for weak and sinful souls:

> There are people, ungrateful towards grace, who attribute much to our poor and wounded nature. It is true that man when he was created was given great strength of will, but by sinning he lost it. He fell into death. The robbers left him on the road half-dead. A passing Samaritan lifted him onto his beast of burden. He is still undergoing treatment. ... You will remember, beloved, the man half-dead who was wounded by robbers on the road, how he is consoled, receiving oil and wine for his wounds. His sins, it is true, were already forgiven; and yet his sickness is cured in the inn. The inn, if you can recognize it, is the Church. While in the inn, let us submit to treatment; let us not boast of health while we are still weak. ... Say to your soul, say this: you are still in this life, the flesh is still weak; even after complete forgiveness [in baptism] you were prescribed prayer as a remedy; you still have to say, until your sickness is cured, 'Forgive us our tresspasses.' (S. 131.6.6) (As quoted in Price, *Augustine*, p. 60).

Indeed, throughout St. Augustine's writings there are passages that show us how the Lord seeks to establish an intimate, personal union with the human soul, so that even the first taste of that intimate union in the soul's depths leads to an insatiable hunger and thirst for more. In his *Confessions*, St. Augustine offers himself as a paradigm of this mysterious courtship of the human soul by the merciful God:

> Late have I loved you, O Beauty so ancient and so new, late have I loved you! And behold, you were within me and I was outside, and there I sought for you, and in my deformity I rushed headlong into the well-formed things that you have made. You were with me, and I was not with you. Those outer beauties held me far from you, yet if they had not been in you, they would not have existed at all. You called, and cried out to me and broke open my deafness; you shone forth upon me and you scattered my blindness; you breathed fragrance, and I drew in my breath and I now pant for you; I tasted and I hunger and thirst; you touched me, and I burned for your peace (*Confessions* 10.27).

Saint Augustine's mature doctrine can be found in his *Enchidrion* (Handbook of Christian Doctrine on Faith, Hope, and Love) written between 419 and 422. He starts out the section entitled "Faith in Christ the Redeemer" by apportioning credit (and blame) for the human condition: "We must in no way doubt that the only cause of good things that come our way is the goodness of God, while the cause of our evils is the will of changeable good falling away from the unchangeable good, first the will of an angel [Satan], and then the will of a human being [Adam]." God alone is the source of the regeneration and sanctification of the elect. Augustine quotes St. Paul in Romans 9:16: "So it comes not from the one who runs, but from God who shows mercy." St. Augustine comments:

> Since there is no doubt whatever that a man, if he is already old enough to have the use of reason, cannot believe, hope, or love unless he wills to do so, nor can he win the reward of God's high vocation unless he

runs it willingly, how can it depend not upon human will or exertion, but on the God who shows mercy unless the will itself is prepared by the Lord? ... It remains for us to recognize that the words "So it comes not from the one who wills or runs, but from the God who shows mercy" are said truly, that all [glory] may be given to God, who makes the good will of man ready for His help, and helps the will He has made ready. ... For in sacred scripture we read both "His mercy shall go before me" (Ps 59:10) and "His mercy shall follow me" (Ps 23:6): it goes before the unwilling that they may will, and it follows the willing, that they may not will in vain (no. 32).

For Augustine, the sending of Christ into the world was a gift of pure, undeserved grace (no. 75): "That one great sin [the fall of Adam] which was committed in a place and state of life of such happiness with the result that the whole human race was condemned originally and, so to say, at root in one man, is not undone and washed away except by the one mediator between God and humanity, the man Christ Jesus, who alone was able to be born in such a way that he had no need to be reborn."

Saint Augustine tells us in his *Enchidrion* that God's mercy is expressed especially in the practice of penance:

But we should not despair of God's mercy for the forgiveness of actual crimes, however great, in the holy Church for those who do penance, each in a way appropriate to his sin. But in works of penance, when a sin has been committed of such a kind that he who committed it is also cut off from the Body of Christ, time should not be measured so much as sorrow, since God does not despise a broken and contrite heart (no. 65).

He continues in the same work:

Penance itself, when there is a good reason for doing

it according to the custom of the Church, is often neglected because of weakness, for shame brings with it a fear of being ill thought of when we care more for the good opinion of others than for the righteousness that leads a person to humiliate himself in penance. So we need God's mercy not only when we do penance, but in order to do penance (no. 82).

In fact, Augustine writes, forgiveness of sins is so readily available in the Church that the only unforgivable sin — the sin against the Holy Spirit — is not to believe that sins are forgiven in the Church (see no. 83).

The only unfortunate aspect of St. Augustine's treatment of Divine Mercy in his *Enchidrion* comes in his discussion of predestination. Saint Paul says in Romans that God's will is to "have mercy on all" (Rom 11:32), and in his first epistle to Timothy he writes: "His will is for all to be saved and come to the knowledge of the truth" (2:4). It is hard to see how this scriptural teaching about God's offer of mercy to "all" fits with what St. Augustine writes here:

> God makes out of the mass of perdition [that is, out of fallen humanity] that has flowed from [Adam's stock] some vessels of honor and some of dishonor; the vessels of honor he makes through his mercy, those of dishonor through his justice, so that nobody may boast of humanity and consequently nobody may boast of himself. ... That is, he has mercy in his great generosity, and he hardens the heart without any unfairness, so that one who has been set free should not boast of his merits, nor should one who has been damned complain, except of his lack of merits. For grace alone distinguishes the redeemed from the lost, who have been formed into one mass of perdition by a cause common to all from which they draw from their origin. ... So, almighty God either in his mercy shows mercy to whom he will or through justice hardens whom he will, and never

does anything unfairly or unwillingly, and does everything that he wills (*Enchidrion* no. 107, 98, 102).

The underlying thought here is that God wills to have
mercy on some sinners, but not on all of them. Original and
actual sin has left all people worthy only of damnation. By His
eternal decree, however, and as an act of sheer mercy, God has
elected some sinners to be the objects of His mercy, objects of
His (evidently irresistible) saving grace, while others His
mercy has simply passed by. They are treated solely as objects
of His justice, for he leaves them wallowing in sin and its con-
sequences. They have no right to complain, however, because
they are only receiving what they deserve.

What has happened here is that St. Augustine has treated
God's justice and God's mercy almost as alternatives, almost as
if they are two distinct "sides" of God's nature, so to speak. He
reaches out to some sinners with His mercy-side, while other
sinners encounter only His justice-side. Yet it is not at all clear
how God could be said to will the gift of mercy for "all" (Rom
11:32) or will "all to be saved" (1 Tim. 2:4), as St. Paul clearly
taught, if God in fact bestows His mercy only on some, while
others are completely passed by. The damned may indeed only
receive in the end what they truly deserve, but how can God be
said to desire to have mercy on them if He never gave to them,
at some point in their lives, grace sufficient for them to be saved,
if only they would have received and cooperated with it?

This brings us to the centuries-long conflict between the
Jesuits and the Dominicans (and in another way, in the
Protestant world, between the Arminians and the Calvinists)
regarding the whole doctrine of predestination. We certainly do
not have the space to unfold that theological controversy here.
Suffice it to say that the Dominicans generally held to the view
of St. Augustine, while the Jesuits objected to their formulation
of the doctrine. Both points of view are permissible within the
Catholic Church, according to the Magisterium. Quite apart
from the technicalities of that debate, however, is the danger of
seeing God's justice and mercy as alternative ways in which He

relates to His creatures — opposite sides of His "character," so to speak.

A surface reading of St. Maria Faustina Kowalska's *Diary* also might lead us to believe in this two-sided God. For example, St. Faustina heard Jesus say that those who run away from His merciful Heart will fall into the hands of His justice (see *Diary*, 1728) and with regard to purgatory, our Lord told her, "My mercy does not want this, but justice demands it" (*Diary*, 20). On the other hand, there are plenty of passages in her *Diary* where she records Jesus' words of comfort, words that show He is reluctant to punish sinners, tempers his justice with mercy, and withholds the full rigor of His justice until the Judgment Day, giving humanity the maximum opportunity for repentance (see *Diary*, 848, 1160). One of the most poignant of these passages is *Diary* entry 1588. Jesus said to her:

> I do not want to punish aching mankind, but I desire to heal it, pressing it to My Merciful Heart. I use punishment when they themselves force Me to do so; My hand is reluctant to take hold of the sword of justice.

Passages such as these suggest that our experience of the rigors of divine justice is largely self-inflicted, just as a man who leaves the warmth of a fire grows cold through no fault of the fire itself. In *Diary* entry 1728, Jesus said to St. Faustina that when sinful souls "bring all My graces to naught, I begin to be angry with them, leaving them alone and giving them what they want."

In the Church today, much of liberal, dissident theology denies the justice (in the sense of the commutative or penal justice) of God. Thus, there is no hell, no purgatorial punishment, nor does God ever chastise anyone in this life, nor is anything owed to God on the scales of justice because of our sins. It follows that Jesus may have done great things for us, but He did not need to die for our sins in the sense of making "satisfaction" for them, or paying the penalty for them on our behalf.

On the other hand, much of conservative, traditionalist

Catholicism falls into the trap of seeing God's mercy and justice as two distinct sides of His nature. The trick is to activate or respond to His good side and avoid His bad side.

Some of the greatest saints and theologians in the Catholic Tradition, however, have struggled to find a way to fuse together, in a single vision, the justice and mercy of God, without denying either one. How God's justice and mercy are one in the absolute simplicity of the infinite divine nature is, of course, a mystery that we can never completely fathom in this life. It is beyond the capacity of our finite minds, and of our fallen nature, fully to comprehend.

Even in this life, however, we can begin to see that God's justice — His occasional chastisements of us in this life, and His purgatorial punishments of us in the next — are also, at one and the same time, expressions of His mercy toward us. If He sometimes chastises us by permitting us to suffer, it is only to "wake us up," and summon us back to repentance and faith ("Those whom the Lord loves, he chastises," Heb 12:6), and purgatory is not only a place of temporary punishment for half-repented sin; it is also, at the same time, a "purging" that mercifully sanctifies and heals the soul (see *Catechism*, 1030).

More difficult to fathom is how the final damnation of a soul is also, in another way, God's final act of mercy toward that soul. (See the Appendix at the end of this book.) And yet we can know, right from the start, that it must be so: Philosophy shows us that God's nature is absolutely simple and indivisible, so that His justice must always be an expression of His mercy (The simplicity and indivisibility of the divine nature is a truth solemnly defined at the First Vatican Council, *Dogmatic Constitution on the Catholic Faith*, Chapter One). Moreover, the Psalms clearly say that God's mercy is over all His works (see Ps 145:9). Most of all, the Cross of Jesus Christ, as Pope John Paul II clearly taught, is the supreme exposition of both the mercy and the justice of God, at one and the same time (see *Dives in Misericordia*, no. 7-8).

Throughout the rest of this book, we will continue to explore this great mystery of the just Mercy and the merciful

Justice of the infinitely perfect God. Meanwhile, let us not be too hard on St. Augustine for his doctrine of predestination. As we have seen, it forms only one aspect of his teaching on the merciful love of God, and he never claimed to have exhausted the mysteries of divine election, saving grace, and human free will:

> Here also is a lamentable darkness in which the capacities within me are hidden from myself, so that when my mind questions itself about its own powers it cannot be assured that its answers are to be believed. For what is in it is often hidden unless manifested by experience, and in this life described as a continuous trial, no one ought to be overassured that, though he is capable of becoming better instead of worse, he is not actually becoming worse instead of better. Our one hope, our one confidence, our one firm promise is in your mercy (*Confessions* 10.32).

Study Questions

1. What aspects of St. Augustine's teaching on God's grace and mercy generally have been accepted as an authentic expression of the Catholic faith (sometimes described as "moderate Augustinianism")?

2. What aspects of St. Augustine's teaching on God's grace and mercy have not been officially accepted by the Catholic Church as authentic expressions of the Catholic faith?

3. How do both liberal and conservative Catholics tend to misunderstand the justice and mercy of God?

Discussion Starter:

What experiences in his own life probably rein-
forced St. Augustine's belief that all human
beings (in a sense, even infants) are worthy of
damnation, and that only God's predestination
and irresistible ("efficacious") grace could save
a minority of them? Do we sometimes allow
our own subjective, personal experiences to
govern our perspective on God and human
nature, rather than the objective testimony of
the Holy Scripture and Catholic Tradition? Is
this one reason why many Catholics no longer
believe in hell, purgatory, divine chastisement,
or that Jesus made satisfaction for our sins on
the Cross and no longer feel the need to go to
confession? Is the Church in North America
influenced by the "I'm OK, you're OK"
culture in which we live?

CHAPTER TWO

St. Bernard of Clairvaux

Monk, preacher, statesman, diplomat, theologian, and spiritual master, St. Bernard of Clairvaux (1090-1153) was one of the most influential figures of the Middle Ages, and much of his influence flowed from his deep devotion to the merciful love of God.

1. THE LIFE OF ST. BERNARD

We actually know very little about his childhood. His family belonged to the minor nobility of Burgundy, France, and as a boy he attended a cathedral school, where he learned to write beautifully in Latin. We also know that from his youth, he manifested an extraordinary religious sensitivity. On Christmas eve of the year 1100, for example, at the age of 10 he saw in a dream the whole story of the Nativity unfold before his eyes. The memory of this vivid dream remained in Bernard's heart, and as his biographer Msgr Leon Cristiani once wrote: "Even when in later years he reached the top of the mystical ladder, he liked to say that the Savior had appeared to him at the very hour of His birth one Christmas. He liked to talk about it in his sermons" (*St. Bernard of Clairvaux.* Boston: Daughter's of St. Paul, 1983, p.14).

At the age of 21, Bernard decided to join a new religious order of austere Benedictines called the "Cistercians" at their first monastery in Citeaux. Bernard was so zealous for this monastic vocation that he persuaded his uncle, his brothers, and a group of young noblemen to join him. In 1115, at the age of 25, he was sent to found a new monastery for the order at a place called "Clairvaux": really no more than a run-down dwelling in a wilderness. Then, over the next 38 years, St. Bernard founded 68 new Cistercian monasteries. In fact, he was so successful in recruiting men for the order that it was said women would try to lock up their husbands and sons whenever St. Bernard came through their neighborhood on one of his preaching tours, for fear that they might hear him speak and follow him to the next new Cistercian foundation!

Soon people began to write to St. Bernard, asking for his spiritual counsel. Gradually, letters, sermons, and treatises poured forth from his pen: the most famous being his treatises *On the Steps of Humility and Pride, On Loving God,* and *On Grace and Free Will,* and his homilies *In Praise of the Virgin Mother* and *On the Song of Songs.* When one of his Cistercian brethren was elected Pope, St. Bernard even wrote a meditation entitled "On Consideration," containing spiritual guidance on how to be a faithful and virtuous shepherd of the universal Church (a treatise read by newly-elected Popes to this very day). For his extraordinary literary output and its deeply pastoral content, scholars often call St. Bernard "the last of the Fathers of the Church."

One of the things that makes St. Bernard's spirituality so appealing is that he was the first great writer to emphasize the importance of affective devotion to the lowly humanity of Jesus Christ, especially devotion to the Christ Child and to the Passion of Jesus. For Bernard, it is precisely meditation on these mysteries of God's incarnate life that first moves the soul to feelings of compassion for Jesus' sufferings, gratitude for His merciful love, and a fervent desire to follow Him by imitating His life of humble service. These themes became dominant ones in Catholic spirituality for nearly a millennium and deeply influenced the Franciscan, Carmelite, and Jesuit traditions of devotion. As St. Bernard wrote in Sermon 43 from *On the Song of Songs:*

At the start of my conversion, in place of the merits I did not possess, I took care to pick a bouquet of myrrh, and place it on my heart.

I fashioned it from all the anguish and bitter sufferings of my Lord, first His sufferings as a child, then the labors and exhaustion He endured during His journeys and preaching campaigns, His vigils of prayer, His temptations in the desert, His tears of compassion, the dangers He encountered among false brothers, the insults, spittle, blows, sarcasm, ridicule, nails, ... which filled His passion in such abundance.

And among all these tiny stalks of fragrant myrrh I did not forget to place the myrrh which He was given to drink on the cross or the myrrh used to anoint Him for His burial. As long as I live, I shall cherish the memories with which their perfume has saturated me. I shall never forget these mercies, for in them I found life (Cristiani, p. 25).

2. ST. BERNARD'S THEOLOGY OF THE CROSS

In the more "theological" passages in his writings, St. Bernard gathered up the Augustinian heritage and expressed it in a new way. While he accepted that no one can be absolutely sure of his or her own election and salvation, Bernard was sure that the Father's mercy embraces all of humanity. When the Father offers us His mercy, He shows us His own eternal nature of love, but when He judges and condemns us, "in some way we force Him to do so" (5 Nat 3: IV, 268).

The sinful soul, enslaved to the world, the flesh, and the devil, is helpless to rescue itself. Unable to face up to the truth of his own misery, the sinner rationalizes his sin away by imagining that there is no God, or that there is no sin, or that God is without holiness or without mercy. On the cross, however, through the wounds of the Son of God, we see the depths of God's own love for us: "the heart of the Church's Bridegroom opens for us the heart of His Father" (Roch Kereszty, O.Cist., *Fundamentals of Christology.* Alba House, 2002, pp. 454-472). This revelation of His merciful love clears away all misconceptions we may have about God that stand in the way of a deeper relationship with Him:

> My opinion is that all those who lack knowledge of God are those who refuse to turn to Him. I am certain that they refuse because they imagine this kindly disposed God to be harsh and severe, this merciful God to be callous and inflexible, this lovable God to be cruel and oppressive. So it is that wickedness plays false to itself, setting up for itself an image that does not represent Him (*On the Song of Songs*, 38:2).

This is the reason why St. Bernard doggedly pursued the ecclesiastical condemnation of the theologian Peter Abelard. Bernard's role in this affair has been portrayed by some historians as that of a fanatical persecutor of a creative thinker, but St. Bernard rightly understood that the very heart of the Christian faith was at stake in this controversy. For Abelard, God incarnate as Jesus Christ manifests divine love for us in some vague, indeterminate way, and calls us to imitate Him. For St. Bernard, however, that is not nearly enough. If Jesus Christ had not also died on the cross to make satisfaction for our sins, and if He had not thereby overcome the power of the devil's hold on us, then we could not be reunited to the love of God, and consequently we would have no ability to follow Him: "The secret of [Christ's] heart lies open through the holes of His body; the great mystery of love lies open, there lie open the bowels of God's mercy in which the Rising Son from on high has visited us" (61 SC. 4II, 150-151 as quoted in Kersezty, p. 466).

3. ST. BERNARD'S SPIRITUALITY OF GRACE

For St. Bernard there was no "disconnect" between the theology in his head and the devotion in his heart. Primarily as a result of knowledge of the love of God revealed to us through Jesus Christ and His cross, our whole relationship with God takes the form of a response to the divine initiative. In other words: "We love because He first loved us" (1 Jn 4:19). This is sometimes called the principle of "the primacy of grace." Saint Bernard explains this principle in his treatise *On Loving God*:

> When seeking why God should be loved, if one asks what right He has to be loved, the answer is that the main reason for loving Him is that "He loved us first." Surely He is worthy of being loved in return when one thinks of who loves, whom He loved, and how much He loves. … This divine love is sincere, for it is the love of one who does not seek His own advantage. To whom is such love shown? It is written: "Although we were His enemies up to then, we were reconciled to God." Thus God loved, and freely so, His enemies. How much did He love? John answers: God so loved the world that He gave His only-begotten Son" (*On Loving God*, 1).

In short, our love for God is always a response to His prior love for us, especially His love shown to us through the gift of creation itself, and through His earthly life and death for us as Jesus Christ.

The primacy of grace, however, is not only something external to us, but something internal as well. Saint Bernard emphasizes again and again that it is only because God seeks us out first, in the depths of our hearts, that we are enabled and strengthened to seek for Him:

> "I sought Him whom my soul loves"— that is what you are urged to do by the goodness of Him who

anticipates you, who sought you, who loved you before you loved Him. You would not seek Him or love Him unless you had first been sought and loved. ... From this comes the zeal and ardor to seek Him whom your soul loves, because you cannot seek unless you are sought, and when you are sought you cannot but seek. ...

It is so important for every soul among you who is seeking God to realize that God was in the field and was seeking you before you began to search for Him ... there is no worse crime than to take to oneself the credit for even a little of the grace one has received. You could not have sought the Word ... if He had not sought you. ...

Do you awake? Well, He too is awake. If you arise in the nighttime, if you anticipate to your utmost your early awaking, you will find Him awake — you will never anticipate His own awakeness. In such intercourse you will always be rash if you attribute any priority and predominance to yourself; for He loves both more than you love and before you love at all. ...

She [the soul] recognizes that in loving Him, she but returns His love because He first loved her. And so indeed it is! God's love begets the soul's [love] and comes before it; His interest and care for her evoke her care for Him (*On the Song of Songs*).

The importance of this principle to the Catholic Tradition of spirituality can hardly be overestimated. Here, St. Bernard simply takes up and clarifies the teachings of St. Paul and St. Augustine. As a result of the Fall of Adam and Eve, the human nature of all their descendents is in "bondage" to sin (see Rom 5:12-19 and 7:4-25). Fallen humanity, bereft of divine grace, retains "freedom of the will" in the sense of the capacity to choose evil and at best to do an occasional good act (basic works of prudence, such as feeding one's children and planting one's crops on time), but we are too weak and wounded by sin to be able to turn to God for help, or do anything at all that puts us on the road to salvation without the "prevenient" action of the grace of God (that is, without the grace of God that "comes before"). Our problem is that our will is in bondage to our disordered passions and inordinate attachments to earthly things, and our mind is clouded by ignorance of the truth. In other words, we are in bondage to the broken, wounded condition passed down to us from Adam and Eve called "original sin," compounded by our own personal sins. In order for us to be able to turn to God for help and freely cooperate with His grace, our will must first (at least to some degree) be set free from its bondage.

It is therefore a defined doctrine of the Catholic Church (both at the Western Council of Orange in 529 and at the 16th century ecumenical Council of Trent), that no one can turn to God for saving help or do anything at all toward salvation unless prompted, strengthened, and assisted to do so every step of the way by God's grace. On the other hand, God's saving grace is not irresistible. He certainly *enables* our response of faith and love to Him, but He never *compels* that response. To put it another way: setting a person free from bondage in prison and giving him a helping hand to start a new life on the outside does not guarantee that the person will use his new freedom wisely and that he will not end up back in prison again. Yet unless we are first set free by God's enabling grace from our bondage to our fallen condition, we have no capacity freely to cooperate with His grace and attain salvation.

The Catholic Tradition sees two equal and opposite dangers. On the one hand there is "Quietism" and classical "Calvinism": the doctrine that human beings are merely passive under the sway of God's saving grace, which is essentially irresistible. As we have seen, St. Augustine's later writings have sometimes been interpreted in this way. On the other hand there is "Pelagianism": the doctrine that we do not need God's saving grace within; we can just save ourselves by our own efforts by striving to follow the good example of Jesus and the saints. A variant of this is known as "Semi-Pelagianism": the doctrine that while we do indeed need the help of God's grace within our souls, we do not always need God to take the initiative with His enabling grace. As some Eastern theologians have taught (for example, John Cassian), sometimes we freely reach out to God first, and He responds to us, or our seeking of Him meets His seeking of us in a simultaneous "synergy." But all of these doctrines violate some part of the Catholic Tradition that we have received from St. Paul, Orange, and Trent, one that St. Bernard so beautifully summed up for us in his treatise *On Grace and Free Will*:

> "Listen," I replied. "He saves us not because of deeds by us done in righteousness but in virtue of His own mercy. What? Did you imagine that you can create your own merits, that you can be saved by your own righteousness, you who cannot even say 'Jesus is Lord' without the Holy Spirit? Or have you forgotten the words: 'Without Me you can do nothing,' and 'It depends not on the one running, nor the one willing, but on God who has mercy'?"
>
> You ask: "What part, then, does free choice play?"
>
> I shall answer you in a word: it is saved. Take away free choice and there is nothing to be saved. Take away grace and there is no means of saving. Without the two combined the work cannot be done: the One as operative principle, the other as object toward which or in which it is accomplished. God is the author of salvation, the free choice is only capable of receiving it. What, therefore, is given by God alone and to free choice alone, cannot any more happen without the recipient's consent than without the Bestower's grace. Consequently, free choice is said to cooperate with operating grace in its act of consent or, in other words, in its process of being saved. For to consent is to be saved (*On Grace and Free Will*, 1f).

If then God works these three things in us, namely thinking, willing and accomplishing the good, the first he does without us, the second with us, and the third through us. By suggesting the good thought, He goes one step ahead of us. By also bringing about the change of our ill will, He joins it to Himself by consent. And by supplying consent with the faculty and ability, the Operator within makes His appearance outwardly through the external work that we perform. Of ourselves we cannot, of course, take that first step. But He who can find no one who is good, can save no one without His first stepping into the lead. There can be no doubt, therefore, that the beginning action rests with God and is enacted neither through us nor with us. The consent and the work, however, though not originating from us nevertheless are not without us. …

It is this grace which arouses free choice when it sows the seed of the good thought, which heals free choice by changing its disposition, which strengthens it so as to lead it to action, and which saves it from experiencing a fall. Grace so cooperates with free choice, however, that only in the first movement does it go a step ahead of it. In the others it accompanies it. Indeed, grace's whole aim in taking a step ahead is that from then on, free choice may co-operate with it. What was begun by grace alone is completed by grace and free choice together (*On Grace and Free Will*, 46ff).

4. ON MARY AS EXEMPLAR OF HUMBLE CONSENT AND 'AQUEDUCT' OF GRACE

The soul that truly understands and accepts "the primacy of grace" in the Christian life certainly becomes more humble as a result in its walk with Jesus Christ. Moreover, the principle has an important practical application as well: what St. Bernard called the principle of "infusion" before "effusion." In his series of meditations *On the Song of Songs* that he preached to his fellow Cistercian monks, he likened the Spirit of Jesus Christ to waters that flow either through a canal or a reservoir:

> Those who are wise will see their lives as more like a reservoir than a canal. The canal simultaneously pours out what it receives; the reservoir retains the water till it is filled, then pours forth the overflow without loss to itself. ... Today there are many in the Church who act like canals, the reservoirs are far too rare. ... They are more ready to speak than to listen, impatient to teach what they have not grasped, and full of presumption to govern others while they know not how to govern themselves. ...

> The reservoir resembles the fountain that runs to form a stream or spreads to form a pool only when its own waters are brimming over. ... You must imitate this process. First, be filled and then control the outpouring. The charity that is benign and prudent does not flow outward until it abounds within (*On the Song of Songs*, 13:3-4).

Thus, as grace always precedes consent, so the "infusion" of grace in humble prayer always must proceed effective "effusion" of action in the service of our Lord.

Saint Bernard sees the Blessed Virgin Mary as the true exemplar of this whole spirituality of grace. Although she certainly has a unique role to play in God's plan of salvation for the world, at the same time, she is also the exemplar, the living icon, of true humility and free consent to God's gracious calling and initiative:

> The Lord says, "Upon whom shall my Spirit rest, if not upon one that is humble and contrite of spirit?" On the *humble*, he says, not *on the virgin*. Had Mary not been humble, then the Holy Spirit would not

have rested upon her. Had the Holy Spirit not rested upon her, she would not have become pregnant. ... Thus there is no doubt that her virginity was found pleasing because her humility made her so (*In Praise of the Blessed Virgin Mary*, 1:1ff).

You have heard that you will conceive and bear a son. You have heard that it will be by the Holy Spirit and not by a man. The angel is waiting for your reply. It is time for him to return to the One who sent him.

We too are waiting for this merciful word, my Lady, we who are miserably weighed down under a sentence of condemnation. The price of our salvation is being offered to you. If you consent we shall immediately be set free. We all have been made in the eternal Word of God, and look, we are dying. In your brief reply we shall be restored and be brought back to life. Doleful Adam and his unhappy offspring, exiled from paradise, implore you, kind Virgin, to give this answer. David asks it. Abraham asks it. All the other holy patriarchs, your very own fathers, beg it of you, as do those now dwelling in the region of the shadow of death. For it the whole world is waiting, bowed down at your feet. And rightly, too, because on your answer depends the comfort of the afflicted, the deliverance of the damned, the salvation of the sons of Adam, your whole race. Give your answer quickly, my Virgin. My Lady, say this word which earth and hell and heaven itself are waiting for. The very King and Lord of all, He who has so desired your beauty, is eager for your answer and assent, by which He proposes to save the world. Him whom you pleased by your silence, you will now please even more by your word. ... Blessed Virgin, open your heart to faith, your lips to consent, and your womb to your Creator. Behold the long-desired of all nations is standing at the door and is knocking. Oh, what if He should pass by because of your delay and sorrowing, you should again have to seek Him whom your soul loves? Get up, run, open! Get up by faith, run by prayer, open by consent!

"Behold," she says, "I am the handmaiden of the Lord, Let it be done to me according to your word" (*In Praise of the Blessed Virgin Mary*, 4:8f).

Through her total surrender to the grace of God, Mary then becomes the maternal intercessor and "aqueduct" of all the graces of salvation that flow to us from Christ:

> Through you, O Blessed One, finder of grace, mother of life, mother of salvation, through you let us have access to your Son, so that through you He may receive us, He who was given to us through you. ... because such is the will of God who would have us obtain everything through her hands (*Second Sermon for Advent; Sermon for the Nativity of the Blessed Virgin Mary*, 6-7).

You must have guessed, dear brothers and sisters, to whom I allude under the image of an aqueduct which, receiving the fullness of the fountain from the Father's heart, has passed it on to us, at least insofar as we can contain it. You know it was she to whom it was said, "Hail, full of grace."

But how did this aqueduct of ours attain to the loftiness of the fountain? How indeed, except by the ardor of her desires, by the fervor of her devotion, by the purity of her prayer? (*Sermon for the Nativity of the Blessed Virgin Mary*, 6).

Indeed, for St. Bernard, it is the desire that Jesus Christ kindles in our hearts for loving union with Him that moves us forward on our spiritual journey:

It is not with steps of feet that God is sought, but with the desire of the heart. When we happily find Him our desire is not quenched but kindled. Does the consummation of joy bring about the consuming of desire? Rather, it is oil poured on the flames. So it is. There will be a fullness of joy, but there will be no end of desire and therefore no end to the search. Think, if you can, of this eagerness to see God as not caused by His absence, for He is always present. And think of the desire for God as without fear or failure, for grace is abundantly present (*On the Song of Songs*, 84:5).

The final consummation of the spiritual journey in this life is what St. Bernard refers to as the spiritual marriage of the soul with Christ the Word: an intimate, spousal union of love between the soul as Bride and Christ the Bridegroom:

When you see a soul leaving everything and clinging to the Word with all her will and desire, living for the Word, ruling her life by the Word, conceiving by the Word what it will bring forth by Him, so that she can say, "for me to live is Christ and to die is gain," you know that the soul is the spouse and bride of the Word. The heart of the Bridegroom has faith in her, knowing her to be faithful, for she has rejected all things as dross to gain Him. ...

The soul is affected in one way when it is made fruitful by the Word, in another way when it enjoys the Word. In the one it is considering the needs of its neighbor, in the other it is allured by the sweetness of the Word. ...

There may be someone who will go on to ask me, "What does it mean to enjoy the Word?" I would answer that one must find someone who has experience of it and ask that person. Do you suppose if I were granted the experience that I could describe to you what is beyond description? (*On the Song of Songs*, 85:11).

Study Questions

1. In St. Bernard's spirituality, what is the principle of the primacy of grace? How does this principle point to the importance of God's mercy?

2. According to St. Bernard what is the principle of infusion and effusion? See these and other passages from the *Diary of St. Faustina* that illustrate how this spiritual principle helps us understand the operation of Divine Mercy like an overflowing fountain without limit: 309, 327, 367.

3. In St. Bernard's teachings, what role does the Blessed Virgin Mary play for us in our spiritual journey with Christ? What does this role tell us of Mary's place in the mystery of redemption, the mystery of Divine Mercy?

Discussion Starter

Talk about your favorite Gospel scenes from the earthly life of our Lord: which ones really move you the most and make you long to be with Him and to love Him in return? Do any of these scenes shed light on Jesus as The Divine Mercy Incarnate? If so, in what ways?

CHAPTER THREE

St. Thomas Aquinas

The theologian who explained in the greatest depth why Divine Mercy is central to the faith of the Church was the great medieval thinker St. Thomas Aquinas (1225-1274).[1] When he was a young student of Theology under the great Dominican St. Albertus Magnus, Thomas's classmates used to tease him by calling him "the dumb ox" because of his portly stature and peaceful, quiet demeanor. Saint Albertus overheard them one time and prophesied: "You call him a dumb ox; I tell you that this dumb ox will bellow so loud that his bellowing will fill the world!"

1. THE LIFE OF ST. THOMAS AQUINAS

Thomas of Aquino was born in the year 1225 into a very wealthy and influential Italian family. His second cousin was the Holy Roman Emperor, Frederick II, and his father was a knight, a member of the nobility. All six of Thomas's brothers became knights too, and the family's expectation was that Thomas would do the same. However, from his earliest years Thomas showed a marked inclination toward the religious life. Legend has it that at the age of three, he turned and asked his nanny "What is God?" — and thereby began his lifelong

---

[1]The author wishes to thank Fr. John Saward for his meditation on St. Thomas entitled "Love's Second Name: St. Thomas on Mercy," which appeared in the *Canadian Catholic Review* in March, 1990. It was a major source of insight and inspiration for this chapter.

enterprise of asking, and trying to answer, the ultimate questions of the universe. In order that he might follow his religious inclinations, at the age of five he was placed in the Benedictine Abbey of Monte Casino with the idea that he would one day be named the Abbot. The Abbey was later overrun in one of medieval Italy's many minor wars, and so Thomas had to return home at the age of 14. Nevertheless, his father did not give up hope of rapid ecclesiastical advancement for his son.

Saint Thomas, though, had dreams of his own. While studying in Naples and without consulting his noble family, Thomas began the process of joining a new religious order: the order of beggar-evangelists called the "Order of Friars Preachers" (known to us today as the Dominicans). When his family discovered his plans, they were shocked and scandalized. At first they tried to dissuade him from joining the Dominicans by bribing him with high office. His father put pressure on the Pope, who in turn offered to make Thomas the next Archbishop of Naples if he would give up the idea of joining the Dominicans. When Thomas remained unmoved by this offer, his family and the Pope tried compromise: Thomas would be appointed by the Pope the next Abbot of Monte Casino, but Thomas still would be allowed to wear the Dominican habit. Thomas was not looking for high ecclesiastical rank, however, and he certainly did not want to parade around Monte Casino as a fake Dominican!

When neither bribery nor compromise would dissuade him, therefore, his family resorted to kidnapping and imprisonment. They had Thomas abducted while he was on his way to study with the Dominicans in Paris, brought him home, and locked him in the high tower of their castle until he should change his mind. Thomas remained imprisoned there for 17 months — but he would not be moved. At one point, his brothers introduced a prostitute into his chambers to try to entice him away from the religious life, but Thomas chased the girl from the tower with a hot iron he had taken from the fireplace and branded the sign of the Cross on the door of his cell, as if to tell his brothers that he could never be moved from his commitment to Jesus Christ by such a base temptation.

After that incident, it is said that his mother and sisters took pity on him and helped him escape, supplying him with a rope with which he was able to make his exit through a window in the tower. Thomas fled to the protection of the Dominicans in Paris, and his family finally gave up on their attempts to obstruct his vocation.

The motto of the Dominicans was (and is) "*Veritas,*" which means "Truth." Their Constitution states: "The Order of Preachers was principally and essentially designed for preaching and teaching in order thereby to communicate to others the fruits of contemplation and to procure the salvation of souls." This was the vocation of St. Thomas Aquinas, and to that end he wrote his two main scholarly works: the *Summa Contra Gentiles*, setting down the rational grounds for adherence to the Catholic faith, and the massive *Summa Theologiae*, providing a complete exposition of the Christian worldview. In this latter work, as we shall see, he shows that Divine Mercy is at the very heart of the Gospel and the greatest of the divine attributes. In fact, he interprets all of God's work as Creator and Redeemer as expressions of the merciful love of God.

In 1274, St. Thomas was summoned by the Pope to Lyons in France to take part in an ecumenical council for the reunion of Eastern and Western Christendom. Along the way, however, Thomas was stricken by an illness and died at the Cistercian Abbey of Fossanova. It is said that the priest who heard his last confession ran out of the bed chamber when Thomas was finished and whispered in awe that his confession had been as simple and sincere as that of a five-year-old child. Such is the childlike trust of those whose hearts and minds are devoted to the end to God's mercy.

2. THE MEANING OF MERCY

Aquinas defined the virtue of "mercy" in his *Summa Theologiae* as "the compassion in our hearts for another person's misery, a compassion which drives us to do what we can to help him" (ST II-II.30.1). For St. Thomas, this virtue has two aspects: "affective" mercy and "effective" mercy.

Affective mercy is an emotion: the pity we feel for the plight of another. In this respect, St. Thomas says, human mercy is grounded in a "defect" in our nature: the defect of human vulnerability to suffering. We feel pity for those who suffer because we, too, are subject to such miseries. Thus, our affective sympathy for others arises from our capacity for empathy. Saint Thomas notes: "Those who reckon themselves happy and so powerful that no ill may befall them are not so compassionate" (II-II.30.2). To some extent, however, the intensity of our affective mercy for the plight of another also depends upon how closely we are united to others in friend- ship: "The person who loves regards his friend as another self, and so he counts his friend's troubles as his own, and grieves over them as if they were his own" (II-II.30.2). An affective bond, we might say, easily forms between friends, and this renders good friends all the more capable of sympathy for each other's plight. For example, when we hear that a friend or a loved one is about to go through a major surgery, we nat- urally feel compassion for them and we say to ourselves, "I can imagine what anxiety my friend is going through right now on the eve of his operation." We can imagine it because we have been sick and in need of medical treatment ourselves. This sympathetic empathy is what St. Thomas means by "affective mercy."

"Effective mercy," on the other hand, is something that we do, a positive action for the good of another, taking steps to relieve the miseries or meet the needs of others. According to St. Thomas, the Latin word *misericordia* literally means "having a miserable heart" — both affectively and effectively — for another person's misery. For example, when we hear that our friend is on the eve of major surgery, we not only feel sympathetic empathy for him, but we also may plan to go and visit him in the hospital before and after the operation to comfort him. This is "effective" mercy because it actively meets the needs of others. In other words, it is "affective" sympathy translated into "effective" action for the good of another.

Saint Thomas observes that there are three kinds of "misery" in this life. First, there is the suffering that goes against our natural appetite for existence and life, such as the misery of a sick man. Secondly, there is suffering that strikes us suddenly and unexpectedly, such as sufferings arising from accidents. The third kind of suffering, however, is the worst of all: suffering that strikes a person when he consistently pursues the good, yet he meets only overpowering evil. Saint Thomas here has in mind those sufferings and misfortunes that strike those who in no way deserve them, the undeserved miseries of the innocent and the virtuous. In the Old Testament, Job is an example of this form of misery. He was overwhelmed with undeserved grief and sorrows of every kind.

Saint Thomas argues that the human virtue of mercy necessarily will be both affective and effective. However, to be the authentic virtue of mercy, it must manifest two additional characteristics. First, it must be rooted in "right reason" — that is, in the truth about the sufferings of others, and what is in fact the objective "good" for the other whom we seek to help. For example, a drunkard may suffer severe shaking and trembling from a day without alcohol, but "right reason" suggests that the best remedy for his problem is not to give him a glass of liquor, even though that may temporarily relieve his symptoms — and even though he may beg for one! The merciful thing to do is to provide the drunkard what he truly, objectively needs: a few days in a detoxification center. Second, the virtue of mercy is proven in effective action for the good of others, as circumstances permit. If we merely sympathize with the plight of others and "share their pain" without making the best of the opportunities we have to help them, then the virtue of mercy does not abide in us to any significant degree.

Saint Thomas asks two related questions. First, is mercy the greatest of the human virtues? It certainly implies a measure of grandeur and nobility, insofar as effective mercy is the generous relief of the needs and miseries of others out of one's own abundance. We help others out of our store of wealth, knowledge, skill, or strength when we see others in need of such help. In that sense, mercy is an act of condescension from one person who has a greater abundance of some good to another person lacking in some good. If the merciful person has a superior (that is, someone with an even greater abundance of goods to share), then his chief virtue will be what unites him with his superior. In the case of human beings, the virtue of "charity" is what unites us to God (since God is not in need of our mercy): "Since man, therefore, has God above him, charity which unites him to God is greater than mercy, which relieves the wants of others" (II-II.30.4). On the other hand, when we consider which of the virtues should govern our relationships with other human beings, it is clear that mercy directed to our neighbors in need is the supreme virtue in man (II-II.30.4).

Second, St. Thomas asks: Is mercy the greatest attribute of God? Since God is the absolute superior, the perfect and self-existent creator, St. Thomas says, He is never self-seeking, but acts only and always with selfless generosity, pouring good gifts out of His abundance on His creatures. Showing mercy is therefore proper to God in a special way, for it manifests His infinite perfection and His infinite abundance and generosity. Saint Thomas writes: "If we consider a virtue in terms of its possessor, however, we can say that mercy is the greatest of the virtues only if its possessor is himself the greatest of all beings, with no one above him and everyone beneath him" (II-II.30.4). This, of course, is properly true only of God Himself. Thus, mercy is, in that sense, the greatest attribute of God.

What, then, is the mercy of God, according to St.

Thomas? It cannot be an emotion or a passion since God in His infinite, immutable perfection cannot be subject to changing passions that "happen" to Him, "overcome" Him, or reduce His fullness of Being in any way. Thus, St. Thomas argues that God's mercy is "effective," not "affective." In other words, His mercy is expressed in the positive action that His love takes to remedy the miseries and meet the needs of His creatures, communicating to them a share in His own perfections. Aquinas writes: "To feel sad about another's misery is no attribute of God, but to drive it out is supremely His, and by misery here we mean any sort of defect. Defects are not done away with save by an achievement of goodness, and as we have said, God is the first source of goodness" (I.21.3).

According to St. Thomas, it is above all the forgiveness of sins that manifests God's mercy. The forgiveness of our sins is an act of God's omnipotence: God's love showing itself to be more powerful than sin and evil. When human beings forgive one another, we control our anger, curb our resentment, and annul any claims of revenge. But we cannot remit the fault itself. God alone can change the will of the malefactor and turn his heart toward repentance. In this sense, God alone can remit sins. Thus, God's mercy is infinitely powerful to destroy sin and regenerate and sanctify the sinner.

For example, we see the powers of God's mercy at work in the New Testament when Jesus not only forgives the sins of the paralytic who was brought to Him, but shows His divine authority to do so by healing the man's body: "That you may know that the Son of Man has authority on earth to forgive sins ... I say to you, rise, take up your pallet and go home" (Mk 2:11). In fact, St. Thomas claims, "Forgiving men, taking pity on them, is a greater work than the creation of the world"(I-II.113.9). As regards the mode of action, bringing the world into being out of nothing is the greater work, but in terms of the greatness of the work done, the justification of the unrighteous is the greater work, because it has an *eternal effect*. The justified and sanctified soul lives forever in God's kingdom, whereas this created world, as we now know it at least, passes away.

3. MERCY AND JUSTICE IN GOD

Saint Thomas argues that in God's nature, Divine Mercy and Divine Justice coincide: they are one in the simplicity of God's essence. God is always and everywhere just and merciful, at one and the same time. When God acts mercifully, He does not act against justice but, in a sense, goes beyond it. In other words, God's justice always furthers His work of mercy, and never detracts from it. Aquinas writes: "The work of divine justice always presupposes the work of mercy and is based on it" (I.21.4). For example, if God chastised the People of Israel by letting them be taken captive to Babylon, it was only so that they might be brought to repentance and national conversion. In a sense, His justice permitted them to suffer because they deserved it, but His underlying plan was not merely to "get even" with His wayward people but ultimately to restore them to a right relationship with Himself. In this case, His mercy took the form of "tough love."

In his essay "Disputed Questions on Truth," St. Thomas explains that God is more properly merciful than punitive. To articulate this truth, St. Thomas draws upon a distinction made by St. John Damascene between God's "antecedent" and "consequent" will.

Antecedently, that is, from all eternity, God's will "before the foundation of the world" is to make us all His adopted children and sharers of His divine life. His antecedent will is that "all should be saved and come to the knowledge of the truth" (1 Tim 2:4).[2]

God's consequent will, however, is what He wills as a response to the choices made by His human creatures. He gave human beings the freedom to reject His love and spurn His mercy. If we choose to do so, then God's consequent will

---

[2] It would seem that St. Thomas has misinterpreted this passage, for the reference here by St. Paul to God's desire for all to be saved seems to mean, in context (verses 5-7), to be "saved" from sin and its effects, which would appear to relate to God's "consequent," not His "antecedent," will.

is to forgive the penitent and punish the hard-hearted: temporal punishment in this life and for the stubbornly impenitent, eternal punishment in the life to come. Hence, God's antecedent will is grace and mercy for all, while His consequent will is punishment for the wicked. However, even divine punishment, St. Thomas claims, is a work of mercy as well as of justice because God rewards the righteous and penitent far beyond their merits and punishes the impenitent far less than they deserve. Thus, even in His consequent will, Divine Mercy at least tempers Divine Justice.

In his essay "Disputed Questions on Evil," St. Thomas writes: "The tradition of Faith holds that rational creatures would not be able to incur any evil in the soul or in the body unless sin had taken place" (I.4). Saint Thomas here refers to the effects of original sin on the human race. God did not want His people to suffer, so He created Adam and Eve incapable of suffering, along with the gift of bodily immortality. But when Adam and Eve fell from grace, they lost those gifts for themselves and for their posterity by their disobedience to God. As C.S. Lewis once wrote, a new kind of human existence, a kind God had never intended, thereby sinned itself into existence. As a result, Adam and Eve and all of their descendents became subject to suffering and death. All of this was certainly not God's antecedent will for His people. Nevertheless, God permitted the fall of man, with all its tragic effects, because it made possible the most amazing display of His merciful love for us, when He sent us Jesus the Savior to die for our sins on the Cross.

Humanity was certainly in a dire predicament after the fall of Adam and Eve. It is possible for sinners to have a right relationship with God restored only if they make a proper "satisfaction" to God for sin. The problem is that making satisfaction to God for sin is precisely what man, by his own power, could not do. He could not make up for sin (for the past cannot be undone, and a man has nothing "extra" in the present or future to offer to God for his past sins, since a life of perfect obedience was owed by each of us to God our Creator anyway). Besides, man owes to God an *infinite* compensation for sin, since by sin he has betrayed and offended Infinite Love. Yet we have nothing infinite to offer God to make up for our sins. Moreover, human nature, corrupted by sin, needs to be regenerated and renewed, for only a renewed, regenerated soul could possibly offer any pleasing satisfaction to God: but again, the regeneration of the soul is beyond human power.

Given that both the satisfaction for our sins and the regeneration of our sinful souls is entirely beyond our power, the human race is desperately in need of a Savior. Of course, St. Thomas argues that God Himself is our Savior through Jesus Christ our Lord.

Study Questions

1. According to St. Thomas Aquinas, what is the difference between "affective" and "effective" mercy? Why does he hold that God's mercy is effective but not affective?

2. Why does St. Thomas Aquinas believe that mercy is the greatest attribute of God?

3. According to St. Thomas Aquinas, why are fallen human beings unable to restore their relationship with God?

Discussion Starter:

What does "forgiveness" between human beings consists of — and how is it similar to, yet different from, the way God acts to forgive human sins? What can God do that human beings cannot do to bring about reconciliation with those who have offended Him?

4. THE SAVING WORK OF JESUS CHRIST

According to St. Thomas Aquinas, the supreme manifestation of God's mercy is the sending of His divine Son into the world to share our human nature and to make "atonement" or "satisfaction" for our sins, meriting for us superabundant graces of regeneration and sanctification.

The Divine Son Shares our Human Nature

The British theologian John Saward sums up St. Thomas's viewpoint on this matter as follows:

> It is through the mercy, affective as well as effective, of his real human heart that Christ manifests the infinitely effective mercy of God. ... In his manhood the Son of God knows by experience human misery, which as God he knew from eternity by simple knowledge. God incarnate does not just know about human misery; he has felt it ("Love's Second Name: St. Thomas on Mercy," *Canadian Catholic Review*, March, 1990, p. 92).

In other words, in His divine nature the divine Son remained beyond suffering, but in the human condition that He assumed, He could actually experience the depths of human suffering and sorrow. In fact, according to St. Thomas, our Savior experienced every general kind of human suffering. He suffered at the hands of all kinds of people. He suffered desertion by His friends and blasphemies against His good name. He suffered in body and soul, and in all His senses, including the emotions of grief and sorrow. Moreover, according to St. Thomas, our Lord suffered the greatest pain (bodily, emotional, and spiritual) that any human being could possibly experience. Saint Thomas writes:

> His body was superbly put together, for it was formed miraculously by the operation of the Holy Spirit ... and

so his sense of touch, the sense through which we experience pain, was extremely keen. His soul, likewise, by all its interior powers, perceived all the causes of sorrow with the greatest clarity (ST III.46.6).

In addition to His bodily and affective sensitivity, according to St. Thomas, our Lord also possessed a far greater wisdom and love than any other human being. This is the case because Christ's human nature, united to the person of the divine Word, was "full of grace and truth" (Jn 1:13). Thus, through His infused and beatific knowledge, He foresaw prophetically the entire future of the human race — all human sins and miseries for which He was offering His life on the Cross. As Saward puts it: "To remove the vast burden of the world's guilt, the incarnate Son lovingly endures the vast burden of the world's pain" (p. 92). However, Jesus Christ does not just suffer alongside of us. Again, Saward explains:

> Christ's humanity, without losing any of its concrete-ness, has a certain inclusiveness. He is our Head, and we are his members, forming together, as it were, a single mystical Body. As man, but because he is God, Christ our Head is able to identify more profoundly and more completely with human wretchedness than any ordinary man could ever do.

In fact, it is implicit in St. Thomas's understanding of Christ that it is precisely the beatific and infused knowledge of the whole human race — past, present, and future — that Jesus possessed in His human soul, coupled with the infused virtue of charity that He possessed in His human soul, that enabled Him, in a unique way, to "include" all humanity within His own concrete humanity, since He embraced all human beings with such unsurpassable knowledge and love. (See, for example, Gal 2:20.) As Pope Pius XII wrote in his encyclical letter *Mystici Corporis* (1943):

But the knowledge and love of our Divine Redeemer, of which we were the object from the first moment of His Incarnation, exceed all that the human intellect can hope to grasp. For hardly was He conceived in the womb of the Mother of God, when He began to enjoy the beatific vision, and in that vision all the members of His Mystical Body were continually and unceasingly present to Him, and He embraced them with His redeeming love. O marvelous condescension of divine love for us! O inestimable dispensation of boundless charity! In the crib, on the Cross, in the unending glory of the Father, Christ has all the members of the Church present before Him and united to Him in a much clearer and more loving manner than that of a mother who clasps her child to her breast, or than that which a man knows and loves himself (no. 75).

He Makes Satisfaction for our Sins

Saint Thomas states that the purpose for which the Son of God took our frail flesh was not just to identify with our human condition by sharing our pain, but to make "satisfaction" for our sins. "God as man did for man what man by himself could not do" (Saward, p. 93). Saint Thomas explains:

For man to be liberated through the passion of Christ was in harmony both with his mercy and justice. With justice because by his passion Christ made satisfaction for the sin of the human race, and so man was liberated through the justice of Christ. But also with mercy, because, since man by himself could not make satisfaction for the sins of all human nature ... God gave his Son to be the satisfier ... and in so doing he showed a more abundant mercy than if he had forgiven sins without requiring satisfaction (II.1.2).

Saint Thomas obviously sees the suffering, redemptive work of Christ as fulfilling the demands of divine justice — that is, making "satisfaction" (compensation) for human sin — but at the same time as the most stupendous act of merciful love for us. This is so because God does all this for us Himself out of nothing but sheer mercy for us in our plight, since we are unable to help ourselves. In doing so, He manifests His merciful love far more than if He had just forgiven sins by letting "bygones be bygones."

Moreover, St. Thomas insists that rescuing us from our sins in this particular way (that is, by making satisfaction for our sins) was the sole purpose of the Incarnation. This teaching later would be opposed by the "Scotists" (the followers of the Franciscan theologian Bl. John Duns Scotus), who argued that the Son of God would have become incarnate even if humanity had never fallen into sin.

In order to understand St. Thomas's theory of atonement, we need to be clear about what he meant in saying that Jesus Christ makes "satisfaction" for our sins. Often, St. Thomas's theory (and that of his predecessor, St. Anselm) is confused with the theory put forward by John Calvin and Martin Luther, for whom the atonement meant merely a quasi-legal transaction in which Christ suffers the "retribution," "penalty," or "punishment" for sin in the place of sinners. In other words, Christ takes upon Himself what sinners deserve, and in this way He clears our debt to God's vindictive justice.

For St. Thomas, "satisfaction" does indeed involve making up our debt to God's justice for our sins. But what is "owed" is not only punishment. In fact, our moral debt for sin can be made up to God in a way that includes, but goes beyond, mere retribution. Our debt can be cleared by another kind of reparatory or compensatory act, which St. Thomas calls "satisfaction."

The word and concept of "satisfaction" actually derives from ancient Roman law. According to St. Thomas, a person can be said to make satisfaction for an offense when he offers something that the offended party accepts with a delight matching or outweighing his displeasure at the original offense. The offender "does enough to clear the debt." Take for example, the case of someone who in a fit of anger throws a punch at another and breaks his jaw. Retributive justice says that the offender ought to suffer to an extent comparable to the suffering that he has caused. Thus, someone should punch him in the jaw, too ("an eye for an eye"), or at least he ought to be put in jail and suffer a punishment that fits the crime. However, "satisfaction" for the original transgression might be made to the offended party in another way if the offender offers appropriate acts of "reparation" or "compensation." For example, he could offer a sincere apology for his actions, offer to pay the injured man's medical bills (plus a compensatory payment for pain and suffering), and do other acts of help and service to "make up" for his crime. All this would amount to "satisfaction" of the man's moral and legal debt.

Saint Thomas states numerous times that what gives saving value in God's eyes to the life and death of His incarnate Son is the loving obedience of the Son's sacred humanity. That is why St. Thomas can argue that our Lord began to merit our salvation even from His cradle, because even His Holy Childhood was one continuous act of loving obedience to the Father. Moreover, St. Thomas quotes with approval St. Augustine's teaching that what made Christ's Passion acceptable to the Father was the charity out of which He offered Himself up for us (see ST III.48.3). Furthermore, it is important to note that because He is the divine Son in human flesh, all of his human acts are "theandric" (that is, acts done by a divine person through His human nature) and therefore of infinite value. Christ's loving obedience throughout His life and death are therefore not only "sufficient" to "make up" for our sins — in fact, His life and death gains "superabundant" merit. It *more* than makes up for our sins. Saint Thomas sums up his view of all this in the *Summa Theologiae* as follows:

> He atones appropriately for an offense who offers
> whatever the offended party equally loves, or loves

more than he detested the offense. But Christ by suffering out of love and obedience gave to God more than was required to compensate for the offenses of the whole human race. First, by reason of the tremendous charity from which he suffered; second, by reason of the dignity of his life, which he gave up in atonement, for this was the life of one who was both God and man; third, on account of the extent of the passion and the greatness of the sorrows suffered. ... and so Christ's passion was not merely sufficient but a superabundant atonement for the sins of the human race (III.48.2).

We see clearly here that in the theology of St. Thomas, Divine Mercy not only fulfills the demands of divine justice, but goes way beyond those demands, meriting an infinite ocean of graces, which our Savior wants to pour out upon a lost and broken world!

Saint Thomas goes on to say that by requiring satisfaction for sin, God was not only being just, but also merciful. He argues that it is even more merciful for God to ask for reparation for sin than if He had just decided to "let bygones be bygones," so to speak. John Saward sums up St. Thomas's insight as follows:

> God wanted a two-way covenant, one in which man, his free and rational creature, would be a committed partner. In so doing, the Father shows the richness of his mercy and his infinite respect for the dignity of man made in his own image. It was far more glorious for man to restore his nature and destiny by his own acts [to some extent] than purely and simply to receive salvation. ...
>
> This human involvement has two moments.
>
> First, superabundant satisfaction for all human sin is made by the man who is God, by the divine person of

the Son in his human nature, through his human actions and through his sufferings, through his loving human will.

Then he associates human persons in that victory over sin; he gives us, his members, grace to cooperate in our salvation and our brethren's, by making satisfaction for our sins and theirs. We do not render atonement by our own unaided powers (to imagine so would be the delusion of Pelagius). No, the satisfaction of the members draws all its efficacy from the satisfaction of the Head (Saward, p. 93).

In this way the Church is said by modern theologians to be "co-redemptive" in its mission: sharing in Christ's redemptive work, filled with His grace and thereby enriched with His merits. This is a far greater dignity for humanity than if we had just been saved as passive objects of irresistible, coercive grace (as in, for example, the classical Calvinist understanding of salvation).

In short, for St. Thomas not only the *fact* that we are given a Savior but even the *manner* in which we are saved is an expression of God's mercy toward us, restoring the lost dignity of the children of God.

5. MERCY, JUDGMENT, AND MARY

Saint Thomas points to the significance of the fact that when our Lord speaks of His Second Coming as judge of the world, He refers to Himself as the "Son of Man." There are several reasons for this: (1) if He came only in divine form to be our judge, He could not be seen except by the blessed; (2) it is fitting that Christ comes again to judge the world in the same form in which He was judged and condemned by Pontius Pilate; (3) it is in accord with the mercy of God that mankind will be given final judgment by a man. In this regard, St. Thomas refers to Hebrews 4:15: "We have not a high priest who is unable to sympathize with our weaknesses." In other words, as it is in His human form that the Son of God ascends to the Father, so it is in the same compassionate human nature, both affectively and effectively merciful, that He comes again to judge the living and the dead.

Preaching on the Feast of the Purification of Mary, St. Thomas quotes a text from the letter to the Hebrews: "Let us therefore go with confidence to the temple of grace, that we may find mercy at the opportune time" (Heb. 4:16). St. Thomas applies this text to Mary and sees her womb as the temple of grace. In other words, by bringing the merciful Christ into the world, Mary shows mercy to us, her fellow creatures, a mercy that is feminine and motherly. For example, in the *Summa Theologiae*, St. Thomas writes: "At the Annunciation the Virgin's consent was besought in lieu of that of the entire human race" (ST II.30.1). Again, the thought here is that by her "fiat," by her consent in faith and love to the divine plan of the Incarnation, "Mary gave the Son of God in his human nature to the world, and so made possible the supreme revelation of God's mercy" (Saward, p. 94).

According to St. Thomas, the members of Christ's Mystical Body on earth, the Church, are members of one another. What this means in practice is that they are to bear one another's burdens, principally in three ways: (1) by patience with each other's faults and failings, and weaknesses of body and spirit, (2) by relieving one another's needs, whether of body or of spirit, and (3) by making satisfaction (atonement or reparation) for each other, especially by prayer and good works, for the remission of the temporal punishment due to sins. John Saward explains in his essay on St. Thomas:

> Since in Christ we are members one of another, we are enabled, by his grace, in the *communio sanctorum* of his Mystical Body, to make atonement not only for ourselves but for one another. By our prayers and good works, by our sufferings offered up in union with Christ's sacrifice, we can contribute to the salvation of

our brethren. In so doing, we act mercifully (p. 95).

This also leads to the importance of the Beatitude of Mercy: "Blessed are the merciful, for they shall obtain mercy" (Mt 5:7). We must show mercy to others in need in order to be able to receive mercy ourselves from God. In addition, when we show mercy to our neighbors, we are actually showing mercy to Christ Himself, the Son of Man : "For I was hungry and you gave me food, thirsty and you gave me drink. I was a stranger and you welcomed me, I was naked and you clothed me, I was sick and you visited me, I was in prison and you came to me. ... Truly I say to you, as you did it to one of the least of these my brethren, you did it to me" (Mt 25:35-40). We learn in Matthew's Gospel that showing such mercy will be the basis for our judgment on the Last Day.

But we might well ask: "How can this be? How can we give solace and relief to our Savior, who is now in the nearer presence of the Father in heaven, where He surely needs no solace and relief from us? Surely the risen and glorified Christ is impassible and beyond all suffering?"

Saint Thomas answers this question in his commentary on St. Matthew's Gospel by referring to the theological truth: "Head and members are one body." In this sense, the Son of Man, Head of His Church, continues to suffer in the members of His Body, and so in them He can still be the object of our compassion and mercy. Indeed, is not mercy shown toward anyone in some way mercy directed toward the compassionate Christ? We shall discuss this in greater depth in Chapter Five on St. Margaret Mary and devotion to the Sacred Heart.

Even when we fail to be merciful, St. Thomas reassures us that Divine Mercy for the repentant is not just adequate or sufficient for us, but superabundant, as infinite as God's nature itself. He writes of the "infinity of the Divine Mercy, which is greater than any number and magnitude of sins. ... The mercy of God grants pardon to sinners through penance without any limits" (ST III.84.10).

Divine Mercy without any limits: such is the mercy theology of St. Thomas Aquinas!

Study Questions

1. What did St. Thomas mean when he wrote that Jesus made "satisfaction" for our sins by His whole life of obedient, suffering love?

2. How can we mercifully "bear one another's burdens" in the Body of Christ today?

3. What act of mercy did Mary do for the human race at the Annunciation?

Discussion Starter:

Why is it considered part of the "Gospel" (good news) message that the divine Son of God shared our human condition walking through all the joys, sorrows, and pains of the human journey of life and death? Does that make a difference to us in our relationship with God? Read Hebrews 4:15-16 and discuss.

CHAPTER FOUR

St. Catherine of Siena

Catherine Benincasa (1347-1380) was born in Siena, Italy, into a family of no great wealth or social standing. She received little in the way of formal education. At the age of six, she had a vision of Christ in the sky above a Dominican Church, and at age seven, she made a private vow of celibacy to Christ. In fact, as a young girl she was noted not only for her piety, but also for her cheerfulness. She was nicknamed Euphrosyne, which means the classical grace of "merriment."

At the age of 18, Catherine was admitted into the Dominican Third Order — a select group of female tertiaries, mostly widows, called the mantellate. They lived in their own homes or family homes, yet kept religious vows and were permitted to wear the Dominican habit.

Thereafter, Catherine began a most remarkable life of prayer, asceticism, literary production, and public activism. As we shall see, the whole of her spiritual vision centered upon the mercy of God.

1. POLITICAL AND ECCLESIAL ACTIVISM

Catherine's reputation for holiness arose from her frequent efforts at nursing the sick, especially when she and some of her companions heroically practiced this work of mercy as the plague swept through Siena. Catherine then put her reputation to good effect: writing to popes, kings, and

other notable persons, lecturing them on their moral and religious duties in the midst of the confusion and strife of the 14th
century. In particular, she insisted that Pope Gregory abandon
the papal residence in Avignon, France, and return the head-
quarters of the Holy See to Rome, the city of St. Peter. In this
political and ecclesial effort she was largely successful. In part
for this reason, she was named a patron saint of the city of
Rome. However, she failed in one of her other political and
ecclesiastical interventions: her attempt to settle the schism in
the Church caused by the three rival claimants to the papal
throne. Catherine had strongly supported the claims of the
first of the contending popes to be elected, Urban VI, but it
would later take an ecumenical council of the Church to sort
out the mess.

2. PRAYER AND ASCETICISM

Catherine was clearly a mystic of the highest order, and
she lived a life saturated with prayer. For example, in 1370,
when she was 23 years old, Christ answered her earnest prayer
that He take her heart and give her His own instead. She
insisted to her confessor that a mystical exchange of hearts
with Christ actually happened after that, and her companions
testified that they had seen the wound in her side as a sign and
testimony of what Christ had done for her. Obviously, this
outer sign of the wound was symbolic of a deeper, mystical
union with God that Christ had given to her.

Catherine's spiritual teaching can be summed up in a few
lines that she wrote to one of her disciples:

> Build yourself a spiritual cell, which you can always
> take with you, and that is the cell of self-knowledge;
> you will find there also the knowledge of God's
> goodness to you. There are really two cells in one,
> and if you live in one you must also live in the other,

otherwise the soul will either despair or be presumptuous; if you dwelt in self-knowledge alone you would despair; if you dwelt in knowledge of God alone you would be tempted to presumption. One must go with the other, and thus you will reach perfection (as quoted in Thomas Maynard, *Saints for Our Times*, Image Books, 1955, p. 77).

Saint Catherine was also a remarkable ascetic. She wore a hair shirt until she found it impossible to keep it clean. Then she replaced it with a still more painful iron chain around her waist. During her adult life, she usually slept less than one hour every night and took almost no food at all: Holy Communion was often her only sustenance throughout the day. To some extent, she did all this out of penance for her sins and in order to be the master of her bodily appetites and passions. However, her minimal food and sleep seem not to have been voluntary penances at all: rather, she seemed to be guided by God to withdraw herself from the flesh in this way. In any case, by God's grace she did not seem to want or need much of either. She writes in a letter to a friend in Florence: "I have prayed constantly, and do pray God and shall pray Him, that in this matter of eating He will give me grace to live like other creatures, if it is His will — for it is mine" (Maynard, p. 72).

It may be that these deprivations hastened her death (she died at age 33), but it is also a fact that she was a woman of remarkable energy, humility, tenderness, and even, at times, holy imperiousness (that is, "tough love"). She also crowded more "achievements" into her short life than most people who live twice as long. Today we might focus more on interior mortification of the will and on keeping our bodies healthy for the service of the Lord, rather than on bodily mortifications. Nevertheless, it may be that the Lord used extraordinary means with Catherine to produce a saint of extraordinary gifts — including a personality of extreme toughness, since she could courageously stand up to popes, emperors, and kings with the Gospel truth. Moreover, the fact that her soul was so freed from bodily distractions may have helped her to receive special guidance from the Holy Spirit in the mysteries of the spiritual life. More on this point later.

3. LITERARY OUTPUT

In addition to a few hundred personal letters, St. Catherine is also noted for writing a great spiritual masterpiece, *The Dialogue*, which she dictated to three secretaries while she was in a state of mystical ecstasy over a period of five days (from October 9-13, 1378). One of her scribes who was witness to all this and participated in the event gives us the following description of what transpired:

> She dictated now to one, now to another, now hiding her face in her hands, now looking up to heaven with her hands crossed, and at every moment she was rapt in ecstasy, yet she continued dictating. But now it happened that she said some words addressed to only one of us, and each of us thought they were addressed to ourselves in particular, and we all wrote them down (Maynard, p. 68).

It is utterly remarkable that such a document could have been "dictated" at all, given the richness and complexity of its teachings and metaphors — and remarkable too that it could have been accomplished in only five days, since the work is over 300 pages long. *The Dialogue* is distinctive in two additional ways: First, it is a dialogue mostly between her soul and God the Father (rather than with Christ, who is the usual "dialogue" partner for Christian mystics), and second, the work is centered on the theme of Divine Mercy.

We will not outline here the entire teaching of St. Catherine's masterpiece, *The Dialogue*. Rather we will focus on the theme of Divine Mercy as it appears in the book, especially in chapter 3, called "Dialogue," and the central chapter of the work, chapter 4, called "The Bridge."

In chapter 3, St. Catherine makes three petitions to God the Father. First, she asks for mercy upon the Church, the "mystic Body," which is so badly in need of reform and renewal. God the Father responds by reassuring her of the redemptive power of Christ's blood. Second, she asks for mercy upon the world, and God responds by showing her with greater clarity how the poison of selfish sensuality is infecting the world. Third, she asks for grace for her confessor and assistant, Raymond of Capua, that he may follow the truth in all things. God the Father responds by telling her of the central truth of the faith: that He has given Christ to us to be a "bridge" of mercy for the world to cross, so we can be united with His fatherly love. Saint Catherine then asks to know more of this "bridge," and the answer she receives to that request forms the basis of the next chapter of her book.

4. THE BRIDGE OF MERCY

Chapter 4 contains much of the essence of St. Catherine's spiritual understanding. She describes first how the damned are those who try to cross the river of life underneath the bridge. As a result, they are swept away by the raging waters of the world, their own passions, and the Devil. Then she is told that there are three ways to cross the bridge itself. The first is the way of those who approach God primarily out of fear of punishment, and on that basis they begin to be contrite for their sins and seek God's forgiveness. The second way is the way of those who cross the bridge out of "ordinary charity," seeking with patience and perseverance to pray and meditate on the Gospels and practice the virtues, although they are very dependent upon the consolations that God gives to them in prayer (and so their following of Christ is still mixed with a fair degree of self-love). Finally, there is the way of the "perfect," those who are willing to abandon all consolations and accept any suffering, so long as it pleases God and wins souls for Him. This is the way of perfect charity, akin to what other saints (for example, St. Teresa of Avila) will call the way of mystical union with God.

What is it that propels the Christian soul to seek to cross the bridge in the first place and that encourages and assists us every step of the way? The answer is Divine Mercy. It is knowledge of the breadth and depth of Divine Mercy that inspires and comforts the soul on its journey. In one of the most famous passages in the book, St. Catherine breaks into a canticle of praise of The Divine Mercy, which is arguably unequalled in the literature of Catholic spirituality:

> By your mercy we were created. And by your mercy we were created anew in your Son's blood. It is your mercy that preserves us. Your mercy made your Son play death against life and life against death on the wood of the cross. In him life confounded the death that is our sin, even while that same death of sin robbed the spotless Lamb of his bodily life. But who was conquered? Death! And how? By your mercy!

> Your mercy is life-giving. It is the light in which both the upright and the sinners discover your goodness. Your mercy shines forth in your saints in the height of heaven. And if I turn to the earth, your mercy is everywhere. Even in the darkness of hell your mercy shines, for you do not punish the damned as much as they deserve.

> You temper your justice with mercy. In mercy you cleansed us in the blood; in mercy you kept company with your creatures. O mad lover! It was not enough for you to take on our humanity: you had to die as well! Nor was death enough: You descended to the depths to summon our holy ancestors and fulfill your truth and mercy in them. Your goodness promises good to those who serve you in truth, so you went

to call these servants of yours from their suffering to reward them for their labours!

I see your mercy pressing us to give you even more when you leave yourself with us as food to strengthen our weakness, so that we forgetful fools should be ever reminded of your goodness. Every day you give us this food, showing us yourself in the sacrament of the altar within the mystic body of the Holy Church. And what has done this? Your mercy.

O mercy! My heart is engulfed with the thought of you! For wherever I turn my thoughts I find nothing but mercy! O eternal Father, forgive my foolish presumption in babbling on so before you — but your merciful love is my excuse in the presence of your kindness (Paulist Press edition, 1980, no. 30).

5. DIVINE MERCY GREATER THAN SIN AND DESPAIR

For St. Catherine, the merciful love of God so essentially defines who He is that, along with St. Augustine and St. Thomas, Catherine understands that it is precisely *despair* of His mercy that constitutes the only unforgivable sin. It is the offense of considering one's own sin to be greater than God the Father's mercy:

This is that sin which is never forgiven, now or ever: the refusal, the scorning of my mercy. For this offends me more than all the other sins they have committed. So the despair of Judas displeased me more and was a greater insult to my Son than his betrayal had been. Therefore, such as these are reproved for this false judgment of considering their sins to be greater than my mercy, and for this they are punished with the demons and tortured eternally with them.

They are reproved also for their injustice in grieving more for their own plight than for having offended me. They are being unjust in this because they are not giving me what is mine, nor taking for themselves what belongs to them. It is their duty to offer love and bitter heartfelt contrition in my presence for the sins they have committed against me. But they have done the opposite: they have lavished such tender love on themselves and felt so sorry about the punishment they expect for their sins! So you see how unjust they are.

They will be punished therefore on both accounts. They have scorned my mercy, so I turn them over to my justice. I condemn them along with their cruel servant, sensuality, and with the devil, that merciless tyrant to whom they bound themselves as slaves through the mediation of that selfish sensuality of theirs (no. 37).

It would seem that we have here a rigid separation between God's mercy and God's justice. However, St. Catherine makes it clear later that it is not so much that God will destroy those who refuse His mercy; rather, God will permit them to destroy themselves if they do not willingly receive and accept His merciful aid. If we stubbornly will it so, we can cut ourselves off from Him forever. For example, Catherine explains in the words of God the Father that the loving "glance" of Christ will be received differently by different souls on the Judgment Day, depending on their self-chosen dispositions:

His glance will be such a torment and terror to the damned that words cannot describe it. But for the just it will be a cause for reverent fear and great rejoicing. Not that his face will change—for he is one with my divine nature and therefore unchangeable, and even in his human nature his face is unchangeable since it has taken on the glory of his resurrection. But it will seem so to the eyes of the damned. For they will see him with terribly darkened vision. A healthy eye looks at the sun and sees light. But a sick eye sees nothing but darkness when it looks into such lightsomeness—and it is no fault of the light that it seems so different to the two; the fault is in the sick eye. So the damned see my Son in darkness, confusion, and hatred, not through any fault of my divine Majesty with which he comes to judge the world, but through their own fault (no. 39).

For St. Catherine, as we have seen, it is vital to our spiritual health that we come to self-knowledge, especially knowledge of how dependent we are upon God for everything: for existence itself, and for the grace that sets us free from sin. Yet we can only safely arrive at this self-knowledge in the light of God's infinite mercy. Otherwise, in gazing at ourselves and our own sinfulness and nothingness, we could easily fall into despair. Saint Catherine says that this is one of the ways that the Devil tries to deceive and entrap us:

> Now I do not want her [that is, the soul] to think about her sins individually, lest her mind be contaminated by the memory of specific ugly sins. I mean that I do not want her to, nor should she, think about her sins either in general or specifically without calling to mind the blood [of Christ] and the greatness of my mercy. Otherwise she will only be confounded. For if self-knowledge and the thought of sin are not seasoned with remembrance of the blood and hope for mercy, the result is bound to be confusion. And along with this comes the devil, who under the guise of contrition and hatred for sin and sorrow for her guilt leads her to eternal damnation. Because of this — though not this alone — she would end in despair if she did not reach out for the arm of my mercy.

> This is one of the subtle deceptions the devil works on my servants. So for your own good, to escape his

deceit and to be pleasing to me, you must keep expanding your heart and your affection in the immeasurable greatness of my mercy, with true humility. For know this: the devil's pride cannot tolerate a humble mind, nor can his confounding withstand the greatness of my goodness and mercy when a soul is truly hopeful (no. 66).

Finally, St. Catherine gives us a beautiful symbol of the merciful love of God when Christ explains to her why blood and water poured out from His pierced side after His death. The ancient Church Fathers had generally held that these two elements flowing from the pierced side of Christ were symbolic of the graces of Baptism (water) and the Eucharist (blood), graces that Christ won for us on the Cross and from which the Church is born. Without contradicting this ancient testimony, St. Catherine is shown another layer of symbolism in the blood and the water. She asks our Lord: "Why, gentle spotless Lamb, since you were dead when your side was opened, did you want your heart to be pierced and parted?" (no. 75). Jesus replied:

> There were plenty of reasons, but I shall tell you one of the chief. My longing for humankind was infinite, but the actual deed of bearing pain and torment was finite and could never show all the love I had. This is why I wanted you to see my inmost heart, so that you would see that I loved you more than finite suffering could show.

Thus, our Lord tells St. Catherine that His merciful love is so infinitely deep and broad that it could not be adequately expressed even by His (finite) act of dying for us in torment on the Cross — it overflows, so to speak, the boundaries of even that demonstration of His love, for no finite act could ever fully contain or exhaust it! This is the same infinity of God's merciful love that St. Paul was referring to when he wrote in Ephesians of "the love of Christ that surpasses knowledge" (Eph 3:18-19).

And of course, as we shall see, this is also the same symbol — the blood and water gushing forth from His pierced side — that our Lord will choose to sum up His infinite mercy when He appears to St. Maria Faustina Kowalska almost six centuries later and gives to her the Image of The Divine Mercy.

Study Questions

1. What were the two inner spiritual "cells" that St. Catherine of Siena believed we need to dwell in simultaneously in order to advance closer to Christian perfection?

2. According to St. Catherine, what is "The Bridge of Mercy?" What are the raging waters beneath that bridge, and what are the three ways we can safely cross over it?

3. How does St. Catherine describe the union of mercy and justice in the "glance" of Christ, as it is beheld by both the blessed and the damned on the Judgment Day?

Discussion Starter:

Saint Catherine received an explanation from Jesus Christ about the meaning of the symbolism of the blood and water that gushed forth from His pierced Heart after His death. What does this symbolism mean? What other vivid images and symbols of the merciful love of Jesus Christ do we have in the Catholic Tradition — and what do they mean to you?

CHAPTER FIVE

St. Francis of Assisi and the Early Franciscans

In the High Middle Ages, the theme of the merciful love of God was certainly not the exclusive property of St. Thomas Aquinas, St. Catherine of Siena, and the Dominicans. The early Franciscans also contributed to the Church's meditations on Divine Mercy in their own distinctive way.

1. THE LIFE OF ST. FRANCIS

We know from *The Life of St. Francis* written by St. Bonaventure (1217-1274) that one of the divine perfections Bonaventure saw most clearly reflected in St. Francis of Assisi was God's mercy. Saint Bonaventure writes the following lines in the "Prologue" to the biography:

> In these latter days the grace of God our Savior has appeared in his servant Francis to all who are truly humble and lovers of holy poverty. In him they can venerate God's superabundant mercy, and be taught by his example to live in conformity with Christ, and to thirst after blessed hope with unflagging desire (Paulist Press edition, 1978).

Later in the same work, St. Bonaventure tells us that one of the principal intentions of St. Francis's own prayers was pleading for mercy upon the world, on the basis of the sorrowful passion of Jesus Christ:

> When the man of God was left alone and at peace, he would fill the groves with sighs, sprinkle the ground with tears, striking his breast with his fist, and having found there a kind of secret hiding place, would converse with his Lord. There he would answer his Judge, there he would entreat his Father, there he would entertain his Friend; and there also on several occasions the friars who were devoutly observing him heard him groan aloud, imploring the divine mercy for sinners and weeping for the Lord's passion as if it were before his eyes (ch.10, no. 4).

Still later in his biography, St. Bonaventure tells the story of the words of St. Francis about Divine Mercy to a hardened sinner that brought about the man's conversion:

> Another time, a noble woman, devoted to God, came to the saint to explain her trouble to him and ask for help. She had a very cruel husband who opposed her serving Christ. So she begged the saint to pray for him so that God in His goodness would soften his heart. When [St. Francis] heard this he said to her: "Go in peace, and without any doubt be assured that your husband will soon be a comfort to you." And he added: "Tell him on God's part and on my own, that now is the time of mercy, and afterwards of justice." After receiving a blessing, the woman went home, found her husband and delivered the message. The Holy Spirit came upon him (Acts 10:44) making him a new man and inducing him to answer with gentleness: "My lady, let us serve the Lord and save our souls." At the suggestion of his holy wife, they lived a celibate life for many years, and both passed away to the Lord on the same day (ch.10, no. 6).

We know from other sources that the message of Divine Mercy was also on the mind of St. Francis at the time of his death. In a biography entitled *Francis of Assisi: The Man Who Found Perfect Joy* (Sophia Institute Press), Michael de la Bedoyere tells how, as Francis lay dying, he asked his brethren to sing with him the "Canticle of the Sun" that he had composed in praise of the Creator. Brother Elias, seated by his side, protested: "Should you not keep recollected and silent?" St. Francis replied: "O let me rejoice in God, and in praising Him in all my sufferings, since by a wonderful grace, I feel myself so close to my Lord that, in the knowledge of His mercy, I can sing again" (p. 302). As the litter on which he lay was carried out in sight of the city of Assisi, Francis offered up this prayer:

> Lord, whereas this city was in olden times a place inhabited by wicked men, I see now that through Your great mercy, in Your own good time, You have been merciful to it more than to other cities. You have chosen it to be the home of those who acknowledge and give glory to Your holy Name. It is giving the world an example of good report, saintly life, full and pure teaching, and of evangelical perfection. I ask You then, my Lord Jesus Christ, Father of all mercy, to overlook our ingratitude, and always to bear in mind Your great pity, that the city should forever be the home of those who truly know Thee and glorify Thy blessed Name forever and ever. Amen (p. 315-316).

2. THE LITTLE FLOWERS OF ST. FRANCIS

If we turn from these relatively reliable sources on the life of St. Francis to the early legends told about him, as recorded in the delightful 14th century collection known as the *Fioretti*, or *The Little Flowers of St. Francis*, we find several touching and beautiful stories about Divine Mercy. Although some of this material is legendary, it is also traceable in part back to oral testimony from some of the earliest companions of the saint. Thus, the whole collection breathes something of the childlike spirit of the early friars: poor mendicants who lived as "holy fools" for the love of Christ Jesus.

Three examples from *The Little Flowers of St. Francis* will suffice. In each of these examples, the merciful love of God — manifest in His willingness to forgive sins — is the central theme.

The first is entitled "How St. Francis taught Friar Leo to answer, and how he was never able to speak except to say the opposite of what St. Francis desired":

> Once, in the beginning of the Order, St. Francis was with Friar Leo in a place where they had no books for saying the Divine Office. When the hour of matins came, St. Francis said to Friar Leo, "Most dear companion, we have no breviary with which we can say matins, but so that we may spend the time in the praise of God, I will speak and you shall answer as I will teach you. See to it that you do not change the words in any way other than I shall teach you. I will say thus: 'O Friar Francis, you have done so many evils and so many sins in the world that you are worthy of hell,' and you shall answer, 'It is true that you deserve the lowest place in hell.'"

> Friar Leo, with dove-like simplicity replied, "Willingly, Father. Begin in the name of God." Then St. Francis began to say, "Friar Francis, you have done so many evils and so many sins in the world, that you are worthy of hell." And Friar Leo answered, "God shall do so much good through you that, as a result, you shall go to Paradise." St. Francis said, "That isn't what you should say, Friar Leo, but when I say, 'Friar Francis, you have done so many wicked things against God, that you are worthy to be accursed from God,' answer thus: 'Truly you are worthy to be sent among the accursed.'" And Friar

Leo answered, "Willingly, Father."

Then St. Francis, with many tears and sighs and beatings of the breast, said with a loud voice, "O my Lord of heaven and earth, I have committed so many wicked deeds and so many sins against You that I am altogether worthy to be accursed from You." Friar Leo answered, "O Friar Francis, God will make you so that among the blessed you shall be singularly blessed." Now St. Francis, marveling that Friar Leo answered contrary to that he had bidden him, rebuked him saying, "Why do you not answer as I teach you? I will speak thus: 'O Friar Francis, miserable sinner, think you that God will have mercy upon you, seeing that you have committed so many sins against the Father of Mercy?' And you Friar Leo, little sheep, shall answer, 'In no way are you worthy to find mercy.'" But afterward, when St. Francis said, "O Friar Francis, miserable sinner," etc., Friar Leo answered, "God the Father, whose mercy is infinitely greater than your sin, will show you such great mercy, and beyond that will give you much grace."

At this reply, St. Francis, sweetly angered and patiently upset, said to Friar Leo, "And how is it that you have had the presumption to act against your vow of obedience and have already so many times replied contrary to what I have commanded you?" Friar Leo answered very humbly and reverently, "God knows, my Father, that each time I resolved in my heart to answer as you have bidden me, but God makes me speak as pleases Him, and not according to what pleases me."

At this St. Francis marveled and said to Friar Leo, "I beseech you very lovingly that this time you answer me as I have told you." Friar Leo answered, "Speak, in the name of God, because you can be sure that this time I will answer as you would have me." And St.

Francis, weeping, said, "O Friar Francis, miserable sinner, think you that God will have mercy upon you?" Friar Leo answered, "Yea, and not only so, but great grace shall you receive from God, and He shall exalt you and shall glorify you forever, because *whoever humbles himself shall be exalted,* and I cannot speak otherwise in that God speaks through my mouth." And in this way, in that humble strife, with many tears and much spiritual consolation, they kept watch until daybreak (Vintage Books edition, 1998, ch.9).

Our second example is taken from Chapter 26, and describes how St. Francis converted three robbers by preaching to them about God's mercy:

"Let us go," said one [of the robbers], "to St. Francis, and if he gives us hope that we may be able to turn from our sins to the mercy of God, let us do that which he commands us, if by so doing we may deliver our souls from the pains of hell." This counsel was pleasing to the others, and so all three of them being agreed, they went in haste to St. Francis and spoke to him thus, "Father, by reason of the many horrible sins which we have committed, we do not believe that we can turn to the mercy of God. But if you have any hope that God will receive us with mercy, indeed we are ready to do what you shall bid us, and to do penance with you."

Then St. Francis received them lovingly and benignly, with many examples, assuring them of the mercy of God and promising them that of a certainty he would obtain it for them from God, showing them that the mercy of God is infinite, and even if our sins were infinite, the mercy of God is greater than our sins, according to the Gospel. St. Paul the Apostle said, "Christ the blessed came into the world to redeem sinners."

Through these words and similar teachings, the three robbers renounced the devil and his works. St. Francis received them into the Order, and they began to do great penance.

Our final example comes from Chapter 45 of *The Little Flowers of St. Francis*, and tells how a certain Friar Matthew relieved a soul of an inordinate fear of damnation:

> What vexed [Friar John] worst of all was that a demon stood ever before him, holding in his hand a great scroll on which were written all the sins he had ever done or thought. It spoke to him continually, saying, "For these sins which you have committed in thought, word, and deed, you are condemned to the depths of hell." And he began not to remember the good things he had done, or that he was in the Order, or that he had ever been in it; and eventually he truly believed that he was damned, even as the demon had told him. Whenever he was asked how he fared, he answered, "Ill, for I am damned."
>
> Now when the friars saw this, they sent for an aged friar, who was called Friar Matthew of Monte Rubbiano. He was a holy man, and a great friend of Friar John's. Friar Matthew came to him on the seventh day of his affliction and saluted him. He asked him how he fared, to which he replied that he fared ill because he was damned. Then Friar Matthew said, "Do you not remember that I have often heard your confession and that I have wholly absolved you of all your sins? Do you not remember that you have been serving God in this holy Order for many years? Further, do you not remember that the mercy of God is greater than all the sins of the world, and that Christ the Blessed, our Savior, paid to redeem us at an infinite price? Be of good hope that for certain you are saved."

While he was speaking, since the period of Friar John's purgation was now ended, the temptation left him, and consolation came unto him. Then Friar John spoke to Friar Matthew with great joy, saying, "Because you are weary and the hour is late, I pray you go and take some rest." Although Friar Matthew did not want to leave him, in the end, after much urging, he left him and went to lie down. Friar John remained alone with the friar who was caring for him. Suddenly Christ the Blessed came with great splendor and with an exceedingly great fragrance, just as He had promised him that He would appear to him a second time when he had greater need of it. He healed him thoroughly of all his sicknesses. Then Friar John, with clasped hands, gave thanks to God, because he had brought the long journey of the present miserable life to so fair an ending. Commending his soul into the hands of Christ and yielding it up to God, he passed from this mortal life to the eternal life with Christ the Blessed, whom he had so long waited for and desired to behold.

3. ST. BONAVENTURE AND THE TREE OF LIFE

Let us move on now to the works of St. Bonaventure, the great 13th century mystic, philosopher, theologian, and Doctor of the Church. We have already seen how St. Bonaventure traces the theme of God's merciful love in the life of St. Francis. However, he also wrote extended meditations on the life of Jesus Christ, especially in a work entitled *The Tree of Life*. In the New Testament image of "Jesus, the Solicitous Shepherd," St. Bonaventure discerns the merciful love of our Savior:

How great was this devoted shepherd's solicitous care for the lost sheep and how great his mercy, the Good

Shepherd himself indicates with an affectionate metaphor in the parable of the shepherd and the hundredth sheep that was lost, sought with much care, and finally found and joyfully brought back on his shoulders. He openly declares the same thing in an express statement when he says: "The good shepherd gives his life for his sheep" (Jn 10:11). In him is truly fulfilled the prophecy: "Like a shepherd he will feed his flock" (Is 40:11). In order to do this he endured toil, anxiety, and lack of food; he traveled through towns and villages preaching the kingdom of God in the midst of many dangers and the plotting of the Pharisees; and he passed nights in watchful prayer. Fearless of the murmuring and scandal of the Pharisees, he was affable to the publicans, saying that he had come into the world for the sake of those who are sick (Mt 9:12). He also extended fatherly affection to the repentant, showing them the open bosom of divine mercy. As witnesses to this I call upon and summon Matthew, Zacchaeus, the sinful woman who prostrated herself at his feet, and the woman taken in adultery (no. 13).

In the next section of *The Tree of Life*, St. Bonaventure tells us that the truth that Jesus is "the Fountain of all mercy" is manifest by His tears:

To manifest the sweetness of supreme devotedness, the Fountain of all mercy, the good Jesus, wept for us in our misery not only once but many times. First over Lazarus, then over the city [of Jerusalem] and finally on the cross, a flood of tears streamed from those loving eyes for the expiation of all sins. The Savior wept abundantly, now deploring the misery of human weakness, now the darkness of a blind heart, now the depravity of obdurate malice (no. 14).

Finally, in section 20 of the same work, entitled "Jesus Bound with Chains," St. Bonaventure again refers to our

Lord as "the Fountain of mercy," but this time as that Fountain to which the traitor Judas refused to turn in the midst of Judas's final despair:

> Woe to that man who did not return to the fountain of mercy out of hope of forgiveness but, terrified by the enormity of his crime, despaired!

Looking at these early Franciscan references to Divine Mercy, one is struck by their focus on God's merciful love expressed in His willingness to forgive our sins and pour into our hearts that sanctifying grace, which is so much greater than our sins. As we have seen, this focus is the same in the life of St. Francis, the writings of St. Bonaventure, and in the legends of the early Franciscans entitled *The Little Flowers of St. Francis.*

Among the early Dominicans, on the other hand, such as St. Thomas Aquinas and St. Catherine of Siena, Divine Mercy is usually seen as a much broader theological concept: It is God's gracious condescension whereby He seeks to meet the needs and overcome all the miseries of His creatures. As St. Catherine put it: "Wherever I look I find nothing but mercy."

The differences between the two mendicant spiritualities, however, are more of style and of emphasis than of substance. For example, St. Thomas Aquinas admitted that the salvation of a soul through the mercy of God was a greater act than His creation of the whole world, because it has an eternal effect (the everlasting salvation of a soul); whereas, the whole earthly creation is merely a temporal effect of God's omnipotence and wisdom and will one day pass away. Thus, even the greatest Dominican theologian gives a certain "pride of place" to God's mercy expressed in the form of the forgiveness of sins.

Moreover, we need to remember the differing charisms given by the Holy Spirit to these two religious Orders. From the very beginning, the Dominicans' special charism involved the task of preaching and teaching the fullness of Catholic Doctrine. The early Franciscans, on the other hand, originally were devoted primarily to "penance" and to preaching the call to repentance. It is no wonder that in the early Franciscan

writings, it is this expression of Divine Mercy — the mercy of
the Good Shepherd for His lost sheep — that is the heart of
their preaching and writing.

Study Questions

1. In *The Little Flowers of St. Francis*, what
   does the story of Br. Leo and St. Francis
   teach us about the merciful love of God?

2. In *The Little Flowers*, what message did St.
   Francis preach to the three robbers that
   led to their conversion?

3. In *The Little Flowers*, what words of
   comfort did Friar Matthew say to Fr. John
   that cured him of his despair?

Discussion Starter:

Read the 23rd Psalm, "The Lord is My
Shepherd" — and after it St. Bonaventure's
meditation on "Jesus, the Solicitous
Shepherd." In what way does the Psalm make
you think of Jesus? What do each of the
stanzas of the Psalm mean to you, in your
walk with Christ?

CHAPTER SIX

St. John Eudes, St. Margaret Mary, and Devotion to the Sacred Heart

⸺◦◦◦◦◦⸺

Catholic devotion to the merciful love of God expanded dramatically in the 17th century through the special graces poured out upon two chosen souls: St. John Eudes (1601-1680) and St. Margaret Mary Alacoque (1647-1690).

1. ST. JOHN EUDES

⸺◦◦◦◦◦⸺

Saint John Eudes was born into a peasant family in Normandy, France, in 1601. After discerning a call to the priesthood he joined the Oratorians and studied under two of the greatest French Oratorian spiritual masters: Cardinal Pierre de Berulle and Fr. Charles de Condren. Berulle emphasized in his writings a scriptural doctrine that had been neglected too often in the past: the following of Jesus is not a mere "Imitation of Christ" — an external conformity to His example — but a complete surrender to the indwelling of Christ in the depths (*le fond*) of the soul. When He lives within us in our very depths, then He shares with us His grace and virtues, His interior dispositions and sentiments. He lives in and through us the mysteries of His own incarnate life. It is not surprising, therefore, that one of the earliest and most important works to come from the pen of St. John Eudes was entitled *The Life and Kingdom of Jesus Christ in Christian Souls*. The first section of that work bears the subtitle: "The Christian Life Must be a Continuation of the Most Holy Life Which Jesus Lived on Earth."

In 1643, St. John Eudes founded a new religious order
— the Congregation of Jesus and Mary — principally dedicated
to priestly formation and missionary work. Later in his life, he
became noted for his devotion to the Sacred Hearts of Jesus
and Mary and for his strong opposition to the Jansenist heresy
that was plaguing the French Church in his day. The
Jansenists became famous for insisting that no one should
make a sacramental confession without perfect contrition for
their sins nor presume to receive Holy Communion without
having made such a confession. The result was a dramatic
decline in the frequency of the reception of the Sacraments
throughout France and a decline in appreciation for the
merciful love of God.

Saint John Eudes discerned that the best remedy for this
spiritual illness was devotion to the loving, compassionate
Heart of Jesus. In fact, he was the first to seriously develop the
liturgical worship of the Sacred Heart, so that at his canonization in 1909, Pope St. Pius X called him "father, doctor, and
apostle of the liturgical cult of the Hearts of Jesus and Mary."
It is especially in the latter period of the life of St. John Eudes
(that is, post 1643) that we find passages in his works extolling
the merciful love of the Sacred Heart of Christ, above all in his
work entitled *The Sacred Heart of Jesus*. Perhaps no one has
written more movingly of the interior life of Jesus — His dispositions, virtues, sentiments, and affections — than St. John
Eudes did in this book. For example, although he does not use
the word "mercy" in the passage below, it is clear that the
merciful, compassionate love of the Heart of Jesus is precisely
what he is describing when he wrote chapter 8, entitled, "The
Sacred Heart of Jesus Is a Furnace Burning with Love for Us in
His Sacred Passion":

> The first cause of those most painful wounds in the
> Sacred Heart of our Redeemer is our sins. We read in
> the life of St. Catherine of Genoa that one day God let
> her see the horror of one tiny venial sin. She assures us
> that, although this vision lasted but a moment, she saw

nevertheless an object so frightening that the blood froze in her veins and she swooned away in an agony that would have killed her if God had not preserved her to relate to others what she had seen. Wherefore she declared that if she were in the very depths of a sea of flaming fire and it were in her power to be set free, on condition that she should once more behold such a spectacle, she would choose to remain rather than to escape. If the sight of the smallest venial sin brought this saint to such a pass, what must we think of the state to which our Savior was reduced by seeing all the sins of the universe? He had them continually before His eyes, and His vision being infinitely more powerful than that of St. Catherine, He could behold infinitely more horror.

He saw the immeasurable insult and dishonor caused His Father by all sins; He saw the damnation of a countless number of souls resulting from those sins. As He had infinite love for His Father and His creatures, the sight of all those sins rent His Heart with countless wounds, such that if we were able to count all the sins of men, which are more numerous than the drops of water in the sea, we would then be able to count the wounds of the loving Heart of Jesus.

The second cause of His wounds is the infinite love of His Sacred Heart for all of His children, and his constant vision of all the afflictions and sufferings that are to happen to them, especially all the torments that His holy martyrs are to suffer. When a mother watches her beloved child suffering, she feels the pain more keenly than the child. Our Savior's love for us is so tremendous that if the love of all parents were centered in a single heart, it would not represent even a spark of the love for us that burns in His Heart. Our pains and sorrows, ever present to His vision and seen most clearly and distinctly, were so many wounds bleeding in His paternal Heart: *Vere nostros ipse tulit, et aegrotationes nostras portavit.* These wounds were so painful and deep that they would have caused His death a thousand times over, even immediately after His birth, if He had not miraculously preserved Himself, because during His whole earthly life His Sacred Heart was continually pierced by many mortal wounds of love.

Therefore we have the greatest obligation to honor the gracious Heart that sustained so many wounds of love for us. ... With what affection should we embrace, and endure all our afflictions, out of love for Jesus, our Savior, since He first bore them for love of us! Should they not be most sweet to us, since they have already passed through His most gentle and loving Heart? What a horror we should have of our sins that have caused so many wounds and such intense grief to the divine Heart of our Redeemer ... !

Let us learn from the foregoing example that it is not our Redeemer's fault if we are lost. There are hearts so hard that, even if Jesus Himself were to come down from heaven to preach to them and they were to see Him covered with wounds and bathed in His blood, they would still not be converted. O my God, let us not be one of them, but give us the grace to open our ears to the voice of all the sacred wounds of Thy body and Thy heart, which are so many mouths through which Thou dost call us unceasingly: *Redite, praevaricatores, ad cor.* "Return, ye transgressors, to the heart," which means to My Heart that is all yours, since I have given it entirely to you. Return to that most loving Heart of your Father, which is full of love and mercy for you, which will receive you home, heaping upon you blessings (Preserving Christian Publications, 1977 edition).

As St. John Eudes was one of the leading proponents of devotion to the Sacred Heart of Jesus, it is interesting to note that he also discerned a close connection between the Heart of Jesus and Divine Mercy. In his collection of meditations entitled *The Sacred Heart of Jesus*, the saint reflects on mercy as the principal perfection of that loving Heart. In the section of that book bearing the subtitle "The Divine Mercy Should be the Object of our Very Special Devotion," he writes:

> Of all the divine perfections mirrored in the Sacred Heart of our Saviour, we should have a very special devotion to divine mercy and we should endeavor to engrave its image on our heart. To this end three things must be done. The first is to pardon with all our heart and promptly forget the offenses done us by our neighbor. The second is to have compassion on his bodily sufferings, and to relieve and succor him. The third is to be compassionate toward the spiritual misfortunes of our brethren, which are much more deserving of our commiseration than corporal ills. For this reason we ought to have great pity on the numbers of wretched souls who have no pity on themselves, using our prayers, our example, and our teaching to safeguard them from the eternal torments of hell.

2. ST. MARGARET MARY AND DEVOTION TO THE SACRED HEART

The link between the Sacred Heart and The Divine Mercy further unfolded in the extraordinary series of prophetic revelations received by St. Margaret Mary Alacoque between 1673-75. Margaret Mary was a Sister of the Order of the Visitation. She had little in the way of education, natural talents, or anything else that might have made her stand out from the rest of her contemporaries, but it is just such lowly vessels that our Lord seems to prefer to use when He is imparting extraordinary revelations and graces to His Church.

In December 1673, St. Margaret Mary received the first of four great apparitions of the loving Heart of Jesus. In the first one, she experienced a mystical phenomenon we have already seen exhibited in the life of St. Catherine of Siena: a mystical "exchange of hearts" with Jesus Christ. She wrote: "[Our Lord] allowed me to recline for a long time on His divine breast, where He disclosed to me the marvels of His love, and the unutterable secrets of His Sacred Heart."

The second apparition took place shortly afterwards, probably on a First Friday of the month in 1674:

> After that the Divine Heart was shown to me as on a throne of flames, more dazzling than the sun and transparent as crystal, with that adorable wound, and surrounded with a crown of thorns signifying the pricks caused to It by our sins; and above there was a cross, which meant that from the first moment of His incarnation, that is as soon as this Sacred Heart was formed, the cross was planted in It, and that It was filled at once with all the bitterness which humiliations and poverty, pains and scorn, would cause to It, and which His Sacred Humanity was to suffer throughout all His lifetime and His Sacred Passion.

> And He showed me that it was His great desire of being loved by men and of withdrawing them from the path of ruin into which Satan hurls such crowds of them, that made him form the design of manifesting His Heart to men, with all the treasures of love, of mercy, of grace, of sanctification, and salvation which It contains, in order that those who desire to render Him and procure for Him all the honour and love possible, might themselves be abundantly enriched with those divine treasures of which this Heart is the source. He should be honoured under the figure of

this heart of flesh, and Its image should be exposed. He wished me to wear this image on my own heart, that He might impress on it His love and fill it with all the gifts with which His Heart is replete, and destroy in it all inordinate affections. He promised me that wherever this image should be exposed with a view to showing It special honour, He would pour forth His blessings and graces. This devotion was the last effort of His love that He would grant to men in these latter ages, in order to withdraw them from the empire of Satan which He desired to destroy, and thus to introduce them into the sweet liberty of the rule of His love, which He wished to restore in the hearts of all those who should embrace this devotion (*Letters*, no. 133: TAN edition, 1977).

Notice that according to St. Margaret Mary, two of the principal "treasures" which Jesus longs to bestow upon mankind from the veneration of His Heart are His "love" and His "mercy." The tremendous compassion of His Heart is also clearly expressed in this passage, for Jesus states that He longs to bestow these blessings upon humanity even though we have wounded His Heart so often and so deeply by our sins. Finally, in this revelation, He seems to attribute the lost condition of mankind more to the assaults of Satan than to the corrupt will of human beings.

It is not by accident that our Lord Jesus recalled the world to the mercy and compassion of His Heart at this time in history. In the 17th century, the Jansenist heresy in Europe led people to think of God principally in terms of His Divine Justice, while at the same time the Deist philosophers led people to believe that God was merely like a cosmic "Watchmaker" who wound up the mechanism of the world at the beginning of time and now lets it run on its own through the operation of the laws of nature, without any further care or concern or intervention needed on His part. What Jesus Christ revealed to St. Margaret Mary — and through her reminded the whole Church — was that the God of the Catholic faith is a God of merciful, compassionate love, summed up and symbolized by the image of His Son's pierced Heart of flesh, aflame with love.

The third apparition of the Sacred Heart took place in July of 1674:

> One day, as I knelt before the Blessed Sacrament exposed on the altar, after feeling withdrawn within myself by an extraordinary recollection of all my senses and faculties, Jesus Christ, my sweet Master, presented Himself to me, all resplendent with glory, with His five wounds shining like so many suns. From all parts of His Sacred Humanity there issued flames but especially from His adorable breast, which was like a furnace. Opening it, He showed me His loving and lovable Heart as the living source of those flames. Then he revealed to me all the unspeakable marvels of His pure love, and the excess of love He had conceived for men from whom He had received nothing but ingratitude and contempt. "This is more grievous to Me," He said, "than all that I endured in my Passion. If they would only give Me some return of love, I should not reckon all that I have done for them, and I would do yet more if possible. But they have only coldness and contempt for all My endeavours to do them good. You, at least, can give Me the happiness of making up for their ingratitude, as much as you can.

> "First, you are to receive Me in the Blessed Sacrament as often as obedience will allow, no matter what mortification or humiliation it may entail. Moreover, you are to receive Holy Communion on the First Friday of each month, and every night between Thursday and Friday I will make you partaker of that sorrow unto death which it was My will to suffer in the Garden of Olives. This sorrow will reduce you, without your understanding how, to

a kind of agony more bitter than death. To join with
Me in the humble prayer which I then offered to My
heavenly Father in agony you are to arise between
eleven and twelve o'clock, and remain with Me upon
your knees for an hour, with your face to the ground,
to appease the anger of My Eternal Father, and to ask
of Him pardon for sinners. You will thus share with
Me, and in a manner soothe the bitter grief I suffered
when my disciples abandoned Me and I was con-
strained to reproach them that they could not watch
with Me even for an hour. During that hour you are
to do what I will teach you."

Jesus makes it clear to St. Margaret Mary in this revelation that the Holy Eucharist is the principal means by which
He applies His merciful love to her soul. Moreover, she is
asked to keep a "Holy Hour" every Thursday night, and
thereby, in some way, keep our Lord company in His agony in
the Garden of Gethsemane long ago. Indeed, twice in this
revelation Jesus assures her by doing these things she can
bring comfort and consolation to His Sacred Heart, wounded
as it is by the sins of thankless men and women. It appears that
St. Margaret Mary is the first one in the history of Catholic spirituality fully to appreciate that in our relationship with Jesus not
only is His "Heart" the source of His merciful love for us, but
also that we can, in a sense, show mercy to Him and console
Him in the Garden and on the Cross by returning His love
today. Pope Pius XI wrote of this mystery in his encyclical
Miserentissimus Redemptor (1928):

> For anyone who has great love of God, if he will look
> back through the tract of past time may dwell in med-
> itation on Christ, and see Him labouring for man,
> sorrowing, suffering the greatest hardship, "for us
> men and for our salvation," well-nigh worn out with
> sadness, with anguish, nay "bruised for our sins (Isaiah
> liii, 5), and healing us by His bruises. And the minds

of the pious meditate on all these things the more truly, because the sins of men and their crimes committed in every age were the cause why Christ was delivered up to death, and now also they would of themselves bring death to Christ, joined with the same griefs and sorrows, since each several sin its own way is held to renew the passion of Our Lord: "Crucifying again to themselves the Son of God, and making him a mockery" (Heb. Vi.6). Now, if because of our sins also which were as yet in the future, but were foreseen, the soul of Christ became sorrowful unto death, it cannot be doubted that then, too, already He derived somewhat of solace from our reparation, which was likewise foreseen, when "there appeared to Him an angel from heaven" (Luke XXII, 43) in order that His Heart, oppressed with weariness and anguish, might find consolation. And so even now, in a wondrous yet true manner, we can and ought to console that most Sacred Heart, which is continually wounded by the sins of thankless men. ...

And for this reason also there have been established many religious families of men and woman whose purpose it is by earnest service, both by day and by night, in some manner to fulfill the office of the Angel consoling Jesus in the garden; hence come certain associations of pious men, approved by the Apostolic See and enriched with indulgences, who take upon themselves this same duty of making expiation, a duty which is to be fulfilled by fitting exercises of devotion and of the virtues (no. 13).

Indeed, Pope John Paul II extended this insight of Pius XI when he wrote in *Dives in Misericordia (Rich in Mercy)* that God the Father "invites man to have 'mercy' on His only Son, the crucified one," so that when we use our freedom to show merciful love to one another it is "a kind of mercy

shown by each one of us to the Son of the eternal Father."
This is "the position of Christ with regard to man when He
says: 'As you did it to one of the least of these … you did it to
me'" (no. 8).

The (fourth) and final apparition of the Sacred Heart to
St. Margaret Mary took place in June of 1675. This is the
famous revelation in which the saint was told of Christ's desire
for the establishment of the liturgical Feast of the Sacred
Heart (an idea that St. John Eudes was developing independ-
ently, around 1668, in another part of France):

> One day, during the octave of Corpus Christi, when
> being before the Blessed Sacrament, I received from
> my God extraordinary proofs of His love. As I
> earnestly desired to make some return of love, He
> said to me: "You could not show me greater love than
> by doing what I have already so many times
> demanded of you." And [opening] to me His Divine
> Heart: "Behold this Heart which has so loved men
> that It spared nothing, even going so far as to exhaust
> and consume Itself, to prove to them Its love. And in
> return I receive from the greater part of men nothing
> but ingratitude, by the contempt, irreverence, sacri-
> leges and coldness with which they treat Me in this
> Sacrament of Love. But what is still more painful to
> Me is that even souls consecrated to Me are acting in
> this way. Therefore I ask of you that the first Friday
> after the octave of Corpus Christi be dedicated as a
> feast in honour of My Heart, and amends made to It
> in an Act of Reparation offered to It and by the recep-
> tion of Holy Communion on that day, to atone for
> the outrages It has received during the time It has
> been exposed on the Altars. I promise you that My
> Heart will open wide and pour forth lavishly the
> influence of Its Divine love on all who will render and
> procure for It this honour."

The Heart spirituality developed by St. John Eudes and St. Margaret Mary Alacoque gave to the Church a deeper understanding of the Heart of Jesus as the source and symbol of the infinite, generous, and tender love of the Son of God for the entire human race. Thus, the Heart of Jesus began to be seen also as the source of the *merciful* love of Jesus Christ for us. This becomes even clearer and more explicit in the beautiful series of prophetic revelations received by Sr. Josefa Menendez of the Society of the Sacred Heart (1890-1923). Sister Josefa centered her whole life on her desire to console the Sacred Heart: "I made up my mind to accept all to glorify the Sacred Heart of Jesus, to console Him, and to win souls for Him." Moreover, Jesus explicitly revealed to her His desire to unveil the mercy of His Heart to the world more and more:

> How often in the course of the ages have I, in one way or another, made known My love for men: I have shown them how ardently I desire their salvation. I have revealed My Heart to them. This devotion has been as light cast over the whole earth, and today is a powerful means of gaining souls, and so of extending My kingdom.

> Now I want something more, for if I long for love in response to My own, this is not the only return I desire from souls: I want them all to have confidence in My mercy, to expect all from My clemency, and never to doubt My readiness to forgive (from *The Way of Divine Love*, TAN, 1972 edition, p. 349).

Study Questions

1. According to St. John Eudes, what are the two causes of the "wounds" of compassion in the Heart of Jesus?

2. What are the three ways that we should practice a special devotion to the merciful Heart of Jesus, according to St. John Eudes?

3. Why did Jesus ask St. Margaret Mary to keep a "Holy Hour" before the Blessed Sacrament every Thursday night?

Discussion Starter:

How does the traditional image of the Sacred Heart symbolize the merciful love of Jesus Christ? What other images and statues of Jesus do you find helpful in expressing His love for you and for all people?

CHAPTER SEVEN

St. Alphonsus Liguori

We now move forward approximately one hundred years to consider the writings of a saint who had a powerful impact upon the whole Catholic world in the 18th century — reviving, sustaining, and summarizing the mainstream tradition of Catholic spirituality in the midst of a rationalistic age.

1. THE LIFE OF ST. ALPHONSUS

Saint Alphonsus Liguori (1696-1787) was a Neapolitan who founded the Redemptorist Order of priests, a congregation dedicated to providing parish missions, especially to the poor in rural areas. His spirituality was both *affective* and *active*, centered above all on the Passion of Jesus Christ as the principal sign of our Savior's love for us. Saint Alphonsus also encouraged an intimate, personal relationship with Jesus Christ through frequent visits to the Blessed Sacrament. In fact, a book of meditations that he originally wrote for his Redemptorist seminarians entitled *Visits to the Blessed Sacrament* went through dozens of editions and was used all across Europe, remaining a popular guide to Eucharistic devotion to this very day. Saint Alphonsus was also devoted to the Sacred Heart of Jesus as a sign and symbol of Christ's love, and in 1758 he sent a copy of his tract "Novena to the Sacred Heart" directly to the Pope in support of an (ultimately successful) petition to obtain approval for the establishment of the liturgical feast of the Sacred Heart. In short, St. Alphonsus' spirituality was strongly Christocentric — centered on the Passion, the Eucharist, and the Heart of Jesus.

Saint Alphonsus was a master of spirituality in other respects as well. For example, his book *The Glories of Mary* earned him the official ecclesiastical title of "The Marian Doctor of the Church," and he insisted that the Redemptorists defend and promote the doctrine of Mary's Immaculate Conception long before that doctrine was infallibly defined as an article of faith by the Magisterium.

In his famous book *Moral Theology*, St. Alphonsus instructed confessors to be gentle and compassionate with their penitents and to manifest the merciful love of Christ in their mildness of manner and in their willingness to dispense absolution for sin, even in response to the "imperfect contrition" of many of their penitents. As a result of his influence, people began to make confessions more often and to receive Holy Communion more often — another development that St. Alphonsus strongly encouraged. By experiencing the love of God in frequent confession and Communion, St. Alphonsus believed, Catholics would come to love Jesus Christ more intimately and follow Him more devoutly in the practice of the virtues. In one of his last books, entitled *The Practice of the Love of Jesus Christ*, the saint gives us detailed guidance on the Christian virtues and the love of Christ that moves us to practice them.

Clearly, the whole of St. Alphonsus's spiritual teaching centers upon the compassionate love of the Redeemer for sinful humanity, whether that love is expressed through His passion and death for us, through the Eucharistic gift of Himself to us, through sacramental absolution administered compassionately to us, or through the prayers and example of the Blessed Mother that He gave to us. All of His love for us is summed up and symbolized in His Sacred Heart.

In 1775, St. Alphonsus published an essay as an appendix to a book on divine providence. That appendix was entitled "Motives for Confidence in Divine Mercy." This little known work now has been translated into English and published in the book *Alphonsus Liguori*, from the "Classics of Western Spirituality" series by Paulist Press. The essay seems to have been provoked by a letter from someone who was troubled by the teachings of the Jansenist heretics, a group that promoted an extreme Augustinian version of the doctrine of predestination. Saint Alphonsus responds to the anxieties of his correspondent by listing all the reasons he can think of as to why we can trust in God for our sanctification and salvation and how we can receive all the spiritual mercies that God wants to pour out upon us.

Saint Alphonsus begins by reminding his anxious friend that the New Testament does not teach that God arbitrarily or inscrutably predestines some people to everlasting damnation. He cites 1 Timothy 2:3-4, "This is good and pleasing to God our Savior, who wills everyone to be saved and come to knowledge of the truth", and 2 Peter 3:9, "He is patient with you, not wishing that any should perish but that all should come to repentance." From Scripture passages such as these, St. Alphonsus concludes:

> From all this can you now have any doubt that God wishes to save you? From this moment onward never dare to utter again: "I wonder does God wish to save me. Maybe He wishes to see me damned on account of the sins I have committed against Him." Get rid of all such thoughts, once and for all, since you must now realize that God is helping you with His graces and calling you insistently to love Him.

2. LIST OF 'CONSIDERATIONS' ON GOD'S SPIRITUAL MERCIES

What follows is a selection from St. Alphonsus's list of "considerations" on God's spiritual mercies and how we can receive them. They are listed below in order, in the saint's

own words, but without the extended explanation that he
provided for each one.

1. The necessity of obedience to your confessor.

2. When you suffer misfortune of any kind, endeavor
   to accept whatever comes as coming to you from
   the hand of God. ... Say simply, the Lord has permitted me to bear these sufferings not because He
   dislikes me but because He loves me. And shall I
   not therefore accept them with resignation?

3. The Lord is full of goodness to those who seek
   Him. No one has ever trusted in the Lord and
   been rejected.

4. When souls seek to love the Lord, He finds it
   impossible not to love them in return.

5. Souls who love their crucified Lord in the midst of
   their own desolation grow closer to Him in their
   hearts.

6. To advance in the way of holiness it is necessary
   above all else to concentrate one's efforts on
   loving God.

7. In your prayers do not neglect to offer yourself to
   God unreservedly. From your heart say: "My
   Jesus, I give myself to You without reserve. I wish
   to be wholly Yours."

8. When you experience great aridity of spirit, be sure
   then to rejoice unselfishly in the bliss your God
   enjoys in heaven. This is an anticipation on earth of
   that perfect act of love of the blessed in heaven,
   since they do not so much rejoice in their own
   happiness as in the infinite happiness of God
   Himself. They love God much more than they love
   themselves.

9. As regards your prayers and reflections, never neglect to meditate on the Passion of Jesus Christ. There is no other subject more calculated to elicit our love than the thought of the sufferings of Jesus Christ.

10. Place yourself on the Hill of Calvary, where you will find your Lord dying on the Cross, consumed with sufferings. Seeing Him in this terrible condition, is there any way you could refuse to undergo willingly all types of suffering for a God who dies out of love for you?

11. I recommend prayer to you above all else. When you can say nothing else, simply say, "Lord, help me, and help me without delay."

12. When you ask for graces from God, make sure you ask them in the name of Jesus Christ. ... So when you fear that God will send you to hell, think for a moment how could it be possible that one who has said to you that whatever you ask Him [in His name] will be granted, would send you to hell?

13. How is it that you think you are not pleasing to God when you suffer desolation in spirit? Rather than being worried you should feel reassured, since God is dealing with you in the very same way that He treats His most intimate friends.

14. Keep on praying to Him with love and tenderness and have no anxiety that He will abandon you. Say in the words of the apostle ... [nothing can] separate us from the love of God in Christ Jesus our Lord (Rom 8:38-39).

15. When you are oppressed by fears for your salvation or by desolation of spirit, do not neglect to have recourse to Our Lady, who has been given to

us by God as the Consolatrix of those who are afflicted.

16. The more trust we have in the Lord the more we receive from Him. He Himself has declared that He rewards those who trust Him.

17. The Lord has declared that His great joy is to be with us: "And I found delight in the sons of men" (Pr 8:31). ... This thought alone should encourage us to pray to God with all confidence.

18. My God, why is it that scrupulous and anxious souls treat You as if You were a tyrant who demands nothing more from Your subjects than fear and trepidation? The result is they think that God gets angry at every thought that passes through their minds and at every word that slips involuntarily from their lips and wishes to cast them into hell.

19. God's infinite majesty certainly deserves all our reverence and submission, but He Himself prefers to receive from souls desirous of loving Him their love and confidence rather than fear and servility.

20. Frequent reception of the sacraments [St. Alphonsus here directly opposes the teachings of the Jansenist heretics, who demanded near perfect contrition for sin before a soul could dare to go to confession and receive Holy Communion].

21. Your love should be centered above all else on the two great mysteries of our Lord's love, the Holy Sacrament of the Altar and the Passion of Jesus Christ. If the love of all human hearts could be concentrated in one heart it would not approach in the slightest degree to the greatness of the love which Jesus Christ has shown us in these two mysteries.

And so, in short, concentrate all your efforts for the future on love for God, and confidence in His great mercy.

[Quotations from St. Alphonsus' essay "Motives for Confidence in the Divine Mercy" are taken from *Alphonsus Liguori: selected writings*, New York: Paulist Press, Classics of Western Spirituality series, 1999. This list carries on through number 26, but the remaining ones are of minor importance, so we will not record them here].

Although the word "mercy" is only rarely used in this essay, the concept is implied throughout, for this whole treatise by St. Alphonsus is about trusting in Divine Mercy in every circumstance and calling on His mercy with confidence at all times, in the light of our Lord's infinite compassion for the human race.

However, there are several significant *omissions* from this list of "considerations" on Divine Mercy.

First of all, one would think that one of the principal ways of nurturing confidence in God's merciful love would be the simple counting of one's blessings from Him every day: life and health, wholesome food, clean clothes, a cheerful residence, good companionship, the beauties of nature — whatever blessings He has granted to us in His providence each day. Unfortunately, St. Alphonsus does not mention simple Christian thanksgiving as an antidote to lack of confidence in God's mercy (although such thanksgiving is certainly a central theme in the opening chapters of his book, *The Practice of the Love of Jesus Christ*).

Second, it seems rather bold to claim that the "two greatest mysteries" of our Lord's love for us are the Passion of Jesus Christ and His gift of Himself in the Blessed Sacrament. Certainly, the Resurrection of Jesus Christ is integrally related to both mysteries. Without the Resurrection, the Cross never would have been seen as "good news" nor would Christ's Real Presence and self-gift in the Blessed Sacrament even be possible. Moreover, behind the Gospel mysteries of the Death and Resurrection of Jesus lie the even deeper and more fundamental mysteries of the Incarnation — manifested so beautifully in the Nativity of Christ — and the Blessed and Holy Trinity: the mystery that God in His own nature is love given, love received, and love returned from all eternity.

That is why the New Testament can say, on the one hand, that God's love was especially manifest in that "while we were yet sinners, Christ *died* for us" (Rom 5:8), and yet also say that the love of God was especially *manifest in the whole mystery of the Incarnation,* in which the divine Son loved us so much that He came down from heaven and shared our human condition, for it is the Incarnation which made His whole human life and death for us possible: "In this the love of God was made manifest among us, that God sent His only Son into the world, that we might live through Him" (1 Jn 4:9). The Passion of Jesus Christ certainly shows us the depth and extent of Christ's merciful love for us through His incarnate life, but the Cross is only an extension to its ultimate limit (so to speak) of the Incarnation, the mystery that God Himself descended into the very depths of our human condition in order to win us back to His Heart, so that we might share in His eternal Trinity of love (see Phil 2: 6-11).

Happily, in other writings St. Alphonsus goes to great lengths to unfold and celebrate the mystery of the Incarnation; indeed, he probably wrote more meditations of the Nativity of Christ and on the Incarnation than any other saint in the history of the Catholic Church. His essay on "Motives for Confidence in the Divine Mercy," therefore, does not even begin to exhaust the riches of his theology of the merciful love of God.

Study Questions

1. What is the "center" of the spiritual teachings of St. Alphonsus?

2. What biblical passages does St. Alphonsus refer to in order to prove that God desires the salvation of everyone?

3. What does St. Alphonsus claim are "the two greatest mysteries" of our Lord's love for us?

Discussion Starter:

If you were going to make your own personal list of reasons for having confidence in Divine Mercy, what would you include on the list?

CHAPTER EIGHT

St. Therese of Lisieux, the Little Flower

As far as "externals" are concerned, there was nothing very remarkable about Therese Martin (1873-1897). She grew up in a middle-class family in the Province of Normandy, France. Her mother died when she was four, her father and her four older sisters were very devout Catholics, and all five sisters ultimately entered the religious life. Therese herself entered the Carmelite convent in Lisieux at the age of 15. She wrote only one book, under obedience to her religious superiors, in three installments. Together they form her autobiography, entitled *The Story of a Soul*. She died of tuberculosis at the age of 24.

1. THE SPIRITUAL LIFE OF ST. THERESE

Despite this seemingly unremarkable life story, it is probably true that no single person had a more profound and lasting impact upon the spirituality of Catholics in the 20th century than St. Therese of the Child Jesus and the Holy Face: St. Therese of Lisieux, the Little Flower. This is not because she experienced much in the way of extraordinary mystical phenomena (visions, locutions, miracles, etc.). In fact, the only really striking supernatural event in her life occurred when she was a child. At about the age of ten, she contracted a danger-ous fever, and it looked for a while as if she might not pull through. She tells the story herself in her autobiography. She was in a delirium, and called out "Mamma, Mamma!" Two of her older sisters, Marie and Celine, were so distressed by her condition that they knelt down beside her bed, turned toward a little statue of Our Lady in her room, and prayed for her. Therese finishes the story in her autobiography:

> Finding no help on earth, poor little Therese had also turned toward the Mother of heaven, and prayed with all her heart that she take pity on her. All of a sudden, the Blessed Virgin appeared *beautiful to me*, so beautiful that never had I seen anything so attractive; her face was suffused with an ineffable benevolence and tenderness, but what penetrated to the very depths of my soul was "*the ravishing smile of the Blessed Virgin.*" At that instant, all pain disappeared, and two large tears glistened on my eyelashes and flowed down my cheeks silently, but they were tears of unmixed joy. Ah! I thought, the Blessed Virgin smiled at me, how happy I am, but never will I tell anyone for my *happiness would then disappear.* Without any effort I then lowered my eyes, and I saw Marie who was looking down at me lovingly; she seemed moved, and appeared to surmise the favor the Blessed Virgin had given me. Ah! It was really to her touching prayers that I owe the grace of the Queen of Heaven's smile. Seeing my gaze fixed on the Blessed Virgin, Marie cried out: "Therese is cured!" Yes, the little flower was going to be born again to life, and the luminous Ray that had warmed her again was not to stop its favors; the Ray did not act all at once, but sweetly and gently it raised the little flower and strengthened her in such a way that five years later she was expanding on the fertile mountain of Carmel (*The Story of a Soul*, third edition, Washington, D.C., Institute of Carmelite Studies publications, 1996, pp. 65-66).

Some months later, on the day of her First Communion, Therese led all the children in the consecration of their lives to Mary:

In the afternoon, it was I who made the Act of Consecration to the Blessed Virgin. It was only right that I speak in the name of my companions to my Mother in heaven, I who had been deprived at such an early age of my earthly Mother. I put all my heart into *speaking* to her, into consecrating myself to her as a child throwing itself into the arms of its mother, asking her to watch over her. It seems to me the Blessed Virgin must have looked upon her little flower and *smiled* at her, for wasn't it *she* who cured her with a *visible smile*? Had she not placed in the heart of her little flower her Jesus, the Flower of the Fields and the Lily of the valleys (Canticle of Canticles, 2:1)? (p. 78).

Therese enriched her spiritual life with meditations on Holy Scripture, especially on the Gospels. She began to deeply appreciate that the images that we find in everyday life can be expressive symbols of divine and supernatural truths. For example, Therese saw herself like a little ship on the sea, plying its way toward the safe harbor of heaven:

In the evening at that moment when the sun seems to bathe itself in the immensity of the waves, leaving a *luminous* trail behind, I went and sat down on the huge rock with Pauline. Then I recalled the touching story of the "Golden Trail." I contemplated that luminous trail for a long time. It was to me the image of God's grace shedding its light across the path the little white-sailed vessel had to travel. And near Pauline, I made the resolution never to wander far away from the glance of Jesus in order to travel peacefully toward the eternal shore! (p. 48-49).

Another time, when she was on retreat, and she was in the midst of spiritual desolation, she interpreted our Lord's seeming absence as similar to the time in the New Testament when Jesus was fast asleep in the boat during a storm on the Sea of Galilee. In effect, her soul was like that boat, tossed about by the waves, and Jesus was just sleeping in the midst of it. Since He is always present, even when He seems asleep and absent, Therese resolved not to wake Him up with her needless worries and anxieties.

Another metaphor that Therese used to make sense of her spiritual journey was the metaphor of the "little flower." In fact, several times in her autobiography she refers to herself as "the little flower," and this has been her ecclesiastical nickname ever since. She was not trying to be cute or precious; rather, she had loved and cultivated flowers ever since she was very young. She saw that flowers needed constant care and nurture if they were to grow and blossom: symbols of God's personal care for her soul as she grew in spirit. For example, on the day St. Therese asked her father's permission to enter the Carmel of Lisieux — a consent he gave without hesitation — she describes their walk together in the garden with these words:

> Papa seemed to be rejoicing with the joy that comes from a sacrifice already made. He spoke just like a saint, and I'd love to recall his words and write them down, but all I preserved of them is a memory too sacred to be expressed. What I do recall, however, is a *symbolic* action my dear King performed, not realizing its full meaning. Going up to a low wall, he pointed to some *little white flowers*, like lilies in miniature, and plucking one of them, he gave it to me, explaining the care with which God brought it into being and preserved it to that very day. While I listened I believed I was hearing my own story, so great was the resemblance between what Jesus had done for the *little flower and little Therese*. I accepted

it as a relic and noticed that, in gathering it, Papa had pulled all its roots out without breaking them. It seemed destined to live on in another soil more fertile than the tender moss where it had spent its first days. This was really the same action Papa had performed a few moments before when he allowed me to climb Mount Carmel and leave the sweet valley which had witnessed my first steps in this life (p. 108).

What is the common thread that ties together all of these metaphors — "little boat," "little flower," etc.? The common thread is "littleness." Indeed, she called her own understanding of the spiritual life her "Little Way."

2. THE 'LITTLE WAY' OF TRUST IN DIVINE MERCY

Why did St. Therese put so much emphasis on "littleness?" On the one hand, she was the youngest child of the Martin household, and seeing herself as a "little one" surely came naturally to her, so that she also found it easy to see her relationship with God in terms of her own "littleness." However, when the Lord fashions His saints he utilizes their natural dispositions for supernatural purposes. Father Vernon Johnson wrote a classic study of this aspect of the life of St. Therese in his book *Spiritual Childhood*, showing that God had a special purpose in mind in leading Therese to appreciate the meaning and importance of "littleness":

> *Unless you be converted and become as little children, you shall not enter the kingdom of heaven.* ... Our Lord did not merely say that she must be converted and become a child; He said she must become a *little* child. Now a child can have to a certain extent an independent life of its own, calling upon its parent

only in moments of need. A *little* child cannot do this: it has no life of its own; it is completely dependent on its parent and so lives with perfect serenity and trust within that parent's protection. For St. Therese the word "little," which many would like to eliminate from her teaching, is the key to everything. She has made the Fatherhood of God live afresh for thousands of the faithful by calling us back from being children with a more or less independent life of our own, to become, as Our Lord would have us, *little* children, with no independent life at all, but depending absolutely on our heavenly Father. In so calling us to a fresh realization of the fatherhood of God, she enables us to move through life with serenity and confidence which is the prerogative of the childlike soul, for she makes known to us one of those secrets which God hides from the wise and prudent, and reveals only to little ones. It is in this sense that the present bishop of Lisieux is never weary of saying that St. Therese has shed a new light on one of the oldest and most fundamental of Catholic doctrines: God is our Father (Ignatius Press edition, 2001, p. 10-11).

The heart of St. Therese's "Little Way" is therefore the way of spiritual childhood, a way of trust and complete self-surrender. Therese knew that in almost every respect she was not a very remarkable person. She was not an intellectual giant, nor did she have great natural talents, nor was she likely to achieve much of anything in her life. She was not able to be a great missionary, preacher, martyr, or hero for the faith. Yet she did long in her heart to be a saint. As a result, her underlying struggle was: "How can a simple, ordinary person like me become one of Jesus' beloved saints?" It is a question that most of us who follow Christ want to have answered, because like Therese, most of us are not destined for earthly greatness. We are ordinary people with ordinary talents in ordinary circumstances. St. Therese's answer to this dilemma was her "Little Way." She describes her discovery of this in her autobiography:

> You know, Mother, I have always wanted to be a saint. Alas! I have always noticed that when I compared myself to the saints, there is between them and me the same difference that exists between a mountain whose summit is lost in the clouds and the obscure grain of sand trampled underfoot by passers-by. Instead of becoming discouraged, I said to myself: God cannot inspire unrealizable desires. I can, then, in spite of my littleness, aspire to holiness. It is impossible for me to grow up, and so I must bear with myself such as I am, with all my imperfections. But I want to seek out a means of going to heaven by a little way, a way that is very straight, very short, and totally new.
>
> We are living now in an age of inventions, and we no longer have to take the trouble of climbing stairs, for, in the homes of the rich, an elevator has replaced these very successfully. I wanted to find an elevator which would raise me to Jesus, for I am too small to climb the rough stairway to perfection. I searched then in the Scriptures for some sign of this elevator, the object of my desires, and I read these words coming from the mouth of Eternal Wisdom: "Whosoever is a LITTLE ONE, let him come to me" (Pr 9:4). And so I succeeded. I felt I had found what I was looking for. But wanting to know, O my God, what You would do to the very *little one* who answered Your call, I continued my search and this is what I discovered: *"As one whom a mother caresses, so will I comfort you; you shall be carried at the breasts, and upon the knees they shall caress you"* (Is 66:13,12). Ah! Never did words more tender and more melodious come to give joy to my soul. The

elevator which must raise me to heaven is Your arms, O Jesus! And for this I had no need to grow up, but rather had to remain *little* and become this more and more.

O my God, You surpassed all my expectation. I want only to sing Your mercies (p. 207-208).

What is it that enables St. Therese to attain such complete, childlike trust in God? Clearly, it is knowledge of His infinite mercy. Divine Mercy is so central to the spirituality of St. Therese that she literally begins and ends her autobiography in praise of God's merciful love:

It is you, dear Mother, to you who are doubly my Mother, to whom I come to confide the story of my soul. The day you asked me to do this, it seemed to me it would distract my heart by too much concentration on myself, but since then Jesus has made me feel that in obeying simply, I would be pleasing to Him; besides, I'm going to be doing only one thing: I shall begin to sing what I must sing eternally: "The Mercies of the Lord" (Ps 88:2). ...

Most of all I imitate the conduct of Magdalene; her astonishing or rather her loving audacity which charms the Heart of Jesus also attracts my own. Yes, I feel it; even though I had on my conscience all the sins that can be committed, I would go, my heart broken with sorrow, and throw myself into Jesus' arms, for I know how much He loves the prodigal child who returns to Him. It is not because God, in His anticipating Mercy, has preserved my soul from mortal sin that I go to Him with confidence and love (pp. 13 and 258-259).

For St. Therese "confidence and love" in The Divine Mercy is the foundation of her whole relationship with Jesus

Christ. Father Vernon Johnson emphasizes this strongly in his classic study of her spirituality, *Spiritual Childhood*:

> On a certain occasion during her life in Carmel, St. Therese was asked: "Tell us what we must do to be as little children. What do you mean by keeping little?" She replied: "When we keep little we recognize our own nothingness, and expect everything from God just as a little child expects everything from its father. Nothing worries us." In those words she reveals to us the foundation of her confidence. By looking at her heavenly Father's love for her, she learns a secret which is hidden from the wise and prudent and revealed only to little ones, namely that whereas, in heaven, the love of God goes out to those who are most like Himself — the saints, Our Lady, the only-begotten Son, on earth His love goes out to those who are farthest off — the weak, the outcast, the sinful. In other words, the love revealed to St. Therese in the Person of our Lord was a merciful love, and it is as the "Merciful Love" that she always speaks of it. From her earliest days she had a special knowledge of the Divine Mercy, and one may say that this was the great light of her life and the grace proper to her mission. No one, it would seem, was ever more attracted than she was to this infinite mercy; no one penetrated further into its unfathomable secrets; no one better understood the immensity of the help that human weakness can draw from it. "The mercy of God was the illuminating sun of her soul, that which, to her eyes, threw light upon all the mystery of God in His relations with man." That this was so she tells us herself. "All souls cannot be alike. They must differ so that each divine perfection may receive special honour. To me He has manifested His infinite mercy, and in this resplendent mirror I contemplate His other attributes. There each appears radiant with love" (p. 90-91).

This last passage quoted by Fr. Johnson occurs near to the end of the first part of *Story of a Soul*, as a summarizing statement of her understanding of the spiritual life up until that moment of her journey with Christ. Here St. Therese tells us that all of God's perfections are expressions of His merciful love, even His divine "justice"! His justice takes account of our weaknesses and involuntary imperfections, and in that sense His justice is suffused with mercy toward us:

O my Dear Mother! After so many graces can I not sing with the Psalmist: "How good is the Lord and His mercy endures forever!" (Ps. 117:1). It seems to me that if all creatures had received the same graces I received, God would be feared by none but would be loved to the point of folly; and through *love*, not through fear, no one would ever consent to cause Him any pain. I understand, however, that all souls cannot be the same, that it is necessary there be different types in order to honor each of God's perfections in a particular way. To me He has granted His *infinite Mercy*, and *through it* I contemplate and adore the other divine perfections! All of these perfections appear to be resplendent *with love*, even His Justice (and perhaps this even more so than the others) seems to me clothed in love. What a sweet joy it is to think that God is Just, i.e., that He takes into account our weakness, that He is perfectly aware of our fragile nature. What should I fear then? Ah! must not the infinitely just God, who deigns to pardon the faults of the prodigal son with so much kindness, be just also toward me who "am with Him always?" (Luke 15:31) (Johnson, p. 180)

Therese then gives thanks for the opportunity she was given by her Mother superior to offer herself as an oblation to God's merciful love. She concludes this section of *Story of a Soul* with an expression of complete trust and joy in the merciful care of Jesus for her, no matter what the future may bring:

> You permitted me, dear Mother, to offer myself in
> this way to God, and you know the rivers or rather
> the oceans of graces that flooded my soul. Ah! since
> the happy day, it seems to me that Love renews me,
> purifying my soul and leaving no trace of sin within
> it, and I need have no fear of purgatory. I know that
> of myself I would not merit even to enter that place
> of expiation, since only holy souls can have entrance
> there, but I also know that the Fire of Love is more
> sanctifying than the fire of purgatory. I know that
> Jesus cannot desire useless sufferings for us, and that
> He would not inspire the longings I feel unless He
> wanted to grant them.

> Oh! How sweet is the way of Love! How I want to
> apply myself to doing the will of God always and with
> the greatest self-surrender!

> Here, dear Mother, is all that I can tell you about the
> life of your little Therese; you know better than I do
> what she is and what Jesus has done for her. You will
> forgive me for having abridged my religious life so
> much.

> How will this "story of a little white flower" come to an
> end? Perhaps the little flower will be plucked in her
> youthful freshness or else transported to other shores. I
> don't know, but what I am certain about is that God's
> mercy will accompany her always, that it will never cease
> blessing the dear Mother who offered her to Jesus; she
> will rejoice eternally at being one of the flowers of her
> crown. And with this, dear Mother, she will sing eter-
> nally the new canticle of Love (p. 181-182).

Finally, although her total oblation to God's merciful
love would require great heroism and her "Little Way" of spir-

itual childhood would require a radically humble spirit, St. Therese was well aware of the fact that she could not live out such ideals and aspirations by her own strength and efforts alone. She assures us that it is only the grace of Jesus Christ Himself, dwelling in our hearts, that can turn such dreams of sanctity into reality, enabling us to love God with all our hearts and our neighbors as ourselves:

> When the Lord commanded His people to love their neighbors as themselves, He had not as yet come upon the earth. Knowing the extent to which each one loved himself, He was not able to ask of His creatures a greater love than this for one's neighbor. But when Jesus gave His Apostles a new commandment, HIS OWN COMMANDMENT, as He calls it later on, it is no longer a question of loving one's neighbor as oneself but of loving him as *He, Jesus, has loved him,* and will love him to the consummation of the ages.

> Ah! Lord, I know you don't command the impossible. You know better than I do my weakness and imperfection; You know very well that never would I be able to love my Sisters as You love them, unless *You,* O my Jesus, *loved them in me.* It is because You wanted to give me this grace that You made your *new* commandment. Oh! How I love this new commandment since it gives me the assurance that Your will is *to love in me* all those You command me to love! (p. 220-221).

Study Questions

1. What makes St. Therese such an appealing saint — one of the most popular saints today?

2. According to Fr. Vernon Johnson, what is the importance of the concept of "littleness" in the spirituality of St. Therese of Lisieux?

3. Why did St. Therese have confidence in Jesus that He could, and would, make her a saint?

Discussion Starter:

Explore the connection between St. Therese's "Little Way" and trusting more in God. What are the implications of her "Little Way" for your own life?

CHAPTER NINE

Bl. Dina Belanger of Quebec

W hat is the best "head-start" that a child can have on the road to sanctity? A little known Canadian daughter of the Church probably had as good a "head-start" as anyone could wish for any Catholic youth.

1. THE CHILDHOOD OF BL. DINA

Dina Belanger (1897-1929) was born in Quebec City, the only child of a fairly wealthy family. In so many ways, she was surrounded by love and showered with blessings right from the start. Her parents provided her with tender care, religious formation, and a solid example of Christian virtue. She says of them in her autobiography:

> Only in heaven shall I fully understand the vigilance, devotedness, and love of my father and mother. It is one of God's greatest blessings to be born and brought up in an atmosphere of peace, union, and charity, edified by the sublime examples of constant conformity to God's good pleasure. ...
>
> All my life I have had before my eyes the example of parents who generously relieved the poor, giving alms on every side, and bestowing comfort wherever they passed. ... How often have I heard them say, "Do not put down my name," or "This is for you, but do

not say anything about it." How many anonymous
gifts they made. ... Nursing the sick was a real mission
for my mother, a task which my father shared by
approving and assisting her kindly ministrations. This
conduct on his part often entailed heroic sacrifice.
How many outings forfeited? How many plans sacri-
ficed to relieve some needy family, either among our
relatives, or total strangers, by day or night, close at
hand or far away, whether the need was certain, or
only probable? (*Autobiography of Dina Belanger*,
Religious of Jesus and Mary, 1984 edition; p. 19, 24).

Dina's mother was her first catechism teacher. Her father
sometimes assisted with this, and provided extra affection and
care. Dina wrote of him:

How happy I was when my father entered the house
in the evening! He seldom could come home at
noon. He would take me in his arms, kiss me, and
' [play with] me before his supper, although he then
must have been quite worn out with his day's toil. I
was his idol. He would spend hours playing with me
and answering my endless questions. His greatest joy
was to procure pleasant surprises: a walk, or a trip,
some little present, a rosary, a statue, some toy or
piece of jewelry. Speaking of the latter, the first I
remember were a tiny golden heart and a little cross.
A heart, symbol of the gift of my own to Jesus, and
of my love for Him, and a cross: emblem of Jesus'
love for me (p. 22).

This is not to say that Dina's parents spoiled her. She makes
it quite clear in her autobiography that her parents knew the
importance of loving correction and discipline. She wrote:

How I thank my good parents for having loved me
in the true sense of the word, for real love supposes
correction of faults; what should I have become, left

to my pride, my stubbornness, my whims and fancies, my mischievous tricks? No doubt I should have developed into a sulky, unbearable child, all the more so as I was brought up without the salutary contact of other children. Later on, I should have been unable to agree with anybody, or get on without making those around me suffer. My God, I thank Thee for having given me parents who taught me to obey (p. 22-23).

We are spending some time on the nurturing of Bl. Dina as a child for good reason. For Bl. Dina, like St. Therese of Lisieux and St. Faustina (as we shall see), was blessed with loving and devout parents who gave her religious instruction as well as a shining example of Christian virtue. In other words, St. Therese, St. Faustina Kowalska, and Bl. Dina were the *objects* of God's merciful love *through their parents* before they could even understand it. *God's mercy came first.* Their lives of holiness — of trust and surrender to God's merciful love — was but a response to the divine initiative, which began from the earliest days of their childhood.

This is also a wonderful example to follow for those of us who are parents. Sometimes we think that being devoted to The Divine Mercy means taking on an elaborate regimen of pious practices — chaplets, novenas, pilgrimages, and so on. Such piety can indeed be a good thing, a channel of graces to our souls, but these graces are not supposed to stagnate and collect in our hearts; rather, they are meant to flow *through* us to our neighbors in need — and as parents, who is more in need of our merciful love every day than our own children? God's merciful love, channeled through us, can make a bigger difference to our children than to anyone else in our lives. Blessed Dina, for example, was so deeply moved by her parents' love for her that she wrote these words (and how would you feel as a parent if your child wrote these words about you?):

To prove my gratitude, I am duty bound to become a saint. ... Only thus can I make a fit return for their past and present solicitude. Yes, I will become a saint. I will become holy in the degree God has marked out for me. Thus may I repay [my parents] for the pains they have taken for my education, and console them in their grief over our separation (p. 19-20).

Dina felt herself called to an intense life of prayer from an early age. At the age of 13, she consecrated her whole life to Jesus through the Blessed Virgin Mary. Dina wrote: "Would that I might consecrate all souls to [Mary]. It is she who leads us to Jesus; it is she whom we must allow to live in us in order that Christ may substitute Himself in place of our nothingness." How similar were the sentiments of St. Faustina: "O Mary, my Mother and my Lady, I offer you my soul, my body, my life and my death, and all that will follow it. I place everything in your hands" (*Diary*, 79).

Dina was especially enthralled by the radiant glory of God, shining through the beauties of nature — and those who have ever been to Quebec will appreciate that such beauty was all around her. She wrote:

I spent the summer in the country with my parents. Nature with its varied charms exerted a powerful spell over me; dusk settling down over the landscape, moonlight shimmering on the water, flowers, the forest, the river, butterflies, birds all enraptured me. The warm caressing breath of the wind, the whispered murmur of the leaves, the deep silence of the night, the aspect of the stars ravished my soul. This reverie, all unknown to me, was a sort of pious meditation, which was to deepen and become a real contemplation rendering me speechless, and inflaming me with gratitude and love for the Infinite God and consuming me with the desire to possess the unique, ideal Beauty (p. 39).

We find similar sentiments in St. Faustina. Just look at the marvelous canticle of praise of the merciful Creator found in her *Diary*, entry 1750, or her prayer recorded in entry 1612:

> I adore You, Lord and Creator. ... I adore You for all the works of Your hands, that reveal to me so much wisdom, goodness and mercy, O Lord. You have spread so much beauty over the earth, and it tells me about Your beauty, even though these beautiful things are but a faint reflection of You, Incomprehensible Beauty.

Dina was gifted with natural musical talent. She advanced rapidly in piano and in musical composition, so that even her spiritual guides encouraged her to glorify God by pursuing a music career. At the age of 19, therefore, her parents sent her for musical studies to a conservatory in New York, where she lodged with two friends from Quebec at a convent of the Religious of Jesus and Mary. All the while, Dina was deepening in prayer and growing in virtue. She would go to the convent chapel often to visit Jesus in the Blessed Sacrament. She wrote: "How often, late in the evening, by the pale flickering of the sanctuary lamp, have I come close to Jesus and there, leaning against the altar rail, listened to His voice and poured forth the secrets of my heart!"

Dina also became a promoter of the Apostleship of Prayer, deepening her devotion to the Sacred Heart, and her desire to make reparation to Him for all the evils of the world. She wrote:

> At the outbreak of the World War, in 1914, I offered myself to Our Lord entirely, body and soul, in a spirit of reparation and love to console Him and to save souls. I was especially distressed at the moral evil threatening the world. The light that illumined me was so vivid that I could not see Jesus suffer and not wish to dry His tears by every means at my disposal (p. 58).

Besides the virtue of piety, Bl. Dina also excelled in the virtue of humility. She relates one humorous incident, which Canadians especially will appreciate. It occurred at the end of one of her many concerts for charity:

> Once [at a recital] I was granted the joy of a slight failure. In a crowded hall I was supposed to close a literary and musical entertainment by playing the national hymn, 'O Canada.' The last line should have been repeated, but by some slip I played it only once. Everybody noticed my mistake. I was very grateful to God for this small humiliation. It was something better to offer Him than the beautiful bouquets with which I had been presented (p. 64).

Dina also learned the art of turning her daily work into prayer and a loving offering to God. She wrote:

> Before each one of my exercises in harmony, from that far off day to this, before reading a single line or writing a single note, I have recited a *Veni Sancte* and a Hail Mary. I do not recall ever having omitted this pious practice. Consequently, if my poor musical compositions have no value from an artistic point of view ... they are a real chain of prayers (p. 66).

In addition to piety and humility, God schooled Bl. Dina in complete surrender, complete abandonment to His divine providence. Such abandonment was especially needed when she first asked permission of her parents and her spiritual director to enter the religious life. Much like St. Therese, the Little Flower, and St. Faustina, this desire of Dina's heart to enter the convent would have to wait some time for its fulfillment. And yet, in retrospect, she saw in this delay the loving plan of God. She wrote:

> God enlightened my superiors and according to their judgement I was to remain in the world. It was too

soon for me to leave my devoted parents whose sole
joy was to have their only child with them. ... Our
Lord saw fit to leave me to their affection several years
more. ... My God, I thank Thee for the happiness
granted my parents, I thank Thee for having clearly
revealed to my soul Thy ineffable designs (p. 56).

Dina's heavenly Father continued to nurture and sanctify
her soul and her work. At the same time, Jesus began to give
her extraordinary graces and consolations to draw her even
closer to His Heart. Just one example will suffice. On
Christmas night, at the age of 21, Bl. Dina was given an
intimate union with the Christ Child. She wrote:

On Christmas night during my thanksgiving after
Holy Communion, I was inundated with divine consolations. ... After receiving the Sacred Host, I was
suddenly transported to Bethlehem like the
Shepherds on the first Christmas night. Our Lady
held up to me the Infant Jesus who gave me a kiss of
loving tenderness and His Heart communed with
mine, Oh! How sweetly! This intimate colloquy with
the Holy Family filled me with an inexplicable happiness. The joys of Heaven of which God sometimes
gives us a foretaste can be felt, but they cannot be
described (p. 94).

Once again, Bl. Dina's experiences here were so very like
those of St. Faustina, who also enjoyed the most intimate
union with the Christ Child. As Faustina wrote in her *Diary*,
in entry 1442:

After a while, I was left alone with the Infant Jesus
who stretched out His little hands to me, and I
understood that I was to take Him in my arms. Jesus
pressed His head against my heart and gave me to
know, by His profound gaze, how good He found it
to be next to my heart.

Dina Belanger was admitted into the postulancy of the Religious of Jesus and Mary in 1921 at the age of 24. As she stepped through the door of the convent, she heard the words in her soul, "This is Home." And home it would be for the rest of her short life.

2. RELIGIOUS LIFE AND 'DIVINE SUBSTITUTION'

The religious order Dina had joined was a teaching order, and her primary role in the community was as a music teacher. She wrote:

> I still continued my teaching. How I loved my pupils! It has been the same for all the children who have since been confided to my care. I loved them with an affection which sought their welfare. ... I identified Jesus personally with each one of my pupils and pictured Him at their age, coming to me for a lesson (p. 115).

During her postulancy and novitiate, Jesus continued to deepen His relationship with Dina's soul. At this time, she had an experience in prayer very similar to those of St. Catherine of Siena and St. Margaret Mary Alacoque, an experience known in the Catholic Tradition as a spiritual "exchange of hearts" with Christ. She described the experience like this:

> It was the second night of [a] retreat. During our free time before the preparation for the morrow's meditation, I went to chapel. Darkness was falling and deep silence pervaded the sanctuary. Jesus made me hear the sweet tones of His voice and I felt myself enraptured. Peace, love, and confidence enveloped me. Then, the dear Lord removed my poor heart as easily as one picks up something and puts it else-

where, and, O joy! Replaced it by His own, and that
of His Immaculate Mother. This was symbolical also,
but there certainly took place in me a mystical operation that no pen can describe (p. 102).

More and more, Jesus began guiding Dina with His own
voice, through inner locutions, the authenticity of which, in
part, she learned to recognize by the deep peace and silence
that accompanied His words in her soul. She wrote:

The Saviour makes Himself heard only in hours of
deep recollection, peace, and silence. His voice is
soft, so soft that in the soul *all must be hushed*; it is a
melodious voice, while that of the devil is noisy,
abrupt, and discordant, and his words are uttered in
the midst of agitation and tumult (p.86).

One time, Bl. Dina received a prophecy from the Lord
— a prophecy which took her completely by surprise. She
recorded it as follows:

On a first Friday, while Our Lord was communing
with my soul, I asked Him the following question:
"What can be the object of my musical studies?" For
I had always retained the intimate conviction that I
should never excel in them, yet I was urged by some
irresistible power to labour persistently at my music.
Jesus said "... You will do good particularly by your
writings." These words filled me with amazement:
"Do good by my writings!" Had I understood
aright? Jesus continued: "Yes, in the convent you will
devote yourself to *literary* work" (p. 96).

From the testimony of her superiors, we know for a fact
that Dina believed this prophecy referred to the poems and
other pious compositions that she wrote for her sisters in
religion. Dina had absolutely no idea that the prophecy might
refer to the *autobiography* she was writing under obedience to
her Mother Superior.

The very first paragraphs of Bl. Dina's autobiography sum up the center of her spirituality:

> O Jesus, I promised not to think back to the past anymore so as to concentrate only on You, in the present, and now, out of obedience, I must submit to it lovingly. My only pleasure is to Let You Have Your Way. I have abandoned myself completely to Your action, so that, without hindrance, You may be able to fulfill Your designs in me, poor as I am; to act freely, always and in everything. You have given me the grace to abandon myself to Your love, You have blotted me out, and in the purest transport of gratitude I cry out: 'I live now not with my own life, but with the life of Christ who lives in me. ...
>
> You have plunged me into the immensity of Your grace and Your mercy, like a tiny sponge in the ocean. Countless times, when I was cold, forgetful, ungrateful, You multiplied Your invitations and caresses. ... The perfect bliss of a soul here on earth is To Love You and Let You Have Your Way (quoted from the third edition, 1997, p. 39-40).

These introductory words from Bl. Dina's autobiography show us what was *central* to her spiritual life. "To Love, and let Jesus Have His Way" was actually Dina's chosen motto; it summarizes for us her understanding of what she called the mystical "*substitution*" of Jesus Christ for her soul. In other words, His mystical indwelling that enabled Him to live in her and through her at every moment. This idea of mystical "substitution" was not intended by Bl. Dina to be a doctrinal novelty, but simply a vivid way of expressing St. Paul's teaching from Galatians 2:20: "It is no longer I who live, but Christ lives in me."

In one of the most famous passages from her autobiography, Bl. Dina describes in greater detail what she meant by mystical "substitution":

If I left everything in the care of Jesus, what would happen? Jesus, in return, undertook to do everything: to think, speak, act, not only with me but in my place. He substituted Himself for me and I let Him have His way. Oh! What a choice gift it is to understand how to let the Savior live within oneself! I wish I could obtain this grace for every soul (third edition, p. 156).

This idea of Christ's mystical "substitution"— in other words, His mystical indwelling and intimate union with the soul that is completely surrendered to Him — also finds an echo in the teachings of the Polish mystic St. Faustina Kowalska. In her *Diary*, entry 1784, for example, Jesus said to Faustina:

> **How much I desire the salvation of souls! My dearest secretary, write that I want to pour out My divine life into human souls and sanctify them, if only they were willing to accept My grace. The greatest sinners would achieve great sanctity if only they would trust in My mercy. ... My delight is to act in a human soul, and to fill it with My mercy. ... My Kingdom on earth is My life in a human soul.**

At other times, St. Faustina came very close to expressing her own union with Christ in terms of mystical "substitution." For example, as she wrote in her prayer in *Diary* entry 163:

> I want to be completely transformed into Your mercy, and be Your living reflection, O Lord. ... O my Jesus, transform me into Yourself, for You can do all things.

For St. Faustina, as we shall see, the principal means which Jesus uses to deepen his mystical indwelling in the soul is the Holy Eucharist. The Eucharist was the center, the wellspring, of her whole life in Christ. As she wrote in her *Diary*, in entry 223:

O living Host, my one and only strength, fountain of love and mercy, embrace the whole world, fortify faint souls. Oh, blessed be the instant and the moment when Jesus left us His most merciful Heart!

Through mystical revelations, Jesus impressed upon the soul of St. Faustina that in the Blessed Host she can find His Sacred Heart, overflowing with mercy. At the Three O'clock Hour each day, for example, Jesus encouraged her to **"at least step into the chapel for a moment and adore in the Blessed Sacrament, My Heart, which is full of mercy"** (*Diary*, 1572). Again, when our Lord appeared to Faustina one time just after she received Holy Communion, He said to her with great kindness:

> **My daughter, look at My merciful Heart.** As I fixed my gaze on the Most Sacred Heart, the same rays of light, as are represented in the image as blood and water, came from it, and I understood how great is the Lord's mercy! (*Diary*, 177).

Thus, for St. Faustina, it is in the Eucharist that we can find the living Heart of Jesus Christ, overflowing with the rays and graces of Divine Mercy for us, and this marks the center and wellspring of our whole life in Christ.

Not only do we find a similar teaching in Bl. Dina's autobiography, we find it especially in her account of a vision she received. This vision seems to pull together all those same images that St. Faustina loved — the Sacred Heart, the Blessed Host, divine rays, flowing graces — it pulls them all together into one extraordinary manifestation of the merciful love of Christ in the Eucharist. Dina wrote:

> This morning when I arrived in Chapel, a little before six o'clock, I found Our Lord pleased. He seemed consoled. ... Finally, during the Communion of the Community at Mass, I found it impossible to resist the force of this divine light any longer so I abandoned

myself to the action of Our Lord. My Savior made me see His adorable Heart in the Sacred Host. I did not look upon His sacred countenance, but His Heart and the Host captivated me. The two, His Heart and the Host, were perfectly united, so much so that I cannot explain how it was possible for me to distinguish one from the other. From the Host there radiated a vast number of rays of light. From His Heart there sprang an infinity of flames which escaped with irresistible force. The Blessed Virgin was there close to Our Lord, so close that she seemed lost in Him and yet I could distinguish her from Him. ... All the rays of the Host and all the flames of the Heart of Jesus passed [through] the Immaculate Heart of the most Holy Virgin. ... I cried out:

"O Eucharistic Heart of Jesus, I entreat Thee, by Our Lady of the Eucharistic Heart, reign over all souls as Thou desirest."

Our Lord then showed me ... the rays of the Host and the flames of His Sacred Heart, passing [through] the heart of the Blessed Virgin, descend[ing] upon the nuns of our Congregation and from them were radiated upon a countless multitude of souls who surrounded them on every side, as far as the eye could reach, and were turned towards them, Our Lord said:

"My Heart overflows with grace for souls! Bring souls to My Eucharistic Heart" (1984 edition, p. 313-314).

This vision alone established Bl. Dina and St. Faustina as kindred spirits, devoted to the Heart of Christ, present and overflowing with graces for us in the Eucharist. This is not to say, however, that Bl. Dina's spiritual teachings are identical to St. Faustina's. There is certainly a difference in *emphasis* between the two. Dina's way emphasizes the indwelling of

Christ in the soul that brings the soul into the life of the Blessed Trinity, and that leads the soul to undertake a life of reparative suffering, in and with Christ. Faustina has all of these elements in her spirituality too, as we shall see, but her emphasis lies more on the merciful love of God that makes all of this possible, and on the response of trust that He asks from every soul in order to open our hearts to all the graces that He wants to pour out upon us.

Nevertheless, the similarities between the teachings of these two holy souls of the Church are so numerous and profound that sometimes, when reading their writings side-by-side, we can feel as if we have uncovered something like a conspiracy between the two!

3. DINA AND FAUSTINA: TEACHERS OF DIVINE MERCY

Here are ten examples of the remarkable similarities between the teachings of Bl. Dina Belanger and her near contemporary, St. Maria Faustina Kowalska.

(1)   On suffering with Christ for the good of souls (reparative suffering), Bl. Dina wrote:

> I have no words to express my thirst for suffering. ... Love is the unique motive of my desires; I would have Jesus crucified reproduced in me that I may resemble Him more closely, and then by Him, apply to souls His inexhaustible merits. Nonetheless, I submit my boundless desires to His good pleasure. As He wills, no more, no less! (p. 258).

On the same subject, St. Faustina wrote:

> I united my sufferings with the sufferings of Jesus and offered them for myself and for the conversion of souls who do not trust in God. ...

O my Jesus, may the last days of my exile be spent totally according to Your most holy will. I unite my sufferings, my bitterness, and my last agony itself to Your Sacred Passion; and I offer myself for the world to implore an abundance of God's mercy for souls (*Diary*, 323 and 1574).

(2) Blessed Dina wrote:

If the angels could desire anything, it seems to me that they would envy us our privilege of suffering, as well as the priceless gift of the Eucharist (p. 106).

Similarly, St. Faustina wrote:

If the angels were capable of envy, they would envy us for two things: one is the receiving of Holy Communion, and the other is suffering (*Diary*, 1804).

(3) Saint Faustina had a vision of the Risen Christ, His right hand raised in blessing, His left hand touching His garment at the breast, with red and pale rays streaming from the area of His Heart. This was the pattern she received for the painting of the great Image of The Divine Mercy (see *Diary*, 47-48).

Blessed Dina wrote:

At times it seemed to me that Jesus appeared laden with graces. They flowed out of His hands and from His Sacred Heart like impetuous torrents. It was His desire that I should apply these treasures to save souls (p. 120).

(4) Saint Faustina received from Christ the revelation of the Chaplet of Divine Mercy:

Eternal Father, I offer You the Body and Blood, Soul and Divinity of Your dearly beloved Son, Our Lord Jesus Christ in atonement for our sins, and those of the whole world. ... For the sake of

**His sorrowful Passion, have mercy on us, and on
the whole world** (*Diary*, 476).

And Jesus promised to St. Faustina: **"Through the
Chaplet you will obtain everything, if what you ask for is
compatible with My will"** (*Diary*, 1731).

Now compare with this the form of prayer that God gave
to Bl. Dina, on the other side of the world, just a few years
prior to Faustina. Dina wrote:

> When a soul in whom [Jesus] lives freely and divinely,
> offers Him to His Father for His glory, the Eternal
> Father can refuse nothing to His Son; moreover, He is
> satisfied with this offering. ... This is how I make the
> offering each time: "Eternal Father, through Mary and
> Thy Spirit of Love, I offer Thee the Eucharistic Heart
> of My Jesus (p. 293, 252-253).

(5) Jesus taught St. Faustina that He has a special compassion and love for the lost and the broken, in other words,
for those who are most in need of His mercy. Jesus said to her:

**My daughter, write that the greater the misery of
a soul, the greater its right to My mercy** (*Diary*,
1182).

Now listen to what Bl. Dina wrote on the same subject:

> If I could pour boundless confidence into all those
> poor souls who mistrust their heavenly Father! Infinite
> Mercy is exercised on our behalf in the measure that it
> finds us miserable and unworthy (p. 199).

(6) Jesus said to St. Faustina:

Oh, how much I am hurt by a soul's distrust!
(*Diary*, 300).

Blessed Dina wrote in her autobiography:

> To give God a chance to exercise His mercy by our

repentance and confidence causes Him joy. Nothing wounds His Heart so much as a lack of trust (p. 199).

(7) The center of St. Faustina's spiritual way is the virtue of trust in The Divine Mercy. Jesus said to her:

> **You see what you are of yourself, but do not be frightened at this. If I were to reveal to you the whole misery that you are, you would die of terror. ... Because you are such great misery, I have revealed to you the whole ocean of My mercy ... you are a daughter of complete trust** (*Diary*, 718).

Similarly, Bl. Dina wrote:

> I am penetrated with my nothingness, I feel myself poor, weak, and powerless. But because of this, my confidence in Jesus is like a shoreless ocean, engulfing the abyss of my misery. I spring up with faith and love into the regions of infinite Mercy, the goodness of God being my firm assurance and my unalterable peace (p. 231).

(8) Through St. Faustina, we learn that during His Agony and Passion, the soul of Jesus was consoled by His prevision of all devout souls of all future generations. Jesus said to her in the Novena he taught her:

> **Today bring to Me all devout and faithful souls, and immerse them in the ocean of My mercy. These souls brought Me consolation on the Way of the Cross. They were that drop of consolation in the midst of an ocean of bitterness** (*Diary*, 1214).

And Bl. Dina wrote:

> I long to console my Jesus: oh, what suffering was His in the Garden of Olives. ... What a mysterious privilege to be specially chosen to console Him. ...

[And Jesus said to her]: Very few souls wish to compassionate My Agony. ... I confide precious secrets to souls who are willing to console Me in My agony (p. 242-244).

(9) Saint Faustina learned from Jesus that His Heart rejoices especially when He is able to indwell and sanctify human souls:

How very much I desire the salvation of souls! My dearest secretary, write that I want to pour out My divine life into human souls and to sanctify them, if only they are willing to accept My grace. ... My delight is to act in a human soul and to fill it with My mercy. ... My kingdom on earth is my life in the human soul (*Diary*, 1784).

Jesus said to Bl. Dina:

My happiness is to reproduce Myself in the souls that I created through love. The more a soul allows me to reproduce Myself truly in itself, the more happiness and repose I feel in it. The greatest joy a soul can give Me is to let Me raise it to the Divinity. Yes, My little spouse, I feel an immense pleasure in transforming a soul into Myself, in deifying it, in absorbing it entirely in the Divinity (p. 307).

(10) Finally, both St. Faustina and Bl. Dina died of the same disease — tuberculosis — and both died of it at the age of 33.

Now what are we to make of all this? Clearly, Jesus Christ communicated a remarkably similar treasury of spiritual wisdom to these two women of prayer, Bl. Dina and St. Faustina, religious who were almost contemporaries of each other, living on opposite sides of the world, and who were completely unknown to each other.

I see three lessons for us here.

First, when God has an extraordinary, prophetic message to give to the world, He usually does not entrust it to just one great mystic, but often, in varying degrees, He entrusts it to several mystics and spiritual writers in the same era — just to make sure that the message permeates the Church as much as possible. We see this in the history of devotion to the Sacred Heart, when, in the late Middle Ages, the revelations given to St. Gertrude the Great were, in a sense, corroborated and amplified in the writings and meditations of a whole series of religious, especially of Carthusian monks and spiritual writers, for the next few centuries.

Perhaps we can discern the hand of divine providence at work in a somewhat similar way here. As we shall see in our next chapter, St. Faustina was given a new way to proclaim to the world the ageless Gospel of Divine Mercy. Through her, we receive from God a clearer focus on the merciful love of God and new forms for entreating and experiencing that mercy: the Image, the Chaplet, the Feast, and the Hour of Great Mercy. Through Faustina, therefore, the Gospel of Divine Mercy has been proclaimed to the modern world in a way that people of all nations and cultures seem to be able to comprehend and embrace. The international spread of this message and devotion is proof enough that this is so.

Second, about the same time, Jesus communicated a similar message to the world through Bl. Dina. Of course, Bl. Dina was not destined to have the same central role in God's plan as St. Faustina, but her witness corroborates and amplifies what we find in St. Faustina. To those who might not know of St. Faustina, or who, for some cultural or psychological reason, are not moved by The Divine Mercy message and devotion, it just may be that these souls will be touched and refreshed by similar teaching reaching them through Bl. Dina. After all, Christ is the sower in His parable, the one who went out to sow and scattered the seed everywhere (see Mt 13:3-9).

With regard to Bl. Dina in particular, it may be that the Lord of Mercy has a special place in His plan for her, for if you compare Dina's autobiography with Faustina's *Diary*, you cannot help being struck by the vast *literary* difference between the two. Faustina, after all, had only three semesters of formal education. She was not a polished literary stylist, nor an educated intellectual; she was a devout Polish peasant girl, filled to overflowing with the wisdom of God. Her writings are simple, direct, even childlike in style — and therefore accessible to all people, the world over.

However, the hardest people to reach with the message of God's mercy are surely in our modern world the Western intelligentsia, the literati, the intellectuals. They wear an almost *impenetrable* armor of skepticism and misinformation, blocking them from believing and trusting in God's merciful love — and the French-speaking intelligentsia may be the most armor-plated of all. In Bl. Dina, however, the Lord has raised up from among them — I mean from among the well-educated, artistically sensitive Francophones — a purified soul, a clear witness to the merciful love of God. Her autobiography is a literary masterpiece; it is sincere and springs from her heart, yet it is also intellectually reflective; she carefully analyzes the different types of mystical experiences that Jesus gives to her and the spiritual insights into which He leads her. In short, Bl. Dina might be able to communicate the message of God's merciful love to those who are unable or unwilling to hear it in any other way. For those who need and appreciate beautiful nuances of literary expression and clear intellectual reflection on God's mystical union with the soul, Bl. Dina's writings may be just the right channel of grace.

Third, I find Bl. Dina helpful because I believe she amplifies St. Faustina on a central point of Mercy spirituality. The essence of Mercy spirituality, after all, is complete trust in The Divine Mercy: "Jesus, I trust in You." It is a wonderful summary and simplification of the underlying response that Jesus asks of us, so that He can pour His grace into our hearts. Trust: it is so simple to understand and so simple to appreciate — and yet, let's be honest, it is not at all simple to live! To trust in Jesus in the midst of grief or sorrow, injustice or oppression, struggle or strife, debilitating disease or financial ruin — trust in Jesus at such times can be an act of sheer spiritual heroism.

Saint Faustina herself was well aware of this. She wrote in her *Diary*, entry 1489:

> Jesus, do not leave me alone in suffering. You know, Lord, how weak I am. I am an abyss of wretchedness. I am nothingness itself; so what will be so strange if You leave me alone and I fall? I am an infant, Lord, so I cannot get along by myself. However, beyond all abandonment I trust, and in spite of my own feeling I trust, and I am being completely transformed into trust, often in spite of what I feel.

However, Bl. Dina adds something to St. Faustina's realism here. First, she echoes that realism in her autobiography when she writes: "My Jesus, do everything Thyself, for Thou seest how hard it is" (p. 309). And yet, by speaking of the indwelling of Christ as a kind of mystical "substitution" of Jesus for the soul, she reassures us that trusting in Him is not something we have to do all on our own. On the contrary, Christ Jesus loves us so much that *He Himself, dwelling within us, is the one who enables us to trust in Him for everything.* As she explained in her autobiography:

> If I can say: "I let Jesus have His way and concern myself only with Him," it is because, through trust, I count on Him alone so as to refuse Him nothing and to correspond always to His inspiration. And my trust in God is not a human trust — wavering, insecure, such as might spring from my weakness, certainly not; it is the trust of God Himself which I borrow, which I make my own (third edition, p.189):

Again, among the last words that Bl. Dina wrote were the following:

> Jesus, be my life, my Divine Substitute forever! Keep my whole being, with all its frailty, and its weakness,

annihilated in Thee, in Thy love and Thy mercy!
(1984 edition, p. 334).

Let me close by putting Bl. Dina's teaching in a prayer, in
my own words:

Lord Jesus, we know through St. Faustina that all we
really need to do is trust in You — but You know, Lord,
how hard that is for us and that we cannot do it on our
own. So, Lord Jesus, *substitute* Yourself for us, as You
did for Bl. Dina. Dwell within our hearts; and then live
in us and through us the very trust that we need to be
Yours, and to belong to You forever. Amen.

Study Questions

1. Describe some of the elements of the spiritual life of Bl. Dina from the time she was
   13 years old until she entered the convent
   at age of 24.

2. What did Bl. Dina mean by mystical "substitution" of Jesus Christ for her soul? How
   did she describe it?

3. What central point of Divine Mercy spirituality is amplified in the autobiography of
   Bl. Dina?

Discussion Starter:

Discuss the similarities in spirituality between
Bl. Dina and St. Faustina. Is there a particular
aspect of their shared spirituality that you find
attractive?

PART THREE

Divine Mercy Today:
St. Faustina, Pope John Paul II,
and on to the Third Millennium

CHAPTER ONE

Divine Mercy in the Life and Witness of St. Maria Faustina Kowalska

In order to understand the life of St. Maria Faustina Kowalska and the remarkable spread of her devotion to The Divine Mercy throughout the world, it helps to begin by learning the story of someone else first: a priest. His name was Fr. Michael Sopocko, and he was born in Vilnius in Poland (now Lithuania) in 1888. Ordained a diocesan priest in 1914, he joined the army as a military chaplain during the First World War. After the war, he continued his studies and obtained a doctorate in theology at the age of 35. Father Sopocko quickly became a favorite of his archbishop, who recognized his academic brilliance and pastoral zeal and soon gave him many tasks to do for the Church. He was also awarded a chair in pastoral theology at the local university. Thus, Fr. Michael Sopocko was a learned, energetic, and well-respected priest when, in 1933, he was appointed to be the usual confessor to the convent of the Sisters of Our Lady of Mercy in Vilnius.

Little did he know that the Lord was about to turn his life "upside down" in the most supernatural way.

1. THE LIFE OF SR. FAUSTINA

One day, when Fr. Sopocko was hearing confessions at the convent, a sister entered the confessional by the name of Sr. Faustina of the Most Blessed Sacrament. Father Sopocko had heard her confessions before, and he had admired her honesty and her love for Jesus. But this time he was completely stunned by what she had to say. She told him:

> In the evening, when I was in my cell, I saw the Lord Jesus clothed in a white garment. One hand [was] raised in the gesture of blessing, the other was touching the garment at the breast. From beneath the garment, slightly drawn aside at the breast, there were emanating two large rays, one red, the other pale. In silence I kept my gaze fixed on the Lord; my soul was struck with awe, but also with great joy. After a while, Jesus said to me, **Paint an image according to the pattern you see, with the signature: Jesus, I trust in You. I desire that this image be venerated, first in your chapel, and [then] throughout the world. I promise that the soul that will venerate this image will not perish. ... I am offering people a vessel with which they are to keep coming for graces to the fountain of mercy. That vessel is this image. ... By means of this image I will grant many graces to souls** (*Diary*, 47-48, 327, and 742).

At this point in the story, it helps to imagine oneself in the place of Fr. Sopocko. Sister Faustina was in his confessional pouring out this tale about an apparition of the Lord Jesus, and Jesus was supposedly asking for a new image of Himself to be painted and venerated throughout the world. Father Sopocko asked her the obvious question: Could she paint? No, she said, she could not paint — and even if she could paint, how could she possibly disseminate the image "throughout the world," as Jesus supposedly had commanded? After all, she was a religious sister, confined mostly to the convent. The whole thing sounded terribly improbable. As a result, Fr. Sopocko was not inclined to believe her at first. He wondered whether she might be imagining things or whether she had simply misinterpreted the Lord's message to her.

Then the situation became worse.

The religious sister later went on to tell him that one of her previous confessors would not believe her, but that Jesus had told her not to worry, because He was going to send her a confessor who would help her to fulfill God's will in these matters. In fact, Jesus had given her a vision of this priest, and the priest in that vision had looked just like him — Fr. Sopocko — and that was why she was confiding all these things to him now. Moreover, Jesus not only wanted a new image of Himself to be painted and spread throughout the world, He also wanted a new feast day in the liturgical calendar: a Feast of The Divine Mercy, to be celebrated on the first Sunday after Easter by the whole Church.

Once again, we can imagine ourselves in Fr. Sopocko's predicament. On the one hand, he knew very well that the Lord does, on rare occasions, give extraordinary private revelations and prophecies to chosen souls for the good of the whole Church. In the 17th century, for example, as we have seen, St. Margaret Mary received from Jesus Himself the special revelations of His Sacred Heart. These revelations were meant to rekindle in the hearts of the faithful an appreciation of His ardent, tender love for souls in an age in which an arid rationalism — if it did not destroy belief in God altogether — portrayed Him merely as the indifferent "Watchmaker" of the universe (Deism) or the Supreme Governor of a system of strict justice and predestination (Jansenism, Calvinism). Sometimes, God does indeed send prophetic revelations to His Church to return His people to the truths of the Gospel.

On the other hand, Fr. Sopocko knew that for every such authentic revelation or prophecy, there are many false ones.

Besides, given the obvious practical difficulties in fulfilling the Lord's alleged requests this time, the odds seemed all against authenticity in the case of Sr. Faustina. Hence, Fr. Sopocko did what any devout and prudent pastor would do in such a circumstance: He inquired about Sr. Faustina's character with the superiors of her religious order, and he also sent her to a psychiatrist for a complete mental health exam.

It turns out that the psychiatrist who examined Sr. Faustina gave a positive opinion that she was in perfect mental health. Moreover, the references from Sr. Faustina's superiors were also overwhelmingly positive. They told Fr. Sopocko that Sr. Faustina (Helena Kowalska) was brought up in a family of peasant farmers. Although she had loved her parents dearly, without their permission and without a penny to her name, she had journeyed to the Mother house of the order in Warsaw to follow a vocation to the religious life. Sister Faustina had then endeared herself to almost everyone because of her cheerfulness, her sincerity, and her hard-working nature. "She is a happy child of God," one of her superiors said. In fact, her superiors knew that she had a special devotion to Jesus in the Eucharist (hence her chosen religious name: Sr. Maria Faustina of the Most Blessed Sacrament), and they had also helped guide her through "the dark night of the soul," so they knew she had a deep and rich mystical life as well. In short, they looked upon Faustina as an extraordinary and model sister.

Father Sopocko was then torn within himself. Evidently, this sister who had reported to him these extraordinary revelations from Jesus Christ was not only perfectly sane; she was also one of the most prayerful and virtuous nuns in the order. What could he do?

He decided to withhold judgment. He prayed for more light. He also put her to the test. Yet she was always willing to obey him, and she told him that Jesus had expressly commanded her to entrust herself completely to his spiritual direction.

Then Fr. Sopocko did a very wise thing, for which future generations will always be grateful. He asked Sr. Faustina to begin to write down, in a diary, all the conversations between herself and the Lord, beginning from the very first stirrings of the spiritual life within her. This she did under obedience, although she found it very difficult to express herself in writing, since she had barely three years of formal education. As a result, she wrote very plainly and without ornament, like a child.

Nevertheless, Fr. Sopocko became more and more astonished at what she was writing. Some years later, he wrote:

> I was amazed that she, a simple nun, with hardly any education, and without the time to read ascetic works, could speak so knowledgeably of theological matters, and such [difficult] ones as the mystery of the Holy Trinity, or the Divine Mercy and other attributes of God, with the expertise of a consummate theologian (as quoted in the biography of St. Faustina by Maria Tarnawska, *Saint Sister Faustina: Her Life and Mission*, 4th edition, p. 425).

On page after page, the *Diary* of St. Faustina proclaims the message of God's merciful love as the very heart of the Gospel. It was not a new teaching, of course. It is just a new expression and a clear focus on the center of the Catholic faith: the loving kindness and compassion of God. In private revelations recorded in her *Diary*, Jesus had spoken to her words such as these:

> **I am love and mercy itself. ... Let no soul fear to draw near to Me, even though its sins be as scarlet. ... My mercy is greater than your sins, and those of the entire world. ... I let My Sacred Heart be pierced with a lance, thus opening wide the source of mercy for you. Come then with trust to draw graces from this fountain. ... The graces of My mercy are drawn by the means of one vessel only, and that is trust. The more a soul trusts, the more it will receive** (*Diary*, 1074, 699, 1485, 1578).

Sister Faustina's devotional life was driven by her sincere desire to put her complete trust in the Lord's mercy in every aspect of life. For her, Jesus was "Mercy Incarnate," and the Lord had given her a mission: to proclaim this message of The Divine Mercy throughout the world, especially by spreading the Image of Mercy and the celebration of the Feast of Mercy. Moreover, this message and devotion was to be a fresh call to her, and to all people, to be merciful to one another. Jesus had said to her:

> **My daughter, look into My Merciful Heart and reflect its compassion in your own heart, and in your deeds, so that you who proclaim My mercy to the world may yourself be aflame with it** (*Diary*, 1688).

As a result, Sr. Faustina was noted in her community for her special care of the poor who came to the convent seeking food, of the sick and infirm, and of the dying. She was also especially beloved by the destitute girls whom the sisters trained and educated at their religious houses.

Faustina's devotion to Jesus Christ found its center and wellspring in the Holy Eucharist. As she wrote in her *Diary*:

> All the good that is in me is due to Holy Communion. ... Herein lies the whole secret of my sanctity. ... One thing alone sustains me and that is Holy Communion. From it I draw my strength; in it is all my comfort. ... Jesus concealed in the host is everything to me. ... I would not know how to give glory to God if I did not have the Eucharist in my heart. ...
>
> O living Host, my one and only strength, fountain of love and mercy, embrace the whole world, and fortify faint souls. Oh, blessed be the instant and the moment when Jesus left us His most merciful Heart! (1392, 1489, 1037, 223).

In short, for Sr. Faustina, the Eucharist is the fountain of all graces because the merciful Jesus is uniquely present there. As Mercy Incarnate, He pours out all His graces upon us from His merciful Heart.

Faustina regarded the Mother of Jesus, the Blessed Virgin Mary, as the most trustworthy guide to the Heart of her Son. She therefore consecrated to the Mother of God all her concerns:

> O Mary, my Mother and my Lady, I offer you my soul, my body, my life, my death, and all that will follow it. I place everything in your hands. O my Mother, cover my soul with your virginal mantle and grant me the grace of purity of heart, soul, and body. Defend me with your power against all enemies (*Diary*, 79).

It would be fair to say, therefore that three words — Mercy, Eucharist, and Mary — summarize the very essence of the spiritual teaching to be found in Sr. Faustina's *Diary*. The more that Fr. Sopocko read, as it flowed from her pen week by week, the more impressed he became by this message.

However, he was still not entirely convinced of the authenticity of her revelations. After all, Fr. Sopocko was a well-trained theologian, and some of the things that Sr. Faustina wrote were so striking that he wondered whether they were entirely orthodox.

First, Faustina claimed that Jesus had insisted that God is not only merciful to sinners — in fact, in a sense, He is even more merciful to sinners than to the just. Faustina wrote:

> All grace flows from mercy ... even if a person's sins were as dark as night, God's mercy is stronger than our misery. One thing alone is necessary: that the sinner set ajar the door of his heart, be it ever so little, to let in a ray of God's merciful grace, and then God will do the rest (*Diary*, 1507).

Jesus said to her:

Let the greatest sinners place their trust in My mercy. They have the right before others to trust

> in the abyss of My mercy. ... Souls that make an
> appeal to My mercy delight Me. To such souls I
> grant even more graces than they ask (*Diary*,
> 1146).

Clearly, the message of Christ to Sr. Faustina was a message of extravagant love: He said He pours out a veritable ocean of graces upon contrite souls who come to Him with trust — even more than they ask. In fact, He has a special compassion for the worst sinners, because they are most in need of His mercy.

Jesus also promised to Sr. Faustina that the message of Divine Mercy, and its spread throughout the world, would be a harbinger of His Second Coming to the earth to bring the final triumph of the kingdom of God:

> Speak to the world about My mercy; let all
> mankind recognize My unfathomable mercy. It is
> a sign for the end times; after it will come the day
> of justice. ... You will prepare the world for My
> final coming (*Diary*, 848 and 429).

Jesus said all this not to frighten Faustina and those who would read these messages, but to convince them of the urgency of this evangelistic work of mercy. Jesus had promised in the Gospels that the good news of God's merciful love would first be preached throughout the whole world before the end times would come (see Mk 13:9). The spread of The Divine Mercy message seems to play an important role in the fulfillment of that prophecy:

> Today I am sending you with My mercy to the
> people of the whole world. I do not want to
> punish aching mankind, but I desire to heal it,
> pressing it to My merciful Heart. I use punish-
> ment when they themselves force me to do so; My
> hand is reluctant to take hold of the sword of
> justice. Before the Day of Justice, I am sending

the Day of Mercy. ... I am prolonging the time of mercy for the sake of [sinners]. But woe to them if they do not recognize this time of My visitation (*Diary*, 1588 and 1160).

In His messages to St. Faustina, Jesus elaborated on another prophecy He had made in the Gospels about the end times: the prophecy about the "sign" that would appear in the heavens just prior to His return (Mt 24:30). Jesus told her it would be a final sign of mercy for the world, a final call to repentance and forgiveness before the Day of Judgment:

Write this: Before I come as the just Judge, I am coming first as the King of Mercy. Before the day of justice arrives, there will be given to people a sign in the heavens of this sort:

All light in the heavens will be extinguished, and there will be great darkness over the whole earth. Then the sign of the cross will be seen in the sky, and from the openings where the hands and the feet of the Savior were nailed will come forth great lights which will light up the earth for a period of time. This will take place shortly before the last day (*Diary*, 83).

Further, all of this should be considered in the broader scriptural context of how we will be judged on the Last Day, based on how we have shown mercy to others out of love for Jesus (see Mt 25:31-46). As Jesus told St. Faustina, "I demand from you deeds of mercy, which are to arise out of love for Me" (*Diary*, 742).

Father Sopocko was most amazed, however, by one of our Lord's messages to Sr. Faustina above all the others. Consequently, he made it the final testing-ground of the authenticity of all her revelations. This testing-ground was the claim that "mercy is the greatest attribute of God." Jesus had actually said this to Faustina several times, but one time He said it in a message that was intended directly for Fr. Sopocko — which certainly made him pay close attention! Jesus said to her:

> **I desire that the first Sunday after Easter be the Feast of Mercy. Ask of my faithful servant [Fr. Sopocko] that on this day, he tell the whole world of My great mercy; that whoever approaches the Fount of Life on this day will be granted complete remission of sins and punishment. Mankind will not have peace until it turns with trust to My mercy. ... My Heart rejoices in this title of Mercy. Proclaim that mercy is the greatest attribute of God. All the works of My hands are crowned with mercy** (*Diary*, 300).

Father Sopocko's response to this message is found in his own recollections, written some years later. He wrote:

> There are truths of the faith which we are supposed to know and which we frequently refer to, but we do not understand them very well, nor do we live by them. It was so with me concerning the Divine Mercy. I had thought of this truth so many times in meditations, especially during retreats. I had spoken of it so often in sermons and repeated in the liturgical prayers, but I had not gone to the core of its substance and its significance for the spiritual life; in particular, I had not understood, and for the moment I could not even agree, that Divine Mercy is the highest attribute of God, the Creator, Redeemer, and Sanctifier. It was only when I encountered a simple holy soul who was in close communion with God, who, as I believe, with divine inspiration told me of it, that she impelled me to read, research, and reflect on this subject. ...

> I began to search in the writings of the Fathers of the Church for a confirmation that this is the greatest of

the attributes of God, as Sister Faustina had stated, for I had found nothing on this subject in the works of more modern theologians. I was very pleased to find similar statements in St. Fulgentius, St. Idelphonse, and more still in St. Thomas and St. Augustine, who, in commenting on the Psalms, had much to say on Divine Mercy, calling it the greatest of God's greatest attributes. From then onwards, I had no serious doubts of the supernatural revelations of Sister Faustina (Tarnowska, p. 167, 201).

With all reasonable doubt removed, Fr. Sopocko began putting the Lord's requests to Faustina into action. First, he commissioned an image of The Divine Mercy to be painted. Then, for the Sunday after Easter in 1935, he had this image displayed over the famous Ostra Brama gate to the city of Vilnius, and in the nearby church, he preached the message of mercy to the Catholic populace. Sister Faustina was given permission to be there, too. And toward the end of the service, when the priest took the Blessed Sacrament to bless the people, she saw the Lord Jesus Himself, as He is represented in the Image of Mercy, and Christ Himself gave His blessing while the rays from His Heart extended over the whole world.

This event marked the beginning of the spread of the great devotion to The Divine Mercy, a devotion that is now having a profound impact upon the Church in our time. However, at first, it did not spread rapidly. Rather, it spread slowly and steadily all over Poland, assisted by the grace of God in the hearts of the people.

Father Sopocko saw very little of Sr. Faustina after that great exposition of the Image at the Ostra Brama gate. She remained in Vilnius for another year, but then she was transferred to Krakow. Nevertheless, she remained in contact with Fr. Sopocko and continued to write her *Diary*, not so much for him, but as Jesus said, she was to be the "apostle" and "secretary" of His mercy for the whole world.

Sister Faustina lived for only two more years. Her body was gradually ravaged by tuberculosis, and she was not spared any of the terrible sufferings caused by that disease in its final stages. The last chapter in her life became one of extreme suffering. She offered up all her sufferings in union with Christ's Passion for mercy upon all lost sinners, and especially those near death. She prayed: "Transform me into Yourself, O Jesus, that I may be a living sacrifice, and pleasing to You. I desire to atone at each moment for poor sinners" (*Diary*, 908).

And Jesus responded to her prayers:

Know, My daughter, that your silent, day-to-day martyrdom in complete submission to My will ushers many souls into heaven. And when it seems to you that your suffering exceeds your strength contemplate My wounds (*Diary*, 1184).

Father Sopocko visited her in late September 1938, just ten days before she died. He always brought her news of the printing and dissemination of the Image and of the spread of the devotion. But this time she had very little to say. As he later recalled, she was just too busy "communing with her heavenly Father."

Sister Faustina died on October 5, 1938, but her mission was far from over. In fact, it was only just beginning. "My mission will not come to an end upon my death," she had said in her *Diary*, "[for] I will draw aside for you the veils of heaven to convince you of God's goodness" (281).

Study Questions

1. How did Fr. Sopocko test the authenticity of Sr. Faustina's alleged revelations from Jesus Christ?

2. What finally convinced Fr. Sopocko to accept the authenticity of these revelations?

3. What three words summarize the essence of the spiritual teaching of found in St. Faustina's *Diary*, and what did she teach regarding these three words?

Discussion Starter:

If you or someone you know seemed to receive an extraordinary revelation from Jesus Christ, what criteria would the Church most likely use to test its authenticity?

2. THE SPREAD OF THE MERCY DEVOTION

Throughout World War II, the people of Poland turned more and more to the Image of Mercy, and to the prayer called the Chaplet of Divine Mercy, to give them comfort and hope in the midst of the raging conflict and the horrors of the Nazi occupation.

One Polish priest, Fr. Joseph Jarzebowski, MIC, in danger of being murdered by the Gestapo, made a dramatic escape across Stalin's Russia and fascist Japan, promising the Lord that if he made it to safety in the USA, he would spend the rest of his life spreading the mercy message. In fact, Fr. Jarzebowski did make it to safety (without proper traveling visas!). True to his word, in 1944, he and his associates in the Congregation of Marians of the Immaculate Conception established The Mercy of God Apostolate on Eden Hill in Stockbridge, Massachusetts, now the National Shrine of The Divine Mercy.

Meanwhile, Fr. Sopocko was busy himself spreading the devotion and in the process suffered much ridicule and loss of reputation. The hardest blow, however, came in 1959 when the Vatican, having received an erroneous and confusing translation of the *Diary* into Italian, forbade the spreading of the mercy devotion in the forms proposed by Sr. Faustina. That ban would last nearly twenty years. Father Sopocko, however, consoled himself with the knowledge that all this was in fulfillment of a prophecy made by Sr. Faustina. She had written:

> There will come a time when this work [of mercy], which God is demanding so very much, will be as though utterly undone. And then God will act with great power, which will give evidence of its authenticity. It will be a new splendor for the Church, although it has been dormant in it from long ago (*Diary*, 378).

In 1965, the Archbishop of Krakow, Karol Wojtyla, knowing full well that the Vatican had received faulty translations of the *Diary*, began the official process of investigation into Sr. Faustina's life and virtues. He asked one of Poland's leading theologians, Fr. Ignacy Rózycki, to prepare a critical analysis of the *Diary* as part of that process. Father Rózycki, however, did not want to waste his time analyzing what rumor told him were merely the hallucinations of an uneducated nun. Yet just before sending his letter of refusal to the Archbishop, he picked up the *Diary* and casually began to read a few pages "just to pass the time." His prejudice against it was immediately shaken. Then he read the whole thing through, and afterward he decided to devote the rest of his life to the study and propagation of Sr. Faustina's message.

In 1978, the Vatican's Congregation for the Doctrine of the Faith, having received the results of Fr. Rózycki's research as well as more accurate translations of the *Diary*, informed the Congregation of Marians that the ban on Sr. Faustina's devotion had finally been lifted. In a letter explaining this decision, the Vatican Congregation wrote: "There no longer exists, on the part of this Sacred Congregation, any impediment to the spreading of the devotion to The Divine Mercy in the authentic forms proposed by the Religious Sister [Faustina]." Finally, there it was: the "*Nihil Obstat*" from the Vatican itself! A few months later, that same Cardinal Archbishop of Krakow who had initiated this process, Karol Wojtyla, became Pope John Paul II.

Still, the lifting of a ban is not yet the Church's full, positive approval and encouragement, a process that usually happens more gradually. Meanwhile, with the ban rescinded, the Image, the *Diary*, the Chaplet, the marking of the Feast Day, and the Three O'clock Hour of Mercy prayers spread quickly throughout the world.

The Chaplet especially became very popular. Here was a form of prayer invoking God's mercy upon the whole world, and extending the Eucharistic offering of Jesus Christ with an intercessory intention:

> **Eternal Father, I offer You the Body and Blood, Soul and Divinity, of Your dearly beloved Son, Our Lord Jesus Christ, in atonement for our sins and those of the whole world; for the sake of His sorrowful Passion, have mercy on us and on the whole world** (*Diary*, 476).

In fact, Jesus had attached the most extraordinary promises to the sincere and devout recitation of this Chaplet. As He said to Sr. Faustina:

> **Encourage souls to say the Chaplet I have given you. ... Whoever will recite it will receive great**

mercy at the hour of death. ... Even if there were a sinner most hardened, if he were to recite this Chaplet only once, he would receive grace from My infinite mercy. ... Through the Chaplet you will obtain everything, if what you ask for is compatible with My will (*Diary*, 1541, 687, 1731).

To these promises about the Chaplet, Jesus added more about the devout practice of intercessory prayer at the three o'clock hour each day, "The Hour of Great Mercy." He said to Sr. Faustina:

As often as you hear the clock strike the third hour, immerse yourself completely in My mercy, adoring and glorifying it; invoke its omnipotence for the whole world, and particularly for poor sinners; for at that moment mercy was opened wide for every soul. In this hour you can obtain everything for yourself and for others for the asking: it was the hour of grace for the whole world — mercy triumphed over justice (*Diary*, 1572).

In the mid-1980s, for example, the people of the Philippines, struggling and suffering under the dictatorship of President Ferdinand Marcos, turned as a nation to The Divine Mercy through a daily nationwide broadcast of the Three O' clock Hour of Mercy prayers and the Chaplet. They pleaded with the Lord for a peaceful and just settlement of their national conflict. Almost miraculously, a non-violent revolution took place and democracy was restored to that poor, yet faithful country.

Meanwhile, convincing evidence of a miracle of healing attributed to Sr. Faustina's intercession removed the last obstacle to the recognition of her sanctity by the universal Church. As a result, on April 18, 1993, on the Sunday after Easter (Mercy Sunday), she was declared "Blessed" at a Mass at St. Peter's Basilica in Rome. In his homily at that beatification, Pope John Paul II exclaimed:

Her mission continues and is yielding astonishing fruit. It is truly marvelous how her devotion to the Merciful Jesus is spreading in our contemporary world, and gaining so many human hearts! This is doubtless a sign of the times, a sign of our 20th century. The balance of this century that is now ending ... presents a deep restlessness and fear of the future. Where, if not in the Divine Mercy, can the world find refuge and the light of hope? Believers understand that perfectly.

On January 23, 1995, the Vatican Congregation for Divine Worship granted to the bishops of Poland — the first group of bishops to make the request — the right to celebrate the liturgical Feast of Divine Mercy on the Sunday after Easter, the very day in the liturgical calendar that the Lord had requested of Sr. Faustina. Then, on the Sunday after Easter in 1995, the Holy Father himself celebrated "Mercy Sunday" in the city of Rome, establishing at the same time an international center for the devotion at the Church of the Holy Spirit in Sassia (just a few hundred yards away from St. Peter's Basilica) and blessing an image of The Divine Mercy for that church.

10 years before JPII death [handwritten marginal note]

If there remained doubt in anyone's mind about the general approval of this message and devotion by the See of St. Peter, that doubt was removed by the Pope's visit to the tomb of Sr. Faustina in Lagiewniki, near the city of Krakow, in the summer of 1997, and by the remarkable address he delivered there at the convent of the Sisters of Our Lady of Mercy. In that address, he not only explained the importance of this message and devotion to all souls seeking for God, he also told how important it had been to him personally in his own spiritual journey:

> There is nothing that man needs more than Divine Mercy — that love which is benevolent, which is compassionate, which raises man above his weakness to the infinite heights of the holiness of God. In this place we become particularly aware of this. From

here, in fact, went out the message of Divine Mercy that Christ Himself chose to pass on to our generation through Blessed Faustina. And it is a *message that is clear and understandable for everyone.* Anyone can come here, look at this image of the merciful Jesus, His Heart radiating grace, and hear in the depths of his own soul what Blessed Faustina heard: *"Fear nothing. I am with You always."* And if this person responds with a sincere heart: *"Jesus, I trust in You,"* he will find comfort in all his anxieties and fears. ... On the threshold of the third millennium *I come to entrust to Him once more my Petrine ministry — "Jesus, I trust in You!"*

The message of Divine Mercy has always been near and dear to me. It is as if history had inscribed it in the tragic experience of the Second World War. In those difficult years it was a *particular support and an inexhaustible source of hope,* not only for the people of Kraków but for the entire nation. This was also my personal experience, which I took with me to the See of Peter and which in a sense forms the image of this Pontificate. I give thanks to divine Providence that I have been enabled to contribute personally to the fulfillment of Christ's will, through the institution of the Feast of Divine Mercy [in Poland]. Here, near the relics of Blessed Faustina Kowalska, I give thanks also for the gift of her beatification. I pray unceasingly that God will have "mercy on us and the whole world."

On almost every occasion that Pope John Paul II spoke of Sr. Faustina, or about The Divine Mercy message and devotion, he stressed that this is a remedy especially suited to meet the critical needs of our age. In a world in which, at times, darkness seems to be enveloping almost everything, a world now full to overflowing with apostasy, the persecution of Christians, the breakdown of the family, the exploitation of the poor, the murder of unborn children, the horrors of ethnic cleansing and international terrorism, where, indeed, if not to The Divine Mercy, can the world turn to find refuge and the light of hope?

As the human race wanders further and further away from its Savior, He has not abandoned it to its fate nor failed to find new ways to bring His lost sheep home. Every aspect of The Divine Mercy message and devotion that Jesus fashioned proclaims loud and clear the same Gospel message: God is not just waiting patiently for the world to come back to Him! Rather, *His mercy always takes the initiative* — without any merit or deserving on our part — *to seek us out and find us.*

The Image of The Divine Mercy revealed to Sr. Faustina is a vivid expression of this Gospel message. Everything about this Image speaks of the risen Lord taking the initiative and seeking out the lost and the brokenhearted with the rays of His merciful love. In this Image, Christ is shown walking toward the viewer, coming to find us. The rays of merciful love flowing from His Heart spread out to embrace the viewer, and His hand is raised with a blessing of peace even before we ask for it. In an age in which the visual image — whether through television, films, or the computer screen — has become the most powerful medium of communication, Jesus Christ has fashioned for us an image of Himself that awakens our trust in Him and calms our fears. As He once said to Sr. Faustina: **"Be not afraid of your Savior, O sinful soul. I make the first move to come to you, for I know that by yourself you are unable to lift yourself to Me"** (*Diary*, 1485).

The Feast of Divine Mercy proclaims this same Gospel message. It is not a new feast. According to St. Augustine, St. Gregory Nazianzen, and *The Apostolic Constitutions*, the early Church celebrated the Sunday after Easter, or Octave Day of Easter, as a great feast day (called in the West *Dominica in Albis* — the Sunday in White). It was a rounding out of the eight days of Easter celebrations, and a day that St. Augustine is reported to have called "the compendium of the days of mercy." In other words, on this day the Church gives thanks to God for His merciful love shining through all the great acts by which He won our salvation, especially the Cross and Resurrection of His Son.

As Pope John Paul II said in his *Regina Caeli* address on Mercy Sunday in 1995, "The whole Octave of Easter is like a single day," and the Octave Sunday is meant to be a day of "thanksgiving for the goodness God has shown man in the whole Easter mystery." For this reason, the opening prayer, psalms, and readings appointed for that Sunday already proclaim the message of mercy and did not need to be changed for the official institution of the Feast. The whole of Mercy Sunday is meant to manifest Jesus Christ, reaching out to sinful humanity with His prevenient, unmerited mercy. As Jesus' words to Sr. Faustina put it:

> I desire that the Feast of Mercy be a refuge and shelter for all souls, and especially for poor sinners. On that day the very depths of My tender mercy are open. I pour out a whole ocean of graces upon souls who approach the fountain of My mercy (*Diary*, 699).

The Chaplet of Divine Mercy also proclaims this message of mercy. The Chaplet is a pleading for God's mercy upon the world, but a pleading upon the basis of God's supreme act of mercy for us all, namely, His Son's "sorrowful Passion." Although not first in time on the linear scale of human history, the Cross is first in the order of grace, for it is the basis for all the graces that the Lord has poured out upon humanity — past, present, and future. "While we were yet sinners," St. Paul wrote, "Christ died for us." "While we were still sinners": the perfect expression of prevenient, undeserved Divine Mercy.

Even The Divine Mercy Novena intentions dictated to St. Faustina by Jesus Himself convey this Gospel message (see *Diary*, 1209-1229). Each day, Faustina was instructed to bring "into His merciful Heart" a different group of people, including those who do not believe in God or know Him, those who have become "lukewarm" in their love for God, and the souls suffering in purgatory. All are to be "immersed" in His mercy, freely poured out upon them, and are to draw from Him "strength and refreshment," and whatever else they need in the hardships of life, and, especially, at the hour of death" (*Diary*, 1209).

Finally, God's mercy is not only meant to be received with trust. It is also to be shared through love. The practice of the works of mercy, both spiritual and corporal, are the goal and fruit of this devotion, as well as a Gospel command: "Be merciful even as your Father is merciful" (Lk 6:36). Sister Faustina knew very well that it is only hearts that have been transformed by the mercy of Jesus Christ that are fully equipped to share it with others, so she prayed constantly for the gift of a merciful heart:

> O Jesus, I understand that Your mercy is beyond all imagining, and therefore I ask You to make my heart so big that there will be room in it for the needs of all souls living on the face of the earth ... and the souls suffering in Purgatory. ... Make my heart sensitive to all the sufferings of my neighbor, whether of body or soul. O my Jesus, I know that You act toward us as we act toward our neighbor. ... Make my heart like unto Your merciful Heart (*Diary*, 692).

Here is the divine remedy for a world full of cold hearts and broken hearts: the Merciful Heart of Jesus, which can transform human hearts so that they become "living reflections" of His own (*Diary*, 163). With approximately one billion people now living in the most abject material poverty, and billions more living under the reign of false and oppressive ideologies, surely, the time is right for the advent of a worldwide apostolate of Divine Mercy, fashioned by Christ's own Merciful Heart. This is also the earnest plea of Pope John Paul II, who asked the faithful on Mercy Sunday in 1995, to "trust in the Lord and be Apostles of Divine Mercy, and follow the invitation of Bl. Faustina."

Sister Faustina was canonized at St. Peter's Basilica in Rome on Mercy Sunday 2000. She was the first saint of the Great Jubilee Year of the Incarnation, which ushered in the third millennium. May it be a millennium of Divine Mercy. Saint Faustina, pray for us!

Study Questions

1. In his address at Sister Faustina's tomb in 1997, what did Pope John Paul II tell us were some of the reasons he valued the message of Divine Mercy that Faustina received from Jesus Christ?

2. What are the roots of "Divine Mercy Sunday" in the early history of the Church?

3. What is the "goal and fruit" of The Divine Mercy message and devotion?

Discussion Starter:

The message and devotion to The Divine Mercy, received from Jesus Christ by St. Faustina, has spread more rapidly throughout the Church than any other set of revelations ever given directly by our Lord to a saint. Why do so many people welcome this mercy message? What urgent needs of the human heart does it fulfill?

CHAPTER TWO

The Legacy of Pope John Paul II

Of all the Catholic saints and theologians who have written about the merciful love of God, none has done so with more public and universal impact than the Servant of God Pope John Paul II. Listing all the things that John Paul II did to confirm and strengthen The Divine Mercy message and devotion leaves one without any doubt that Pope Benedict XVI was "on the mark" in saying: "The mystery of God's merciful love was at the center of the pontificate of my venerated predecessor" (*Regina Caeli* address, April 23, 2006).

1. THE GREAT MERCY PONTIFICATE

A list of the principal acts of Divine Mercy evangelism by Pope John Paul II would certainly include the following:

- In 1981, Pope John Paul II wrote an entire encyclical dedicated to The Divine Mercy entitled *Dives in Misericordia* (*Rich in Mercy*), illustrating that the heart of the mission of Jesus Christ was to reveal the merciful love of the Father.

- In 1993, he beatified Sr. Faustina, stating in his homily: "Her mission continues and is yielding astonishing fruit. It is truly marvelous how her devotion to the merciful Jesus is spreading in our contemporary world, and gaining so many human hearts!"

- In 1997, he visited Bl. Faustina's tomb in Lagiewniki, Poland, and proclaimed: "There is nothing that man needs more than Divine Mercy. ... From here went out the message of Mercy that Christ Himself chose to pass on to our generation through Bl. Faustina."

- In 2000, he canonized Sr. Faustina — making her the first canonized saint of the preparatory Jubilee Year for the Third Millennium — and established "Divine Mercy Sunday" as a special title for the Octave Sunday of Easter for the universal Church. At the canonization, he said that he was passing the message of Divine Mercy on to the new millennium.

- In his homily on Mercy Sunday in 2001, Pope John Paul II called The Divine Mercy message given to St. Faustina "the appropriate and incisive answer that God wanted to offer to the questions and expectations of human beings in our time, marked by terrible tragedies. ... Divine Mercy! This is the Easter gift that the Church receives from the risen Christ and offers to humanity at the dawn of the third millennium."

- In Lagiewniki, Poland, in 2002, at the new Shrine of The Divine Mercy, the Holy Father consecrated the whole world to The Divine Mercy, saying: "I do so with the burning desire that the message of God's merciful love, proclaimed here through St. Faustina, may be made known to all the peoples of the earth and fill their hearts with hope."

- As Pope Benedict XVI pointed out, "Providence decided that he should die right on the eve of that day [Mercy Sunday] in the arms of Divine Mercy." Indeed, just before his death on Saturday, April 2, 2005, Pope John Paul II received the Holy Communion of the Vigil Mass for Divine Mercy Sunday.

- Among John Paul II's last written words as Pope were those of the *Regina Caeli* message that he had prepared to deliver the next day, that is, on Divine Mercy Sunday itself (April 3, 2005):

> As a gift to humanity, which sometimes seems bewildered and overwhelmed by the power of evil, selfishness, and fear, the Risen Lord offers His love that pardons, reconciles, and reopens hearts to love. It is a love that converts hearts and gives peace. How much the world needs to understand and accept Divine Mercy!

> Lord, who reveals the Father's love by Your death and Resurrection, we believe in You and confidently repeat to You today: Jesus I trust in You, have mercy upon us and upon the whole world.

Pope John Paul II was truly "The Great Mercy Pope," as the title of a recent book so accurately phrases it (Rev. George Kosicki, CSB, *John Paul II: The Great Mercy Pope*, Marian Press, Stockbridge, MA, revised edition, 2006). He preached about God's mercy, wrote about it, and most of all *lived* it — offering forgiveness to the man who shot him in St. Peter's Square and doing everything in his power to heal the wounds caused by the historic conflicts between Catholics and other Christian communities, as well as with the Jewish people.

What many people do not realize, however, is that Pope John Paul's interest in St. Faustina and the message of Divine Mercy stretches right back to the days of his youth. In his foreword to Fr. Kosicki's book, Fr. Ron Pytel — healed himself by the prayers of St. Faustina in a miracle investigated and substantiated by the Church — outlines the early history of Karol Wojtyla with The Divine Mercy devotion:

> As a young college student in Krakow, he witnessed man's inhumanity to man during World War II in occupied Poland. He saw many people rounded up and sent to concentration camps and slave labor. In

his hometown of Wadowice, he had many friends of the Jewish faith who would perish in the Holocaust. Death and danger surrounded the young Wojtyla. He experienced the need for God's mercy and humanity's need to be merciful to one another.

It was during this horrible period in human history that the young Karol Wojtyla decided to enter Cardinal Sapieha's clandestine seminary in Krakow. This decision further jeopardized his life, for he could be executed [by the Nazis] if caught. It was also during this time that another seminarian, Andrew Deskur, now a retired Cardinal at the Vatican, introduced Karol to the message of the Divine Mercy, as revealed to the mystic nun, now St. Maria Faustina Kowalska, the great suffering soul, who died at the age of 33 in 1938. St. Faustina wrote a diary entitled *Divine Mercy in My Soul*, in which she recorded the revelations given to her by Jesus about the greatness of God's mercy. The message of God's mercy, as recorded by Sister Faustina, would be a beacon of light and hope for the people of Poland during this dark time in their history.

In his years as a young priest, and later as Bishop and Archbishop of Krakow (now under the oppression of a Communist regime), Karol Wojtyla would reflect and meditate upon the message of God's mercy. He would often visit the convent in Lagiewniki where Sister Faustina was buried for private times of prayer, and to lead the Sisters in reflective retreats.

2. DIVINE MERCY SUNDAY

Perhaps the most surprising act of Pope John Paul II in promoting The Divine Mercy message was his proclamation at the canonization of Sr. Faustina in St. Peter's Square in 2000: "From now on, throughout the Church [this Sunday] will be called Divine Mercy Sunday." Many of the Church's pastors and liturgists were stunned by this announcement. Some wondered: "Why is the Holy Father doing this? Is he simply creating a new feast because of his personal devotion to the private revelations of a Polish mystic?"

Pope John Paul II was well aware that the visions of Christ received by St. Faustina, and the messages and devotions flowing from them, remain in the official category of "private revelations." The Church's doctrine of Divine Mercy and her liturgical practices are not based on any such revelations; they are based on Holy Scripture, the faith handed down from the apostles, and on the liturgical traditions rooted in the worship life of the ancient, apostolic communities. Saint Faustina's revelations can add nothing new to the deposit of faith nor anything novel to the official liturgy of the Church. Moreover, it is also true that the Holy Father did not establish Divine Mercy Sunday to commemorate St. Faustina's mystical experiences. Thus, it remains true to this day that no one is *required* by the Holy See, on Mercy Sunday, to pray the Chaplet of Divine Mercy, venerate the Image of The Divine Mercy, or do anything else that springs from St. Faustina's revelations. No priest could be called a "heretic" or in any way disobedient to liturgical law for ignoring these things entirely.

Nevertheless, what makes St. Faustina's revelations striking is the way that they so powerfully express the central truths that lay at the heart of the Gospel: the merciful love of God, manifest especially in the Passion and Resurrection of His Son. Indeed, some of the devotional forms that come from her "private revelations" (such as the Chaplet and the veneration of

the Image) are especially vivid ways of contemplating and celebrating the Paschal Mystery: the mystery that lies at the very
heart of the "public revelation" passed down to us from the
apostles, as well as at the very heart of the ancient liturgical traditions for the eight days of the Easter Octave.

In short, what is not strictly required — that is, what is not
a matter of law or precept — can still be a matter of good
counsel. Pope John Paul II, the chief pastor and shepherd of the
Church, strongly encouraged Catholics to pay heed to the
messages and revelations given to St. Faustina as a special call to
our time to turn back to the God of merciful love. Given that
this same Pope also recommended the Image and the Chaplet as
helpful means to that end and that he even established "Divine
Mercy Sunday" for the whole Church, surely it would be rash
and imprudent to ignore these pastoral and liturgical directives
from the Vicar of Christ.

In his homily on Mercy Sunday, 2001, Pope John Paul
II again stressed the importance of Christ's call to the world
through St. Faustina:

> We are celebrating the Second Sunday of Easter,
> which, since last year — the year of the Great Jubilee
> — is also called "Divine Mercy Sunday." It is a great
> joy for me to be able to join all of you, dear pilgrims
> and faithful who have come here from various nations
> to commemorate, after one year, the canonization of
> Sr. Faustina Kowalska, witness and messenger of the
> Lord's merciful love. The elevation to the honors of
> the altar of this humble religious is not only a gift for
> Poland, but for all humanity. Indeed, the message
> she brought is the appropriate and incisive answer
> that God wanted to offer to the questions and expec-
> tations of human beings in our time, marked by
> terrible tragedies. Jesus said to Sr. Faustina:
> "Humanity will not have peace until it turns with
> trust to My mercy" (*Diary*, 300). Divine Mercy!
> This is the Easter gift that the Church receives from

the risen Christ and offers to humanity at the dawn of the third millennium. ...

Today the Lord also shows His glorious wounds and His heart, an inexhaustible source of truth, of love and forgiveness. ... Saint Faustina saw coming from this Heart that was overflowing with generous love, two rays of light that illuminated the world. "The two rays," according to what Jesus Himself told her, "represent the blood and the water" (*Diary*, 299). The blood recalls the sacrifice of Golgotha, and the mystery of the Eucharist; the water, according to the rich symbolism of the Evangelist St. John, makes us think of Baptism and the Gift of the Holy Spirit (cf. Jn 3:5; 4:14).

Through the mystery of this wounded Heart, the restorative tide of God's merciful love continues to spread over the men and women of our time. Here alone can those who long for true and lasting happiness find its secret.

3. A MESSAGE FOR OUR TIME

Why did Pope John Paul II so strongly recommend that we pay heed to The Divine Mercy message and devotion — even the Image and the Chaplet — given to the world through St. Faustina? Clearly, he did so because he saw all this as more than just a collection of "private revelations." Rather, he saw them as *prophetic* revelations. In other words, he saw them as revelations given to us by God to proclaim the heart of the Gospel — the Gospel of the merciful love of God, shining through the Death and Resurrection of His Son — in a way especially suited to meet the needs of our era.

Throughout the modern era, false, secular ideologies have

taken a stranglehold on large portions of the world, threatening the peace and freedom of the nations. In his last book, *Memory and Identity*, Pope John Paul II explained that the message of mercy from St. Faustina is an antidote to these poisonous falsehoods:

> Everything I said in the encyclical *Redemptor Hominis* I brought with me from Poland. Likewise, the reflections offered in *Dives in Misericordia* were the fruit of my pastoral experience in Poland, especially in Krakow. That is where Saint Faustina Kowalska is buried, she who was chosen by Christ to be a particularly enlightened interpreter of the truth of Divine Mercy. For Sister Faustina, this truth led to an extraordinarily rich mystical life. She was a simple, uneducated person, and yet those who read the *Diary* of her revelations are astounded by the depth of her mystical experience.
>
> I mention Sister Faustina because her revelations, focused on the mystery of Divine Mercy, occurred during the period preceding the Second World War. This was precisely the time when those ideologies of evil, nazism and communism, were taking shape. Sister Faustina became the herald of the one message capable of off-setting the evil of those ideologies, the fact that God is mercy — the truth of the merciful Christ. And for this reason, when I was called to the See of Peter, I felt impelled to pass on those experiences of a fellow Pole that deserve a place in the treasury of the universal Church. ...
>
> I have chosen here to speak of Sister Faustina and the devotion to the merciful Christ which she promoted, because she too belongs to our time. She lived in the first decades of the twentieth century and died before the Second World War. In that very period the mystery of Divine Mercy was revealed to her, and

what she experienced she then recorded in her *Diary*. To those who survived the Second World War, Saint Faustina's *Diary* appears as a particular Gospel of Divine Mercy, written from a twentieth century perspective. The people of that time understood her message. They understood it in the light of the dramatic buildup of evil during the Second World War and the cruelty of totalitarian systems. It was as if Christ had wanted to reveal that the limit imposed upon evil, of which man is both perpetrator and victim, is ultimately Divine Mercy. Of course, there is also justice, but this alone does not have the last word in the divine economy of world history and human history. God can always draw good from evil. He wills that all should be saved and come to the knowledge of the truth (cf. 1 Tim 2:4): God is Love (cf. 1 Jn 4:8). Christ, crucified and risen, just as he appeared to Sister Faustina, is the supreme revelation of this truth.

Here I should like to return to what I said about the experience of the Church in Poland during the period of resistance to communism. It seems to me to have a universal value. I think that the same applies to Sister Faustina and her witness to the mystery of Divine Mercy. The patrimony of her spirituality was of great importance, as we know from experience, for the resistance against the evil and inhuman systems of the time. The lesson to be drawn from all this is important not only for Poles, but also in every part of the world where the Church is present. This became clear during the beatification and canonization of Sister Faustina. It was as if Christ had wanted to say through her: "Evil does not have the last word!" The Paschal Mystery confirms that good is ultimately victorious, that life conquers death, and that love triumphs over hate.

Above all, Pope John Paul II stressed again and again that Divine Mercy is not just a doctrine to be believed by the mind, or another "devotion" involving acts of piety. Rather, it is a *personal encounter with the merciful Savior Himself.* The Image, the Feast, the Chaplet, and even the doctrinal message, are just means to enable us to *personally experience* the love of Jesus Christ. Only if we have experienced His love for ourselves, the Holy Father insisted, are we adequately prepared to share His love effectively with others.

For example, on April 10, 1994, on the Second Sunday of Easter (Mercy Sunday), Pope John Paul II stated in his *Regina Caeli* address:

> What is mercy if not the boundless love of God, who confronted with human sin, restrains the sentiment of severe justice and, allowing Himself to be moved by the wretchedness of His creatures, spurs Himself to the total gift of self, in the Son's cross … ?

> Who can say he is free from sin and does not need God's mercy? As people of this restless time of ours, wavering between the emptiness of self-exaltation and the humiliation of despair, we have a greater need than ever for a regenerating experience of mercy.

In his *Regina Caeli* address on Mercy Sunday in 1995, the Holy Father spoke of the whole octave of Easter as like "a single day" of celebration and the Sunday of the octave (Mercy Sunday) as the special day of thanksgiving for God's mercy. He concluded:

> Dear brothers and sisters, we must *personally experience* this [tender-hearted mercy of the Father] if, in turn, we want to be capable of mercy. Let us learn to forgive! The spiral of hatred and violence that stains with blood the path of so many individuals and nations can only be broken by the *miracle of forgiveness.*

We have already seen how the Pope testified to the impact that message of mercy had upon him personally. Here again is a portion of his speech at the tomb of St. Faustina in Lagiewniki in June of 1997:

> The message of Divine Mercy has always been near and dear to me. It is as if history had inscribed it in the tragic experience of the Second World War. In those difficult years, it was a particular support and an inexhaustible source of hope, not only for the people of Krakow, but for the entire nation.
>
> This was also my personal experience, which I took with me to the See of St. Peter, and which, in a sense, forms the image of this Pontificate.

On another occasion, the Pope expressed his wish that *everyone* would be able to experience God's merciful love in a personal way and so be empowered to transmit that love to others. In his evening prayer on Divine Mercy Sunday 2000, from the papal balcony on St. Peter's Square, the Holy Father made this earnest appeal:

> Dear brothers and sisters, on this Second Sunday of Easter, on which I had the joy of enrolling Sister Faustina Kowalska — Apostle of Divine Mercy — among the saints, I urge you always to trust in God's merciful love revealed to us in Christ Jesus, who died and rose again for our salvation. May the personal experience of this love commit everyone to becoming, in turn, a witness of active charity towards his brothers and sisters. Make Sister Faustina's beautiful exclamation your own: "Jesus, I trust in You!"

4. CONSECRATING THE WORLD TO THE DIVINE MERCY

Perhaps the most stirring example of Pope John Paul II's witness to Divine Mercy came on August 17, 2002, when he consecrated the whole world to Divine Mercy. In his homily that day at the new International Divine Mercy Shrine in Lagiewniki, Poland, the Holy Father explained that the whole story of God's merciful love for mankind — a story we have traced in this book from Genesis to the 21st century — culminates in an urgent need for Christians everywhere to proclaim, pray for, and practice merciful love. This is truly the only hope for the future of the human race. May these powerful words of John Paul the Great, the Pope of Divine Mercy, echo in hearts and minds throughout the world, paving the way for the final victory of the merciful love of Jesus Christ over the forces of evil:

Dear Brothers and Sisters ...

Like St. Faustina, we wish to proclaim that apart from the mercy of God there is no other source of hope for mankind. We desire to repeat with faith: *Jesus, I trust in You!*

This proclamation, this confession of trust in the all-powerful love of God, is especially needed in our own time, when mankind is experiencing bewilderment in the face of many manifestations of evil. *The invocation of God's mercy* needs to rise up from the depth of hearts filled with suffering, apprehension, and uncertainty, and at the same time yearning for an infallible source of hope. That is why we have come here today, to this Shrine of Lagiewniki, in order to glimpse once more in Christ the face of the Father: "The Father of mercies and the God of all consolation" (2 Cor. 1:3). With the eyes of our soul, we long to look into the eyes of the merciful Jesus in order to find, deep within His gaze, the reflection of His inner life, as well as the light of grace which we have already received so often, and which God holds out to us anew each day and on the last day. ...

How greatly today's world needs God's mercy! In every continent, from the depths of human suffering, a cry for mercy seems to rise up. Where hatred and the thirst for revenge dominate, where war brings suffering and death to the innocent, there the grace of mercy is needed in order to settle human minds and hearts and to bring about peace. Wherever respect for human life and dignity are lacking, there is need of God's merciful love, in whose light we see the inexpressible value of every human being. Mercy is needed to insure that every injustice in the world will come to an end in the splendor of truth.

Today, therefore, in this Shrine, I wish to *solemnly entrust the world to Divine Mercy*. I do so with the burning desire that the message of God's merciful love, proclaimed here through St. Faustina, *may be made known to all the peoples of the earth* and fill their hearts with hope. May this message radiate from this place to our beloved homeland, and throughout the world. May the binding promise of the Lord Jesus be fulfilled: from here there must go forth "the spark which will prepare the world for His final coming" (*Diary*, 1732).

This spark needs to be lighted by the grace of God. This fire of mercy needs to be passed on to the world. *In the mercy of God, the world will find peace and mankind will find happiness!* I entrust this task to you, dear Brothers and Sisters. ... *May you be witnesses to mercy!*

God, merciful Father, in Your Son, Jesus Christ, You have revealed Your love and poured it out upon us in the Holy Spirit, the Comforter. We entrust to You today the destiny of the world and of every man and woman. Bend down to us sinners, heal our weakness, conquer all evil, and grant that all the peoples of the earth may experience Your mercy. In You, the Triune God, may they ever find the source of hope. Eternal Father, by the Passion and Resurrection of Your Son, have mercy on us, and upon the whole world! Amen.

Study Questions

1. Can you think of at least three reasons why Pope John Paul II can be considered "The Great Mercy Pope"?

2. What was the most surprising act of Pope John Paul II in promoting The Divine Mercy message? Why?

3. What do you think motivated Pope John Paul II to consecrate the world to Divine Mercy in 2002?

Discussion Starter:

Pope John Paul II bequeathed Divine Mercy to the Church as an important part of his legacy. Why did he consider Divine Mercy so important? For background on this, read again the passages from his last book, *Memory and Identity*. Also, see again his last Divine Mercy message, which was written for Divine Mercy Sunday, April 3, 2005.

CHAPTER THREE

Pope Benedict XVI and the Future

U nder the pastoral leadership of Pope Benedict XVI, the "spark" lit by St. Faustina and Pope John Paul II — the message of Divine Mercy — continues to spread throughout the world.

1. A GIFT OF THE DIVINE MERCY THROUGH JOHN PAUL II'S INTERCESSION

Right from the start of his pontificate, Pope Benedict seemed to be aware of the tremendous responsibility God had given him to carry on the mission of his predecessor and that only the gift of God's merciful love would enable him to do so faithfully and effectively. For example, in his first public address as Pope (April 20, 2005), Benedict spoke these moving words to the Cardinals who elected him:

> May grace and peace be multiplied to all of you (cf. Pet 1:2)! In these hours, two contrasting sentiments coexist in my spirit. On the one hand, a sense of inadequacy and of human anxiety before the universal Church, because of the responsibility that was entrusted to me yesterday as successor to the apostle Peter in this See of Rome. On the other hand, I feel very intensely in myself a profound gratitude to God who — as we sing in the liturgy — does not abandon His flock, but leads it through the times, under the

guidance of those whom He Himself has chosen as vicars of His Son, and has constituted pastors (cf. Preface of the Apostles, 1).

Beloved, this profound gratitude for a gift of The Divine Mercy prevails in my heart despite everything. And I consider it in fact as a special grace obtained for me by my venerable Predecessor, John Paul II. I seem to feel his strong hand gripping mine; I seem to see his smiling eyes and to hear his words, addressed at this moment particularly to me, "Be not afraid!" (as quoted in George Kosicki, *John Paul II: The Great Mercy Pope,* second edition, p. 138).

Notice how Pope Benedict describes in endearing terms a personal encounter with John Paul II as he speaks of his "profound gratitude for a gift of The Divine Mercy" that had been obtained for him through John Paul's intercession.

2. WITNESSES TO GOD'S MERCY

Then, on May 26, 2006, Pope Benedict visited the convent of the Sisters of Our Lady of Mercy in Lagiewniki, Poland, and prayed at St. Faustina's tomb there. Later, at the International Shrine of The Divine Mercy, he addressed these words to the sick:

Dear friends who are sick, who are marked by suffering in body and soul, you are most closely united to the Cross of Christ, and at the same time you are the most eloquent witnesses of God's mercy. Through you and through your suffering, He bows down to humanity with love. You who say in silence: "Jesus, I trust in You," teach us that there is no faith more profound, no hope more alive, and no love more ardent than the faith, hope, and love of a person who in the midst of suffering places himself squarely in God's hands. May the human hands of those who care for you in the name of mercy be an extension of the open hands of God (as quoted in Kosicki, p. 142).

Following that meeting with the sick, on May 27, 2006, Pope Benedict met with an estimated 500,000 young people at Blonie Park in Krakow, Poland, where he emphasized the importance of building one's faith on the Rock of Christ. He told the young people of Jesus Christ's personal love for each one of them. The Pope reflected back on his pastoral visit to Poland in his Wednesday General Audience address in Rome on May 31, 2006:

> My next stop, at the Shrine of The Divine Mercy in Lagiewniki, gave me the opportunity to stress that Divine Mercy alone illumines the mystery of man. It was here at the neighboring convent that Sr. Faustina Kowalska, contemplating the shining wounds of the Risen Christ, received a message of trust for humanity which John Paul II echoed and interpreted and which really is a central message precisely for our time: Mercy as God's power, as a divine barrier against the evil of the world.

> Another beautiful experience was my meeting with young people that took place in Krakow's large Blonie Park. I symbolically consigned the "Flame of Mercy" to the crowds of young people who had come so that they might be heralds of Love and Divine Mercy in the world (Kosicki, p. 143).

Clearly, Pope Benedict is calling the world — and especially the young people of the world — to be "heralds," evangelists, of the merciful love of Jesus Christ. In a world growing ever darker through violence, atheism, and despair, Jesus Christ's followers cannot be silent or inactive. God's merciful love has already won the decisive victory over evil through the Cross and Resurrection of Jesus Christ, but unless humanity turns with trust to His merciful love, the world will not be able to receive the peace that He won for us. As Jesus said to St. Faustina: **"Mankind will not have peace until it turns with trust to My mercy"** (*Diary*, 300).

On a more personal note, Pope Benedict decided on Divine Mercy Sunday, April 15, 2007, to celebrate his 80th birthday even though the actual day of his birth is April 16. Harkening back to his election, he again spoke of receiving a gift of Divine Mercy. Benedict said in his homily to mark the occasion:

> In these days illumined in particular by the light of Divine Mercy, a coincidence occurs that is significant to me: I can look back on over 80 years of life. ...

> I have always considered it a great gift of Divine Mercy to have been granted birth and rebirth, so to speak, on the same day, in the sign of the beginning of Easter. Thus, I was born as a member of my own family and of the great family of God on the same day.

Pope Benedict mentions his rebirth in his remarks, since he was baptized with the first water of Easter on Holy Saturday, the very day he was born.

Whether through the personal witness of his 80th birthday or by encouraging the sick and youth in Poland to a witness of mercy, Pope Benedict is following the lead of Pope John Paul II in inviting everyone to spread the Gospel of Mercy to a troubled world. In fact, in his *Angelus* message of September 16, 2007, in commenting on the "parables of mercy" in the 15th Chapter of the Gospel of Luke, he said:

> In our time, humanity needs a strong proclamation and witness of God's mercy. Beloved John Paul II, a great apostle of Divine Mercy, prophetically intuited this urgent pastoral need. He dedicated his second Encyclical to it and throughout his pontificate made himself a missionary of God's love to all peoples.

3. DIVINE MERCY, CENTER OF THE GOSPEL MESSAGE

Perhaps no better summary of Pope Benedict's mercy message can be found than his *Regina Caeli* address on Divine Mercy Sunday, March 30, 2008. In his book, *Pope Benedict's Divine Mercy Mandate* (Marian Press, 2009), David Came points out that this address reads like a "five-star" message that lays out the centrality of Divine Mercy for the Gospel, the life of the Church, and the peace and wellbeing of the world:

> Indeed, mercy is the central nucleus of the Gospel message; it is the very name of God, the face with which he revealed himself in the Old Covenant and fully in Jesus Christ, the incarnation of creative and redemptive love. May this merciful love also shine on the face of the Church and show itself through the sacraments, in particular that of Reconciliation, and in works of charity, both communitarian and individual. May all that the Church says and does manifest the mercy God feels for man, and therefore for us. When the Church has to recall an unrecognized truth or a betrayed good, she always does so impelled by merciful love, so that men and women may have life and have it abundantly (cf. Jn 10:10). From Divine Mercy, which brings peace to hearts, genuine peace flows into the world, peace between different peoples, cultures, and religions.

Divine Mercy is the center of the Gospel message, manifested through the Sacraments and works of mercy done by the Church. It is the only source of true peace for every human heart and every human community. In a nutshell, such is the mercy message of Pope Benedict XVI.

4. PAPAL MANDATE AT FIRST WORLD MERCY CONGRESS

During the week that followed, Pope Benedict opened a new chapter in the story of Divine Mercy. At the request of Cardinal Christoph Schönborn of Vienna, Austria, he had given his blesing for a World Apostolic Congress on Mercy to be held in Rome: a gathering of the hierarchy, clergy, religious, and laity from all over the world to celebrate and reflect on God's merciful love.

Significantly, Pope Benedict inaugurated the first World Mercy Congress by celebrating Mass in St. Peter's Square on April 2, 2008, for the Servant of God John Paul II on the third anniversary of his death. Although more than 40,000 people gathered for the Mass, Pope Benedict singled out in his homily the nearly 4,000 delegates who were present for the opening of the Congress:

> I address a special thought to the participants of the first World Congress on Divine Mercy, which is opening this very day and which intends to deepen [John Paul II's] rich Magisterium on the subject of God's mercy. God's mercy, as he himself said, is a privileged key to the interpretation of his Pontificate. He wanted the message of God's merciful love to be made known to all and urged the faithful to witness to it (cf. Homily at Krakow-Lagiewniki, August 17, 2002).

Then, at the conclusion of the Congress on April 6, 2008, in his remarks after his *Regina Caeli* address, Pope Benedict went beyond exhorting the faithful to proclaim and practice mercy: he actually gave the Church a papal "mandate" to be witnesses of God's merciful love. He said:

> Dear Friends, the first World Congress on Divine Mercy ended this morning with the Eucharistic

Celebration in St. Peter's Basilica. I thank the organizers, especially the Vicariate of Rome, and to all the participants I address my cordial greeting, which now becomes a *mandate*: go forth and be witnesses of God's mercy, a source of hope for every person and for the whole world. May the Risen Lord be with you always! (author's emphasis).

Finally, on Divine Mercy Sunday, April 19, 2009, Pope Benedict focused in his *Regina Caeli* message on how "God's merciful love ... unites the Church." In his message, not surprisingly, he also highlighted the important contributions of John Paul II and St. Faustina Kowalska in spreading the Good News of that merciful love:

Risen, Jesus gave His disciples a new unity, stronger than before, invincible because it was founded not on human resources but on divine mercy, which made them all feel loved and forgiven by Him. It is therefore God's merciful love that firmly unites the Church, today as in the past, and makes humanity a single family; divine love which through the Crucified and Risen Jesus forgives us our sins and renews us from within. Inspired by this deep conviction, my beloved Predecessor, John Paul II, desired to call this Sunday, the second Sunday of Easter, Divine Mercy Sunday, and indicated to all the Risen Christ as the source of trust and hope, accepting the spiritual message transmitted by the Lord to St. Faustina Kowalska, summed up in the invocation "Jesus, I trust in You!"

As we conclude this chapter, the story of Divine Mercy is not finished. It is still being written in the hearts and lives of Christians everywhere. Only the last chapter — when Jesus Christ comes again in glory to establish His merciful reign once and for all — is already guaranteed. Meanwhile, the rest of the tale will be primarily the story of the heroic witness of those who will heed the words of Jesus to St. Faustina and embrace His challenge to her as their own:

> Today I am sending you with My mercy to the people of the whole world. I do not want to punish aching mankind, but I desire to heal it, pressing it to My merciful Heart. ... Before the Day of Justice, I am sending the Day of Mercy (*Diary*, 1588).

Study Questions

1. How has Pope Benedict XVI followed in the footsteps of his predecessor, John Paul II, as an apostle of Divine Mercy?

2. In your personal life, family, and parish, how can you fulfill Pope Benedict's "mandate" to "go forth and be witnesses of God's mercy"? Be as specific as possible. Also, why is such a witness "a source of hope for every person and for the whole world"?

3. How exactly is Divine Mercy the basis for the Church's unity? What does this say about the importance of forgiveness and reconciliation in the life of the Church?

Discussion Starter:

At the end of this journey through the story of God's merciful love, from Genesis to the present, reflect on the path the Church has taken. Are there any aspects of God's merciful love and His merciful plan rooted in Scripture and in the teachings of the saints that are being overlooked today? Can we reach back into the Church's heritage of reflection on Divine Mercy and recover these lost treasures? Are there any aspects of God's merciful love and plan that have yet to receive the full attention and appreciation they deserve from the faithful? Be sure to pray for the Church on its path of mercy in preparation for the Second Coming of the Lord.

Selected Bibliography

Alphonsus de Liguori. *Selected Writings.* New York: Classics of Western Spirituality. Mahwah: Paulist Press, 1999.

Augustine of Hippo. *The Augustine Catechism: The Enchidrion on Faith, Hope, and Love.* Hyde Park: New City, 1999.

Belanger, Dina. *Autobiography of Dina Belanger.* Montreal: Religious of Jesus and Mary, 1984.

_____ *The Autobiography of Dina Belanger.* Third Edition. Canada: Religious of Jesus and Mary, 1997.

Bonaventure. *The Soul's Journey Into God. The Tree of Life. The Life of St. Francis.* New York: Classics of Western Spirituality. Mahwah: Paulist Press, 1978.

Came, David. *Pope Benedict's Divine Mercy Mandate.* Stockbridge: Marian Press, 2009.

Catherine of Siena. *The Dialogue.* New York: Classics of Western Spirituality. Mahwah: Paulist Press, 1980.

Chadwick, Henry. *The Early Church.* Harmondsworth, Middlesex, England: Penguin, 1967.

Cristiani, Leon. *St. Bernard of Clairvaux.* Boston: Daughters of St. Paul, 1983.

Dupre, Louis, and Wiseman, James, O.S.B. *Light From Light: An Anthology of Christian Mysticism.* New York: Paulist Press, 1988.

Eudes, Saint John. *The Sacred Heart of Jesus.* Albany: Preserving Christian Publications, 1997.

John Paul II. *Memory and Identity.* New York: Rizzoli International Publications, Inc., 2005

_____ *Rich in Mercy (Dives in Misericordia)*.
Stockbridge: Marian Press, 2006.

Johnson, Vernon. *Spiritual Childhood: The Spirituality of St. Therese of Lisieux.* San Francisco: Ignatius Press, 2001.

Kereszty, Roch, O.Cist. *Fundamentals of Christology.* New York: Society of St. Paul, 2002.

Kosicki, George. *John Paul II: The Great Mercy Pope.* Second Edition. Stockbridge: Marian Press, 2006.

Kowalska, Saint Maria Faustina. *Diary of Saint Maria Faustina Kowalska: Divine Mercy in My Soul.* Stockbridge: Marian Press, 1987.

Maynard, Thomas. *Saints For Our Times.* New York: Image Books, 1955.

McKenzie, John. *The Two Edged Sword: An Interpretation of the Old Testament.* Milwaukee: The Bruce, 1955.

O'Donnell, Timothy. *Heart of the Redeemer.* San Francisco: Ignatius Press, 1985.

Pennington, M. Basil. *Bernard of Clairvaux: A Lover Teaching the Way of Love.* Hyde Park, N.Y.: New City Press, 1997.

Price, Richard. *Augustine.* Ligouri, MO: Triumph, 1996.

Saward, John. "Love's Second Name: St. Thomas on Mercy." Canadian Catholic Review, March, 1990.

Stackpole, Robert. *Jesus, Mercy Incarnate.* Stockbridge: Marian Press, 2000.

_____, **ed.** *Divine Mercy: The Heart of the Gospel.* Stockbridge: Marian Press, 1999.

_____, **ed.** *Pillars of Fire in My Soul: The Spirituality of Saint Faustina.* Stockbridge: Marian Press, 2003.

Tarnawska, Maria. *Saint Sister Faustina: Her Life and*

Mission. Fourth Edition. London: Veritas Foundation, 2000.

Therese of Lisieux, Saint. *Story of A Soul: The Autobiography of Saint Therese of Lisieux.* Third Edition. Washington, D.C.: Institute of Carmelite Studies, 1996.

Trape, Agostino, "St. Augustine," in J. Quasten, Ed. *Patrology.* Westminster, MD: Christian Classics, vol. IV, 1992.

Ugolino di Monte Santa Maria. *The Little Flowers of Saint Francis of Assisi.* New York: Vintage, 1998.

Woroniecki, Hyacinth, O.P. *Mystery of Mercy.* Stockbridge: Marian Press, 1955.

Heaven, Hell, and Purgatory

HEAVEN

The New Testament tells us many times of the eternal joy that awaits the friends of God. Saint Paul wrote: "I consider that the sufferings of this present time are not worth comparing with the glory that is to be revealed to us" (Rom 8:18). "For this slight momentary affliction is preparing for us an eternal weight of glory beyond all comparison (2 Cor 4:17-18). He wrote in Colossians, "No eye has seen, nor ear heard, nor the heart of man conceived what God has prepared for those who love him" (Col 2:9).

Saint Faustina also found it almost impossible to describe the joys of heaven that she saw in a vision, "Today I was in heaven, in spirit, and I saw its inconceivable beauties and the happiness that awaits us after death. I saw how all creatures give ceaseless praise and glory to God. I saw how great is happiness in God, which spreads to all creatures, making them happy; and then all the glory and praise which springs from this happiness returns to its source; and they enter into the depths of God, contemplating the inner life of God — the Father, the Son, and the Holy Spirit, whom they will never understand or fathom" (*Diary*, 777).

For St. Faustina, to be in heaven is to be immersed in God, in the ocean of His mercy, and embraced by His love forever. "O Lord, immerse my soul in the ocean of Your divinity, and grant me the grace of knowing You; for the better I know You, the more I desire You, and the more my love for you grows. I feel in my soul an unfathomable abyss which only God can fill. I lose myself in Him as a drop does in the ocean" (*Diary*, 605). And: "The more I come to know the greatness of God, the more joyful I become that He is as He is. And I rejoice immensely in His greatness and am delighted that I am so little because, since I am so little, He carries me in His arms and holds me close to His Heart" (*Diary*, 779).

Above all, to be in heaven is to be forever with Jesus, for He promised: "And when I go and prepare a place for you, I will come again and will take you to myself, that where I am you may be also" (Jn 14:2-3). As the *Catechism of the Catholic Church* states, "Those who die in God's grace and friendship and are perfectly purified live forever with Christ. They are like God forever, for they see Him as He is, face to face" (*Catechism*, 1023-1024).

This perfect life with the Most Holy Trinity — this communion of life and love with the Trinity, with the Virgin Mary, the angels and all the blessed — is called "heaven." Heaven is the ultimate end and fulfillment of the deepest human longings, the state of supreme, definitive happiness.

HELL

Saint Faustina writes in her *Diary*, entry 741, of a vision she once had of the terrors of hell. Yet we need to interpret this frightening vision in the context of the rest of her *Diary*. In entry 1588, for example, our Lord told her that He metes out punishment to impenitent souls only with great reluctance, **"I do not want to punish mankind, but I desire to heal it, pressing it to my Merciful Heart. I use punishment when they force me to do so; My hand is reluctant to take hold of the sword of justice"** (*Diary*, 1588).

On another occasion, St. Faustina states that the ultimate punishment — eternal damnation — is essentially a self-chosen state: "I received a deeper understanding of divine mercy. Only that soul who wants it [damnation] will be damned, for God condemns no one" (*Diary*, 1452). This fits perfectly with the *Catechism* definition of "hell" as a "state of definitive self-exclusion from communion with God" (*Catechism*, 1033).

Remember that to deliberately throw away communion with God, the source of all good, is to lose *everything*. The "torments" of hell described by St. Faustina, therefore — loss of God, remorse with no hope of change, fire that penetrates but does not destroy, despair, darkness, stench, the company of Satan, hatred of God, vile words, curses, blasphemies, torments of the senses — all of this is probably a fairly accurate description of what total eternal loss would be like, both spiritually and physically. And this sobering truth is related in the words of Christ in the Gospels and in the *Catechism* (1034-1036).

Saint Faustina does not actually say that *God* is the one who "tortures" the soul in hell or that He is the one who "designed" special torments for each particular kind of sinner. Catholic Tradition has it — through the visions of other saints — that it is Satan and his demons who do that. After all, to reject God is to choose instead the everlasting company of those who reject Him! And yet, in another sense, it is true that this state of irrevocable "self-exclusion" from God, the source of all good, with all its inevitable self-destructive effects, is something that in His justice, God permits. As St. Thomas Aquinas would say, it is God's "consequent will," not His "absolute will."

At one point, St. Faustina says that she saw a "fire that will penetrate the soul without destroying it — a terrible suffering, since it is a purely spiritual fire, lit by God's anger" (*Diary*, 741). God's anger is not an emotion, nor vindictiveness, but His total, unrelenting, active opposition to evil. What burns the soul in a "spiritual" way, we may surmise, is to be unavoidably confronted with the full truth about one's evil deeds and irreversible rejection of God's love, and to hear Christ Jesus Himself ratify that truth with the words, "Depart from me, you cursed, into the eternal fire prepared for the devil and his angels" (Mt 25:41). In the end, "the truth will win out," and God will not be mocked.

Yet, God is so merciful that He has even assumed our human condition, dying on the Cross for us, in order to save us from such an eternal loss. Saint Faustina's teaching about hell, therefore, magnifies God's mercy, for it shows us clearly the greatest evil from which God wants to rescue us.

In fact, as many of the saints teach, even hell itself is tempered by God's mercy (for example, St. Catherine of Siena and St. John Eudes). By allowing souls to reject Him and His love forever, God thereby respects human freedom — the ability He gave us to choose our own destiny.

Moreover, God knows that for souls who truly hate Him, to see Him face to face forever would make them even more miserable than their self-chosen exile. That is why Cardinal Newman wrote: "Heaven would be hell to the irreligious" — and Milton's Satan in *Paradise Lost* voices the sentiments of all damned: "Better to reign in hell than serve in heaven." As C.S. Lewis put it: "The gates of hell are locked from the *inside*."

PURGATORY

The Church's teaching on purgatory is summarized in the *Catechism of The Catholic Church*, paragraph 1030:

"All who die in God's grace and friendship, but still imperfectly purified, are indeed assured of their eternal salvation; but after death they undergo purification, so as to achieve the holiness necessary to enter the joy of heaven."

Elaborating further on the teaching of Church Tradition on this matter, Fr. Kenneth Baker, S.J., wrote in *Fundamentals of Catholicism* (vol. 3), "The souls in purgatory, after their particular judgement, know for certain that they are saved; in this they rejoice. But since they need cleansing, they are separated from God for a time. This separation is most painful to them, since their whole being longs to be united with God."

Clearly, this "purifying" and "cleansing" of souls in purgatory is an expression of the mercy of God and not merely of His justice. On the one hand, it is only just that those who were partially and imperfectly penitent for their sins on earth should make up their debt to divine justice by undergoing "purgatorial or cleansing punishments" after their death (Council of Lyons, 1274). On the other hand, this divine punishment is more remedial than retributive. In other words, God intends it for the healing and rehabilitation of the soul. Much as a person might need to have a tooth pulled in order to restore his dental health, so the soul can only attain full health by the uprooting of its inordinate attachment to creatures, and especially its own pride and ego. This healing process for the soul is painful, but necessary if the soul is ever to be prepared for heaven, and attain "the holiness without which no one will see the Lord" (Heb 12:14). Thus, God purifies imperfect souls by punishing them in a way that heals them, making them holy, and ready for heavenly joy. In this way, the Lord's justice is exercised with great mercy.

The Church has never precisely defined the pains of purgatory. But some of the saints have reasoned that it consists primarily in the spiritual pain of "longing for God," and several saints have had private revelations to that effect as well (for example, St. Catherine of Genoa). Saint Alphonsus Liguori wrote that for the souls in purgatory, "The supernatural love of God with which they burn draws them with such violence to be united to [God], that when they see the barrier which their sins have put in the way, they feel a pain so acute that if they were capable of death, they could not live a moment" (*The Great Means of Salvation*, no. 20).

Nevertheless, the saints do not teach us about the sufferings of the souls in purgatory primarily in order to frighten us, but in order to move us with compassion to come to their aid. As St. Augustine wrote: "One of the holiest works, one of the best exercises of piety that we can practice in this world, is to offer sacrifices, alms, and prayers for the dead" (Homily 16). To pray for the souls in purgatory is truly a work of mercy.

Look up some of the Scripture passages in which the doctrine of purgatory has its roots: 2 Maccabees 12:42-46; Matthew 5:25-26; 12:32; 1 Corinthians 3:11-15; Hebrews 12:14. After reading them, you will see that the doctrine is more implicit in these passages than explicit. These implications were drawn out and clarified in the ancient and medieval eras by the saints, doctors, and Magisterium of the Church. The teachings of the Church and of the saints were confirmed and vividly expressed in a vision of purgatory received by St. Faustina, as she recorded in her *Diary*. It is a summary of the Catholic understanding of purgatory:

> [The next night] I saw my Guardian Angel, who ordered me to follow him. In a moment I was in a misty place full of fire in which there was a great crowd of suffering souls. They were praying fervently, but to no avail, for themselves; only we can come to their aid. The flames which were burning them did not touch me at all. My Guardian Angel did not leave me for an instant. I asked these souls what their greatest suffering was. They answered me in one voice that their greatest torment was longing for God. I saw Our Lady visiting the souls in purgatory. The souls call her 'The Star of the Sea.' She brings them refreshment. ... We went out of that prison of suffering. [I heard an interior voice] which said, **My mercy does not want this, but justice demands it**. Since that time, I am in closer communion with the suffering souls (*Diary*, 20).

Reflecting on his departed wife, C.S. Lewis wrote in *A Grief Observed*, "She was a splendid thing; a soul straight, bright, and tempered like a sword. But not a perfect saint. A sinful woman married to a sinful man; two of God's patients, not yet cured. I know there are not only tears to be dried but stains to be scoured. The sword will be made even brighter. ... But oh God, tenderly, tenderly."

One of the charisms of the Congregation of Marians of the Immaculate Conception is to pray for the poor souls in purgatory. Let us never forget these souls; let us pray for them, and ask them to pray for us when they reach their final reward in heaven.

ACKNOWLEDGMENTS

Excerpts from *Memory and Identity* by Pope John Paul II are reprinted with the permission of Rizzoli International Publications Inc.

Excerpts from *Alphonsus de Liguori*, Edited by Frederick M. Jones, C.SS.R. Copyright © 1999 by the Dublin Province of the Congregation of the Most Holy Redeemer. Paulist Press, Inc., New York/Mahwah, NJ. Reprinted by permission of Paulist Press, Inc. www.paulistpress.com

Excerpts from *Catherine of Siena*, Translated by Suzanne Noffke, O.P. Copyright © 1980 by Paulist Press. Paulist Press, Inc., New York/Mahwah, NJ. Reprinted by permission of Paulist Press, Inc. www.paulistpress.com

Excerpts from *Bonaventure*, Translated by Ewert Cousins. Copyright © 1978 by Paulist Press. Paulist Press, Inc., New York/Mahwah, NJ. Reprinted by permission of Paulist Press, Inc. www.paulistpress.com

Excerpts from *Spiritual Childhood: The Spirituality of St. Therese of Lisieux* by Vernon Johnson are reprinted with permission of The Converts' Aid Society.

All Scripture quotations, unless otherwise indicated, are taken from *The Revised Standard Version* of the Bible, Old Testament copyright © 1952, and New Testament copyright © 1971, National Council of the Churches of Christ, USA.

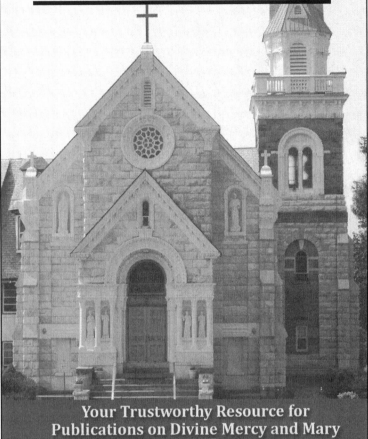
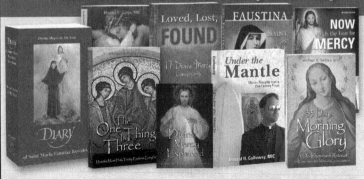

PROMOTING DIVINE MERCY SINCE 1941

Marian Press, the publishing apostolate of the Congregation of Marians of the Immaculate Conception, has published and distributed millions of religious books, magazines and pamphlets that teach, encourage, and edify Catholics around the world. Our publications promote and support the ministry and spirituality of the Marians of the Immaculate Conception. Loyal to the Holy Father and to the teachings of the Catholic Church they fulfill their special mission by:

- Fostering devotion to Mary, the Immaculate Conception.
- Promoting The Divine Mercy message and devotion.
- Offering assistance to the dying and the deceased, especially the victims of war and disease.
- Promoting Christian knowledge, administering parishes, shrines, and conducting missions.

Based in Stockbridge, Mass, Marian Press is known as the publisher of the *Diary of Saint Maria Faustina Kowalska,* and the Marians are the leading authorities on The Divine Mercy message and devotion.

Stockbridge is also the home of the National Shrine of The Divine Mercy, the Association of Marian Helpers, and a destination for thousands of pilgrims each year.

Globally, the Marians' ministries also include missions in developing countries where the spiritual and material needs are enormous.

To learn more about the Marians, their spirituality, publications or ministries, visit www.marian.org, or www.thedivinemercy.org, the Marians' website that is devoted exclusively to Divine Mercy.

Below is a view of the National Shrine of The Divine Mercy and its Residence in Stockbridge, Mass. The Shrine, which was built in the 1950s was declared a National Shrine by the National Conference of Catholic Bishops on March 20, 1996.

© MARIE ROMAGNANO

ESSENTIAL DIVINE MERCY RESOURCES

DIARY OF SAINT MARIA FAUSTINA KOWALSKA: DIVINE MERCY IN MY SOUL

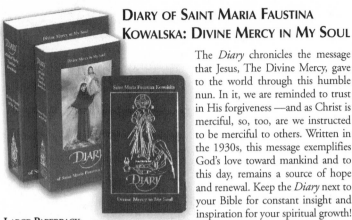

The *Diary* chronicles the message that Jesus, The Divine Mercy, gave to the world through this humble nun. In it, we are reminded to trust in His forgiveness —and as Christ is merciful, so, too, are we instructed to be merciful to others. Written in the 1930s, this message exemplifies God's love toward mankind and to this day, remains a source of hope and renewal. Keep the *Diary* next to your Bible for constant insight and inspiration for your spiritual growth!

LARGE PAPERBACK:
NBFD 9780944203040
768 pages, including 24 pages of color photographs, 5 ½" x 7 ¾".

COMPACT PAPERBACK:
DNBF 9781596141100
768 pages, including 24 pages of black and white photographs, 4" x 7".

DELUXE LEATHER-BOUND EDITION
Treasure this handsome, Deluxe Leather Edition for years to come. Includes a special dedication from the Marian Fathers of the Immaculate Conception in commemoration of the first World Apostolic Congress on Mercy, gilded edges, a ribbon marker, and 20 pages of color photographs. 768 pages, 4 ⅜" x 7 ⅛".

BURGUNDY: DDBURG 9781596141896

DIARY OF SAINT MARIA FAUSTINA KOWALSKA: DIVINE MERCY IN MY SOUL

Audio *Diary* Mp3 replaces the original 27-CD set released in 2010 with three mp3 discs containing the complete *Diary*. Also included is a bonus DVD containing an interactive timeline with links to fascinating details and resources on St. Faustina and Divine Mercy.

Mp3 Audio Disc 30 hours

ADMP3
9781596142930

18225013R00169

Made in the USA
Middletown, DE
26 February 2015